The Power of Place:
How Our Surroundings
Shape Our Thoughts,
Emotions, and Actions

I.D.

I.D.

HOW HEREDITY AND

EXPERIENCE MAKE

YOU WHO YOU ARE

WINIFRED GALLAGHER

RANDOM HOUSE • NEW YORK

All rights reserved under International and Pan-American Copyright Conventions.
Published in the United States by Random House, Inc., New York,
and simultaneously in Canada by Random House
of Canada Limited, Toronto.

Grateful acknowledgment is made to the following for permission to reprint
previously published material:

THE NEW YORK TIMES: Excerpt from "A Nonconformist in a League of His Own"
by Tom Friend (April 20, 1995). Copyright © by The New York Times
Company. Reprinted by permission.

SIMON & SCHUSTER: Excerpt from *Lonesome Dove* by Larry McMurtry. Copyright
© 1985 by Larry McMurtry. Reprinted with the permission of Simon & Schuster.

Library of Congress Cataloging-in-Publication Data
Gallagher, Winifred.
I.D.: how heredity and experience make you who you
are/Winifred Gallagher.
p.   cm.
ISBN 0-679-43018-0
1. Temperament.   2. Nature and nurture.   3. Individuality.
4. Personality.   I. Title.
BF798.G35   1996
155.2—dc20   95-39955

Printed in the United States of America on acid-free paper

24689753

First Edition

To Gal and Annie, Eliza, Tom and Molly

"A Man cannot know himself better than by attending to the feelings of his heart and to his external Actions from which he may with tolerable certainty judge what manner of person he is."

—JAMES BOSWELL, *London Journal*

"Let the cowboy ride."

—VAN MORRISON, "Santa Fe"

CONTENTS

INTRODUCTION

Who am I? Was I born the way I am? Or made? What makes me different from other people? Why do I behave as I do? How does my identity shape my fate?

As long as Homo sapiens has existed, people have asked such questions. Religion, philosophy, and art offer certain answers. In this book, these age-old inquiries are pursued from the different yet converging perspectives of very diverse behavioral scientists—geneticists and psychoanalysts, psychiatrists and psychologists, neuroscientists and primatologists—who are forging history's most sophisticated understanding of who we are and why. Over the past dozen years, their research has provided me with many wonderful things to think about. Some insights have been profound, affecting the way I see and behave with my five children. Others have been amusing as well as instructive.

"O wad some power the giftie gie us / To see oursel's as ithers see us!" wrote Robert Burns. Hoping for a measure of such enlightenment, in the course of my research I took several personality tests—those problematic, fascinating cultural artifacts—and discussed the results with their designers. Having evaluated thousands of such questionnaires, these theorists can zero in on essential, if not always immediately apparent, differences and similarities among people. Pondering my scores, one psychologist said they were along the lines of what he might expect from, say, Beverly Sills, the soprano. Another was reminded of Joe Garagiola, the legendary catcher.

At first, I was dubious about this trio of supposedly kindred spirits. Aside from the differences between the great diva and athlete, my rendition of "Happy Birthday" provokes smirks, and an airborne baseball causes me to protect my head. As I thought more about my alleged soulmates, however, some definitions and distinctions that are important to an understanding of who we are and why came alive.

Just as ability depends on both native intelligence and learned skill, personality has innate as well as acquired components. Its more enduring, biologically rooted, and often inheritable aspects are called temperament, which is the focus of the book's first part. While we may be born equal, we're not born the same, and can be very broadly distinguished by our expression of a few basic traits, or abiding behavioral tendencies. According to our capacities for anxiety, aggression, and involvement in the world, some of us fear the challenges that thrill others; some of us look for the fights that others duck; some of us are the life of the party that others observe. Walking onto the brightly lit stage or playing field would certainly give me the jitters, and I can't match Joe's major-league drive or Bubbles's champagne charm. Like their lives, however, a reporter's wouldn't suit someone who's inherently very uncomfortable with stress, competition, or engaging with others.

An old term that until recently hasn't been used much in the twentieth century, temperament derives from the Latin for "weather," evoking one's typical emotional climate, or mood. In this innate disposition, one's fundamental physiological and psychological reactions to life inextricably mesh. Its biological integers, such as heart rate and neurochemical balances, are mostly invisible. We can glimpse temperament, however, in behavior, particularly a person's reactions to life's archetypal situations, from the stressful—an opera debut or the World Series—to the social—being home alone or one of the gang.

An early master of psychology understood that each temperament has inherent strengths and weaknesses. Of the original hooker with the heart of gold, he said, "Many sins are forgiven her, because she has loved much." Particular attention is paid in these pages to two normal temperaments that are often misunderstood, even maligned, in our increasingly "virtual" world. Although it has come to be discussed as something to be stamped out with Prozac, the sensitive nature that

Hippocrates, the first personality theorist, described as melancholic has given us Chopin nocturnes and Handel alleluias, El Greco virgins and de Kooning viragos. Because my other heroes have always been cowboys, the stand-up disposition that Hippocrates called choleric also has a special place here, as in my heart.

Just as every disposition has its positive and negative aspects, each can, like an artistic form—sonata, ode, cathedral—develop in many different ways. Of the myriad traits that distinguish the opera star, the ballplayer, and me, for example, most have been acquired through our very different experiences. Character, from the Greek for "engrave," is the venerable term for these behavioral patterns that life, particularly early on, impresses on temperament, creating personality. Along with the classic learning influences, such as family, education, and class, this environmental aspect of identity includes all those numberless private experiences that, like those evoked by Proust's famous madeleine, make our memories and selves unique.

It's customary and often convenient to oppose the two ingredients of who we are—temperament versus character, genes versus environment—as if they were oil and water. This book poses a very different analogy for their relationship: the flour and water in bread. After many swings of the ideological pendulum—for nearly a century in the environmental direction—the old "nature or nurture" debate is over. In a living person, the inherited and acquired can no more be teased apart than the effect of Winslow Homer's *Northeaster* can be pinned to the irritable waves, the blowing spume, or the leaden sky; to the grays, greens, and dirty whites, or the drawing beneath them; to God's hand or Homer's.

How do my genes influence who I am? How much depends on what happens to me? How do my biology and experience affect each other? To what extent can parents shape their children? Is there a real me? Which one is it? How does my past haunt the present and augur the future? Does the life I lead suit who I am? To what degree has my identity been formed by culture?

The greatest modern advance in the understanding of why we are the way we are has been behavioral geneticists' confirmation of an ancient scientific premise: like our constitutions, our dispositions are to a significant degree inherited. Having established the importance of genes, researchers are returning to explore the well-trodden subject of how we're molded by the environment, but from a very different perspective—that is the focus of the book's second part. Just as our biology shapes our history, cutting-edge research is demonstrating that our experience is literally as well as figuratively engraved in our nervous systems, sometimes as emphatically as the marks of genes. As a result, at the turn of the millennium, the old definition of temperament as inborn is being rewritten.

Despite the common misconception, we're limited less by our vast genetic potential than by the narrow use that most of us and our environments make of it. Like all temperaments, those of the artists and knights errant who figure in earlier chapters not only "select," as scientists say, but also *attract* certain kinds of formative experience. That our innate dispositions pull us toward or away from situations in a way that make us "more ourselves" is arguably temperament's most powerful effect on who we are—and one that can be deliberately managed.

Far from neuroscientists' labs and geneticists' computers, psychiatrists and psychologists are mapping the behavioral processes by which an individual evolves through experience. We Westerners tend to think of personality as a monolith, an unchanging entity that objectively takes in and processes information and generates consistent responses. This is a heroic idea, but inaccurate. Far from being a solitary, unchanging Rock of Gibraltar, personality is deeply social and inherently multitudinous—elements reflected in the origins of the word itself. *Per* is Latin for "through," and *sonus,* for "sound," recalling classical actors' practice of using small megaphones to project their voices through their characters' masks. On life's stage, personality, like those ancient props, enables us to communicate and collaborate with our fellow players and, when necessary, to "put a good face" on the sensitive hidden self: the insider's view of personality that is one's immediate awareness of being.

Just as a good actor plays many roles—and even in a single one reveals many dimensions and nuances—so does a finely developed personality. Its flexibility, which enables us, unlike the dinosaurs, to

respond to a changing world, derives from its many parts. Like an um-
brella, the term "personality" spans a collection of characteristic traits
and states, or brief psychobiological conditions. Early in life, depending on our temperamental predilections, we react to particular stimuli
with certain ways of being. Over time, each of these trait-modulated
states becomes hooked to the particular self, or consciousness, that per-
ceives it. In turn, these habitual states and selves generate schemas, or
concepts of what the world is like and how we should behave in it.

Less commodity than process, this vast *system,* rising from our innate
tendencies and acquired experience and dynamically existing in memory, is personality. Not some static formulation—Aquarius or Leo, obsessive-compulsive or narcissistic—we are, at any given moment, the
sum of our operative physiological and behavioral parts, reflecting our
species' genetic and historical heritage and our own, and responding to
messages from the outside world and the private three-pound one in
our heads. If the ancient metaphor for personality was the masked
actor, a modern one is the jazz musician: master of his instrument yet
able to play in ensemble, aware of form and structure yet ready to im-
provise, knowing his limits but occasionally stretching them.

*Am I a certain type of person, or unique? Why do I repeat the same mis-
takes? Is the source of my problems inside me or out there in the world? Can
I solve them through insight? Drugs? How much can I really change who
I am?*

Past early adulthood, most of us don't alter much as far as our basic
traits, such as sociability or irritability, are concerned. Because it's made
up of so many parts—more Rube Goldberg than Henry Moore—personality can change, however, which is the subject of the book's third
part. With our diets and fitness regimens, plastic surgery and fashion
overhauls, we're obsessed with becoming different. The billions of dollars we spend each year on psychotherapy and psychopharmacology, as
well as the hundreds of books and courses offering do-it-yourself cures
for personal problems, testify that we're no less interested in internal
makeovers.

Notwithstanding this chronic, postmodern sense of dissatisfaction, scientists insist that most of our personalities are all right in themselves. If anything needs to change, it's often our inability—or society's—to accept both who we are and the fact that no one is perfect. In our urbanized, highly mobile, information-oriented culture, the resilient, assertive, and outgoing among us seem most nearly so. We evolved, however, in tribal groups that more closely resembled small-town communities than the vast electronically connected sprawls in which most of us live. Because no personality exists in a vacuum, some variation on what psychiatrists once derided as a "geographical cure"—whether a move to a new job or a new state—can ease problems that have less to do with who an individual is than where.

Some of us, however, can benefit by modifying who we are. Sometimes we're spurred to do so by the environment. As we live longer lives in an increasingly changeable world, for example, shifts in careers and relationships are becoming more the rule than the exception, which challenges our flexibility. In other cases, we need to change because a normal trait has become rigid and exaggerated, interfering with our comfort and functioning or others'. One reason why we're fascinated by Adolf Hitler, Marilyn Monroe, Napoleon, and other famous and infamous persons who manifest so-called personality disorders is that they're extremes of ourselves—far more hateful, volatile, or self-absorbed than average, but hardly unrecognizable. Some, but not all, personality problems can be smoothed out in psychotherapy, but that process is long, demanding, and costly. Partly for those reasons, society as well as psychiatry is engaged in the question of whether drugs can or should be used to change personality, and at what cost.

Some changes in who we are are part of life. Certain of these, such as the hormonal transitions at adolescence and later adulthood, simply happen. Others involve an element of choice. For those who want to experiment with do-it-yourself change, the wisest course seems to be to accept the basics of who you are, then decide to do something different with them. When we form a relationship, become parents, switch careers, attend college, or embrace a philosophy or religion, our scores in extroversion or aggression may not alter, but our lives do.

Of all the mysteries of the science of who we are, the most profound is manifest in the nearest family album. How does that tiny newborn become that schoolchild, teenager, adult, and grandparent, remaining the same individual, yet becoming different?

A while ago, after I had turned in a long story about the different biologically influenced inclinations of men and women, a fine editor, not coincidentally from the South, asked, "Would this have made sense to my grandmother?" He understood that, despite tremendous social shifts and our fond notions of progress, the foundations of human behavior don't change much. In a figurative if not always literal way, I've found the grandmother gauge very useful in writing this book. The more I learned about the science of personality, the more skeptical I grew of fads and grand unified theories (and there are many); the more respectful I became of information and intuitions that extend or at least resonate with scientific wisdom and my own hands-on experience as child, parent, friend, spouse. I hope the result would have made sense to my grandmothers, who were so quick to get one's number and nearly impossible to surprise.

I wish I could say that everyone should—*must*—think about why we are the way we are. Such knowledge does have a certain practical utility, allowing us, for example, to respond to others in ways that maximize the pleasures and minimize the frustrations of their company, and ours. Like a love for trecento frescoes or Baroque chamber music, however, insight into behavior is not essential to life. Many very bright, successful people have almost no interest in or taste for such things, and even take pride in the fact. Like an appreciation of art, an understanding of people requires not only effort, but also the ability to tolerate complexity, ambiguity, and even contradiction. Like art, too, this knowledge can be disturbing. Like art, however, a sense of what makes us individuals and what we can—and can't—do with and about it adds to our potential and simply makes life more *interesting*.

The experience that has been most important to the shape of this book came, as such things often do, by accident. After many months of reporting, I had accumulated a lot of facts, figures, and theories, but they seemed dry and academic. While attending yet another scientific conference, I noticed that a psychiatrist friend was leading a certain seminar, and stopped in toward the end to say hello. Walking into a darkened auditorium, I saw Monica, a true personality artist, lighting up the movie screen. Like many before me, I was immediately captivated by her complicated smile. Her story, which is described in the following chapter and particularly figures in the book's second part, illustrates in a way that very few could the alchemy of biology and experience that makes each of us one of a kind.

PART I

HOW WE ARE

CHAPTER 1

A DYNAMITE SMILE

In the flickering frames of a 1950s home movie, the big-eyed baby staring out from the steel-barred hospital crib is every sad case from every save-the-child poster designed to break hearts. Although she's fifteen months old, at ten pounds Monica weighs what a big newborn might. Her development has been so perturbed that she can neither sit up nor turn over, as can most babies half her age, much less stand or walk. She makes no attempts at language. More eloquently than any words, her condition speaks of her experience. For much of her life, her world has consisted of whatever she could perceive while lying on her back alone in a bedroom of a desolate, run-down farmhouse.

It takes more than just another traumatized child to move people habituated to images of tiny African starvelings and East European amputees, not to mention the crack babies just around the corner. Like other great heroines of the screen, however, Monica has a special quality that makes others respond to her. In the darkened hall, filled with psychiatrists curious about this unique visual case history, eyes sting, hair prickles, and the atmosphere thickens with fantasies about how to save *this* baby. As the film continues, it becomes clear that this chemistry between Monica's nature and the world defends her against the kind of experience that condemns most of the children it doesn't kill to a stunted life in an institution.

Lying limply in the pediatric ward of a university medical center, pretty little Monica has the fairy-tale charisma of a bewitched princess, and the staff joins forces to rescue her from the elusive evil spell that has frozen her development. The magnet that draws this critical attention is what the innovative American child psychiatrist Daniel Stern, now conducting research at the University of Geneva, later describes to the audience as Monica's "dynamite smile." Radiant yet a little tremulous, demure yet flirty, the baby's shy, potent grin brings to mind one of the twentieth century's most distinctive and reputedly irresistible femmes fatales. Remarking on her predecessor in the White House, Lady Bird Johnson said that, like many others, she felt that Jacqueline Kennedy "came across as a little girl you wanted to help"; from a different viewpoint, an old admirer once described her as "the sort of woman who always gives the car keys to the man." Even as a baby, Monica has this capacity not only to attract others but to have her way with them by making them feel powerful. Surely not coincidentally, the former first lady and Monica have other things in common. Despite vast cultural differences, both come from a line of handsome, high-spirited charmers, and their resilient, exacting mothers and dark, wild-rover fathers left the family when divorce was unusual. Like most people's however, Jacqueline's childhood trials diminish in comparison to Monica's.

In 1952, in a small town in rural New York, Monica was born with a congenital defect called esophageal atresia, which made a flat tape out of part of the hollow pipe connecting her mouth and stomach. Because she couldn't eat, her food had to be poured into a tube inserted into a fistula, or duct, that surgeons had cut into her stomach when she was three days old; to prevent her from choking to death, another fistula in her neck drained her saliva. Because the process of pouring in the formula required two hands, the person in charge couldn't hold Monica, who lay on her back; so experientially remote was she from her own feedings that they could even take place while she slept or cried. Rather than the usual cozy nursing sessions of more or less a half hour that are the focus of a baby's life, Monica's, as they appeared on film, eerily resembled filling up at the gas station. Guilty about the birth defect and fearful of doing something wrong, her teenage mother was nervous about handling her, but a doting grandmother, who had raised many children, held the little girl for hours. To this experienced, nurturing woman, Monica was a good baby who, despite her handicap, did well for her first five months.

The day after her first Christmas, Monica's life went into a protracted downhill skid. Her father, a long-distance trucker with an adventurous streak, moved Monica, her toddler brother, and his newly pregnant wife from his in-laws' home to a remote rural house. Cut off from her own supportive mother during a harsh winter and left alone with two small children for long periods by her wandering husband, the young woman fell into a depression, paralyzed by its hallmarks of helplessness and hopelessness. No one can know exactly how she felt about Monica, but psychiatrists conjecture that on some level she believed her daughter was doomed and that the baby she carried was a "replacement child." What is clear is that, for about six months, her mother more or less gave up on Monica. Except for the few minutes demanded by her odd feedings, the baby was left in dismal isolation at a time when, as neuroscientists increasingly discover, infants totally depend on others not just for sustenance but for the tremendous sensory, intellectual, and emotional stimulation required for normal physical and psychological development. In a ghastly variation on sensory deprivation experiments that would soon be conducted with animals, Monica first became irritable, then passive, then stunted. Her near immobility was merely the most obvious sign of development gone profoundly awry—skewed as surely by experience as it could have been by flawed genes.

By the age of eleven months, Monica's situation was so dire that she was lucky to get the chicken pox. Her mother's depression had run its course, and emerging from her melancholic haze, the young woman took her terribly ill baby to the distant hospital. After staying there more than a month, Monica went home, and at first seemed better. When her new baby sister arrived, however, she became upset, then withdrawn again. On being readmitted to the hospital in her sixteenth month, when the first film was shot, she still weighed just ten pounds. Doctors could only diagnose her strange condition, later called "failure to thrive," as "depression of infancy." They doubted that she would live.

Once again, serendipity intervened on Monica's behalf. In the hospital's cafeteria, a pediatric nurse mentioned her extraordinary new patient to Franz Reichsman, an internist who, with his colleague George Engel, a pioneer in psychosomatic medicine, was interested in the behavioral dimensions of gastric illnesses. On first seeing Monica, the two doctors knew that a simple photograph or verbal description couldn't possibly convey the quality of the pervasive yet elusive pall that hung over the child. In the best tradition of the 1950s fathers they were, they fetched a home movie camera.

There was also a powerful scientific precedent for such a film. In 1945, R. A. Spitz had shot movies of institutionalized infants who, although fed and physically maintained, became withdrawn, stopped gaining weight, developed abnormally, and sickened easily. Although scientists didn't then fully understand the syndrome, they sensed that the children had been starved of adequate human contact and suffered from "skin hunger." Along with making a visual record of someone they already suspected was a "Spitz child," Engel and Reichsman hoped to gain insight into the genesis of gastric illnesses. Having had psychoanalytic training, Engel knew the importance Freud had placed on feeding and what he called development's "oral phase"; his disciples suspected that perturbations of this early experience could contribute to later gastric troubles. Engel and Reichsman reasoned that the highly social interactions of feeding were indeed the infant's primary way of engaging with the world, and so the baby's gastric secretions should ebb and flow in tune with her social experiences. Monica's tender age and the tube that allowed the painless aspiration of her intestinal juices made her the perfect subject for a benign test of their hypothesis. If Monica survived, she would need a long convalescence before surgeons would attempt to restructure her esophagus so that she could eat normally. Tapping their research budget, Reichsman and Engel offered to pay her $14-per-day hospitalization fee and began the study that neither imagined would go on for decades, changing not only her life but theirs.

For most babies, the experience of a long hospital stay is something like Jonah's on being swallowed by the whale. For Monica, it was more like Lazarus's walk from the tomb. Overnight, the doomed isolate became the darling of the pediatric floor (particularly of the nurturing nurse Kathy Dailey), which she commanded from a central position.

Her capacity to draw people with her wonderful smile was one of the first things her doctors noted. Planted at last in fertile ground, this temperamental seed sent up the vital green shoot from which her personality could finally blossom.

Monica's signature magnetism is an economical demonstration of what personality is, and is for: the mask through which one projects the self and its needs to the world. Even this debilitated, speechless baby could convey the essentials of who she was—desperate but *special*—so effectively that some professionals who saw the early films suggested that one of her doctors should adopt her.

The first images of Monica, smiling yet shy, reaching out while holding back, illustrate the futility of trying to pluck apart the threads of heredity and experience so tightly woven into a personality's unique fabric. Judging by histories and films of her kin, her exceptional capacity to attract others and engage them in her behalf came naturally. A special kind of intelligence that enables someone instantaneously to process and react to others' cues—social genius, if you will—plays a part, but her genetic gift also has a temperamental element. By the time certain babies are two or three months old, their ready smiles and babbles and reachings out express an innately sunny disposition that virtually guarantees them lots of social rewards. Through this dynamic, which scientists call gene-environment correlation, we're drawn to the kind of experiences that call out to deep parts of ourselves and further reinforce them. Nature gave Monica this head start on a happy life, but the traumatic environment of her mid-infancy shaped her as well.

Not long after Monica's ordeal, University of Wisconsin psychologist Harry Harlow began a quiet, still-underappreciated revolution in the understanding of the impact of environment on how we develop. When he isolated normal infant monkeys and reared them in a condition of social deprivation, they soon developed severe behavioral problems. When Harlow made slight modifications in the cages, however, such as providing a terry-cloth-wrapped wire surrogate "companion," the babies were spared particular abnormalities. For example, in studies conducted by William Mason, one of Harlow's former students, infants supplied with a mobile surrogate that swung from a string didn't develop the compulsion to rock back and forth that afflicted those caged with a stationary companion. The more such maternal sensory features were provided, the more normal the monkeys' development. Moreover, their response to even a minimally cozy "mother" changed their whole approach to the world. When a toy was put in their cage, for example, infants who clung to a padded companion gradually overcame their anxiety and explored the "monster," while those who hung on to a wire feeding apparatus continued to cower in fear. Harlow concluded that for babies, the "contact comfort" that Monica so lacked was as basic a need as food, and that mothers were the source of much more than calories, and even love. Nurture was not only vital to normal development, but could even transform nature.

The chairman of the Monica seminar and a pioneer in developmental psychobiology, psychiatrist Myron Hofer conducts far more intricate animal experiments, currently at the New York State Psychiatric Institute, which have further expanded the meaning of environment and its impact on who we are. He describes to the audience his research on how each of the different maternal sensory stimuli—tactile, thermal, visual, olfactory, vestibular—precisely control particular elements of the infant's physiology and behavior, from heart rate to appetite to activity level. Like a delicate seedling in a greenhouse, the infant develops within the invisible bubble of what Hofer calls hidden maternal regulation—an interaction of which Monica was severely deprived. From this perspective, the effects of our early environments—relationships—can be glimpsed in some of the most basic neurophysiological underpinnings of individuality.

Long after birth, our brains continue to develop, particularly during life's first two years. For that process to unfold normally, a child must have certain kinds of sensory, emotional, and cognitive experiences at certain times. Research increasingly shows that "formative" experiences that have traditionally been regarded as purely social or psychological actually help forge the neuronal connections that make an individual's brain and the behavioral patterns it generates unique. Along with affecting his neuroanatomy, a baby's "quality of life" also helps establish the hormonal and emotional parameters of his later characteristic stress response—a pillar of temperament. For ethical reasons, manipulative research on how we're affected by our first environment can't be conducted with children. In the late 1980s, however, following a revolu-tion in Romania, a horrifying "natural experiment" there made front-page news around the world. A legion of orphans who had been institutionalized—warehoused is a more accurate term—showed on a vast scale, witnessed by Daniel Stern, that children subjected to se-vere sensory and social deprivation almost invariably die or suffer from profound retardation. Like the responses of experimentally deprived animals and warehoused babies, Monica's reaction to months of un-answered cries, unmet needs, and a world shrunk to a patch of ceiling illustrates environment's power to affect brain and behavior as pro-foundly as heredity.

Soon after Monica's arrival at the hospital, her doctors noticed a striking phenomenon. When confronted by a stranger or left by a friend, Monica reacted to the stress by disengaging from the world. Psy-chologically she turned inward, and physically she turned off. In one scene, when she's approached by an unfamiliar doctor, she faces in the other direction and begins to doze. As soon as the stranger leaves and her beloved Dr. Reichsman returns, however, Monica comes back to life like Sleeping Beauty, smiling and reaching out.

In scientific journals, George Engel later described Monica's peculiar disengaged response as "conservation withdrawal." Like other organ-isms confronting a crisis, he hypothesized, Monica had reacted to her early deprivation by shutting down, thus saving energy needed for sheer survival. When what was meant as a short-term emergency strategy went on and on for months, however, Monica became imprisoned by this state, which eventually evolved into a trait that changed who she was. No longer just the smiling "good baby" of her grandmother's lap and later, the pediatric ward, she was also the withdrawn victim. As Daniel Stern says, "the problem for such a baby isn't so much lack of stimulation as a maladaptive construct of reality. Her experience with a depressed mother became what it's like to be with another person."

The older we get, the more we rely on intellect, and the harder it is even to imagine the first realm of the senses and emotions that shaped us and our vision of reality. Certain casual expressions, however, cap-ture its synthesis of physical and psychological feelings. When we say that fear sends a shiver up our spines or makes our hair stand on end, says Myron Hofer, we allude not only to an affective but also to a thermal-regulation response. Such reactions, and even crying, he suspects, may have evolved as ways to maintain the temperature of a lone infant until its mother returns. "Anxiety may have begun as a response to keep us warm," he says. "Its physiology derives from simpler, more basic body responses that got taken over by this complicated thing we call emotion."

Repeated over time, our joint physiological and emotional responses to a world seen through the lenses of our particular temperament make us who we are. In one of the film archive's most striking sequences, little Monica provides an unsurpassable demonstration of individuality: when Dr. Reichsman and a stranger gently test their small research subject by taking positions on the left and right of her crib, sophisticated Monica responds by animating one side of her body while freezing the other. Although we speak of a person's having "two sides" or even being "two-faced," the sight is unsettling. Who is the *real* Monica? The one blessed by nature with that dynamite smile, or the one turned to stone by hard experience?

From the iconoclastic new perspective on the old "nature or nurture" question, Monica's self-protective withdrawal is, in the sense of being apparent early in life, profound, enduring, and enmeshed in biology, no less a temperamental quality than her innate magnetism. She may have been born with the familial élan, but research now suggests that her harsh experience could have remodeled her nervous system, making it more closely resemble that of someone born with a different, highly sensitive temperament. If nurture can thus be inscribed on nature, trying to separate the two becomes not only futile but absurd.

When she left the hospital after nine months of what amounted to a second gestation, Monica finally had a future. Experience—this time the benign sort—had once again altered who she was. She was no longer depressed, had gained more than six pounds, and could sit up. Thanks to corrective surgery, she could eat normally and even feed herself. Eager to do right, her mother, now also restored to health, welcomed the child home and asked the generous, nearly paternal Rochester doctors who had come to Monica's rescue to continue their special relationship with her. On film, audiotape, and paper over the next forty years, Engel, Reichsman, and many colleagues—most recently Lynne Hofer, a psychoanalyst and researcher who's especially interested in parent-child interactions—interviewed, evaluated, and observed Monica as she defied various expert opinions to walk, talk, love, learn, marry, have four children, and work in the world. It's difficult to overstate the study's historical and scientific importance. Monica is the first person to be followed in multimedia detail from infancy to grandparenthood. Probably the most extensively documented case in psychiatry, the study of her life includes nearly a hundred thousand pages of psychological tests, drawings, reports, and transcribed interviews, in addition to the extraordinary films and tape recordings. Not only is her behavior completely documented in each session with the study's investigators but also theirs and, on occasion, that of members from four generations of her family.

Despite the many theories Monica has inspired, no one can say what her experience was or is really like, much less exactly why she is the way she is. To protect her privacy, only a handful of people have ever known her real name or whereabouts; she is and will remain largely mysterious. Like that of other special smiling ladies, from Mona Lisa to Jackie Kennedy, part of Monica's charm is that she inspires so much guessing. That process is destined to continue, because in 1995 George Engel, retired after a long, distinguished career, settled the vast Monica archive in a permanent home at Radcliffe's Henry A. Murray Research Center for the Study of Lives, where much of the voluminous data awaits scholarly analysis.

Beyond its special value to the scientists who study the dynamics of how nature and nurture make us who we are, Monica's story is a gift to a world that's increasingly intolerant of bad starts and bad genes, mistakes and flaws, lags and lapses. Contradicting the experts' dire predictions at nearly every turn, her life celebrates our often-underestimated resilience and demonstrates that even the harshest experience can add depth and luster to who we are. The empathy that her story inspires, even from the remove of a printed page or movie screen, testifies to the bittersweet awareness that we too have been born and made. We too came into the world with something special and have struggled to make the best of it in circumstances not always ideal. Like this phoenix, we too have risen from the ashes and gone on.

CHAPTER 2

TEMPERAMENT: THE WAY YOU DO THE THINGS YOU DO

Like the ghost in the machine or the mind in the brain, temperament—that profound aspect of who we are that's revealed by our *manner* of behavior—is best seen in action. A few minutes of film say more about Monica's than a pile of scientific abstracts. To Daniel Stern, its defining characteristic is an "animal attractiveness—a passive charisma that's something like sex appeal, but it isn't about sex. This quality, which she still seems to have in her forties and God knows she had as a kid, has bought her a lot. My gaze always goes to her, as happens with some really good actresses. Even if they're not the most beautiful, you can't keep your eyes off them."

That not even what scientists sum up as "massive stimulus deprivation" during infancy stamped out this pervasive, enduring psychobiological characteristic, which Lynne Hofer simply calls Monica's "star quality," speaks of temperament. Along with her innate appeal, however, the flickering images also reflect Monica's hard early experience. Temperament is often most clearly revealed in the process of communication. Even though the traumatized child in the first films can't talk, she employs a special body language that eloquently speaks of who she is. When Monica sees a friend, she radiates smiles and literally as well as figuratively extends herself, unfurling toward her visitor the delicate tendril of a limb—often, a wriggling left leg. To Hofer, this proffered body part, "like a pseudopod, is a primitive extension of her whole essence, stretched to her body's limits, yet contained within its boundaries." When Monica meets the environment in this idiosyncratic way, simultaneously open and reserved, she reveals a distinctive, adaptive personality that, like Elizabeth Barrett Browning's before her, draws the world to the safety of the invalid's couch. When the screen lights up with her smile, the *o-o-ohhh* rippling through the audience testifies to temperament at work—moving people and, sometimes, mountains.

That her special magnetism distinguishes Monica as baby, girl, and woman would not have surprised Hippocrates. For most of history, it was assumed that we are each pretty much "born that way" and stay that way. Until the turn of the twentieth century, scientists regarded different people less as the rugged individuals Americans envision than as variations on a few basic human themes. In the fifth century B.C., the Greek father of medicine defined four temperaments, each of which was linked to a predominant bodily fluid, or humor. The people he called "sanguine" are optimistic and energetic; the "melancholic," moody and withdrawn; the "choleric," irritable and impulsive; the "phlegmatic," calm and slow. However quaint his theory may seem at first, the prototypes Hippocrates described are as familiar today as they were in the agora. Unlike many of his successors, even modern ones, he didn't try to segregate mind from body or disposition from constitution. One of his most prescient intuitions was the connection between biochemistry and behavior. Hippocrates would be surprised neither by the discovery of neurotransmitters—the neurochemicals by which the brain transmits information—nor by potions like Prozac that quell melancholic black and choleric yellow bile.

For more than two thousand years, variations on Hippocrates' theory of constitutions and dispositions dominated science. The twentieth century, however, brought a great decline in scientists' interest in temperament, which has begun to reverse only in the past decade or two. With the dawn of the modern era, political, philosophical, and scientific developments diverted attention from who we are at birth to what others, from mothers to governments, do to us afterward. From very different perspectives, both Freud and behaviorists such as B. F. Skinner asserted that our experience was vastly more important to who we are than our inborn traits. Revulsion at Nazism's doctrine of inferior and superior genetic types converged with the worldwide spread of democratic ideas and civil rights to focus academe on human similarities and the environment's formative power. In this egalitarian intellectual climate of the 1930s and 1940s, the new discipline of personality psychology began its search for a systematic way to describe people according to a set of basic traits that all of us share to varying degrees. By this light, we differ not in quality—being *either* melancholic, say, *or* sanguine—but in quantity—being more, or less, gloomy and hearty than others.

Considering his reputation, it seems ironic that I. P. Pavlov, the dark prince of conditioning, was among the few earlier modern scientists to remain interested in temperament. Of his famous canines, he observed that "the final nervous activity in the animal is an alloy of the features peculiar to the type and of the changes wrought by the environment." "Excitatory," or choleric, dogs were by nature "pugnacious, passionate, and easily and quickly irritated," while the "inhibitory," or melancholic, animal "believes in nothing, hopes for nothing, in everything he sees the dark side." Of the two stabler sorts, one was "self-contained and quiet; persistent and steadfast," the other "energetic and very productive" but easily bored. Nobody paid much attention, but even Pavlov's dogs, those exemplars of environmental conditioning, showed the classical temperaments.

After a long lapse, scientists are again interested in the innate aspects of who we are. The application of the technology that exposed the genetic roots of physical illnesses such as muscular dystrophy and Huntington's disease to the search for the origins of certain mental illnesses, such as depression and schizophrenia, has restored to scientific credibility the idea that nature is a strong influence on behavior. Although it's best conveyed in the flesh or on a movie screen, the researchers who study temperament must try to get it down on paper. In that process, they particularly consider several elements that can sometimes be gauged even in the womb, including an individual's levels of activity and reactivity, rhythmicity, attention span, and mood, or internal state of well-being. The variations in these basic ways in which people react to the world and regulate themselves distinguish the different dispositions. Each arises from constitutional variables in the nervous, circulatory, and endocrine systems that respond to the environment, affect

one another, and change with development and experience, while pre-
serving what psychologist Arnold Buss has prettily described as "the
native individuality that shines through the overlay of learned tendencies." What gleams most brightly is a person's characteristic affective
tone. To sleuth of the intricacies of mood Hagop Akiskal, a professor
of psychiatry at the University of California at San Diego, described by
an admiring peer as both an exacting researcher "and a doctor who
knows and cares about what people are really like," temperament is
"not just a matter of personality but something more basic that has to
do with rhythms, gestures, *emotion.*"

Of all species, Homo sapiens has not only the best brain but the most
heart. A neuroendocrinologist with a literary cast of mind not general
among scientists, psychiatrist Philip Gold describes his research at the
National Institute of Mental Health as "helping people to modify their
prevailing emotional tone, which is temperament, so that their
thoughts are charged with appropriate feelings." Like our ideas, our
emotions, which are physiological as well as psychological events, en-
hance our ability to survive. Just as drives, such as hunger and lust, are
more flexible responses than reflexes, such as the eye blink or knee jerk,
emotions give us more behavioral options than drives do. In large part,
they concern our habitual reactions to things in the world that are
novel, menacing, or otherwise arousing, from strangers to snakes to unfamiliar software.

That our natures are organized around our characteristic reactions to
threat has given the nevertheless ebullient Gold a "tragic view of the
human condition." Physical or emotional, real or imagined, danger
lurks everywhere. From an evolutionary perspective, Gold considers
that our species' great asset—and sometimes individual liability—has
been an extremely sensitive emotional and physiological arousal system
that detects and reacts to threat: the stress, or "fight or flight," response.
The major variations in how it's expressed underlie the classical temperaments.

Because their stress reaction isn't triggered by every little thing and
doesn't stay on red alert longer than necessary, those who have the kind

of disposition that researchers variously describe as bold, uninhibited, or relaxed—Hippocrates' sanguine and phlegmatic sorts—can cope with life's vicissitudes, from a jaguar in the jungle to a fire-breathing boss, in a manner Gold describes as "philosophical. Despite being surrounded by unanswerable questions, ambiguous dilemmas, and the certainty of loss and death, these resilient people are innately disposed to celebrate the beauty of existence and the wonders of an interior life and external connections."

Although they have other special advantages, the people whose nervous systems naturally react to the threatening or merely unfamiliar by preparing to flee have a harder time of it. Because their stress response spikes frequently and ebbs slowly, Hippocrates' melancholics, whom scientists now describe as reactive, inhibited, sensitive, anxious, or fearful, experience the strain of life in flight. To buffer themselves from upsets, they may adopt an avoidant behavioral style that only worsens their plight or become so worn down that they act in what Gold calls "a depressive way. Faced with a setback, for example, such people say it occurred because they're worthless. They're likelier to survive in truly threatening situations, but they have less comfortable lives."

The often-misunderstood people described by Hippocrates as choleric respond to stress not with sanguine élan or melancholic angst but by becoming annoyed and even preparing to fight. To those numbered in this less homogeneous group, whom researchers variously call irritable, impulsive, or aggressive, "the dark possibility of pain and defeat is so intense," says Gold, "that they can't bear to be accountable for it in a depressive way." Instead, they blame it on others and strike out.

The bias toward one of these fundamental emotional tones, or temperaments, "has to do with what a person has learned he has to be in order to be loved," says Gold, "but it also has to do with genetic factors that biologically predispose him to respond in a certain way to the paradigmatic human situations of pleasure and opportunity, danger and loss. In the daily blood-and-guts world of challenges, these variations on the stress response account for the fundamental parameters of what people are like."

The lives of three eminent Victorians speak of how individuals who are strongly flavored by one of these basic temperaments operate in the world. The high-strung queen whose name is synonymous with the effort to dampen arousal describes the clockwork progress of an ideal day in the company of her beloved consort: "We walked in the garden. . . . At twelve o'clock we had prayers in the drawing-room, which were read by a young clergyman, who preached a good sermon. . . . I read to Albert the first three cantos of *The Lay of the Last Minstrel,* which delighted us both; and then we looked over some curious, fine old prints by Ridinger." Yet even the queen had days when novelty intruded on her careful plans, trying her sensitive nerves. Despite the efforts of maids and courtiers in a posh Highland lodge, some missing luggage gave Victoria a very bad night—one signal of a reactive temperament. "I disliked the idea of going to bed without any of the necessary toilette," she wrote in her diary. "However, some arrangements were made which were very uncomfortable; and after two I got into bed, but had very little sleep at first; finally, fatigue got the better of discomfort, and after three I fell asleep."

If Victoria's idea of a rough night illumines the sensitive temperament, the nocturnal arrangements of one of her subjects, the Honorable Jane Digby el-Mezrab, reveal the bold one. Like the queen, this well-traveled, much married lady also doted on her husband—at least her fourth one—but in a manner that would have greatly perturbed Victoria. With Sheik Medjuel el-Mezrab, Jane passed half the year in a Bedouin tent in the Syrian desert, where, Arab robes flying and blue eyes rimmed with kohl, she raced camels and horses, went falconing, and even accompanied her lord and master into battle. Nor did her adventures cease with the setting of the sun. After more than a decade of the flared-nostril life, taken up well past the point at which Victoria had abandoned herself to inconsolable widowhood, Jane wrote, "Sixty-two years of age, and an impetuous romantic girl of seventeen cannot exceed me in ardent passionate feelings."

By the age of nine, the boy who would become Captain Sir Richard Francis Burton, the legendary Victorian explorer, spy, linguist, scholar, swordsman, soldier—and friend of Jane Digby—was, writes his biographer Edward Rice, "virtually a hard-core delinquent" more or less ignored by his parents and known for fighting, shooting at tombstones and church windows, lewdness—and the ability to endure toothache.

A prodigy who mastered twenty-nine languages, Burton nonetheless preferred the army to Oxford. The temperament of the translator of the *Kama Sutra* and the *Arabian Nights* and the proverbial first white man in many parts of Asia and Africa is summed up by his rationale for visiting the forbidden Muslim city of Harar: all Europeans who attempted it had been murdered, so entry was "therefore a point of honor with me." By any standard, he was touchy on that point. At one moment in his youth, he had no fewer than thirty-two affairs of honor pending violent settlement. Had he been born in the gutter rather than in an upper-class milieu that provided acceptable channels for his fighting spirit, "Ruffian Dick" might have followed his aggressive proclivities to the gallows rather than to knighthood. Queen Victoria, Jane Digby, and Richard Burton each engaged in various activities, but *how* he or she went about them was the same, and that is temperament.

To characterize a person as hypersensitive, laid-back, irritable, or aggressive—upset, intrigued, or annoyed by a challenge—is hardly a Henry Jamesian portrait. Unlike writers, however, scientists must have a systematic, economical way to talk about who we are and our differences. Even the great novelist, whose brother William founded American psychology, would have approved of Gordon Allport's pioneering effort, back in the 1930s, to search for personality's attributes in the dictionary. Reasoning that such a book must contain all the terms a particular culture uses to describe its members, he combed through, finding about 18,000 pertinent words, many of which refer to traits, or "generalized and personalized determining tendencies—consistent and stable modes of an individual's adjustment to his environment." (Linguistically minded personality theorist Michael Stone, a professor of psychiatry at Columbia University's College of Physicians and Surgeons, also dug through the dictionary for personality descriptors and found much the same 500 to 700 words, mostly negative ones, in Chinese, Japanese, German, and some of the fifteen other languages he knows.) To make such complexity practical, psychologists began the process of reducing overlapping terms—garrulous and friendly, say, or hostile and angry—to personality's least common denominators. Their successors are still searching for the ideal "model," or formula of the basic qualities that all human beings share in different measures, that can systematically describe each of us in the same terms.

The author of the most enduring model and the father of the modern biological study of personality is psychologist Hans Eysenck, who conducts his research from the Institute of Psychiatry in London. "We've done our studies in thirty-six countries," he says, "and everywhere we find the same few ways in which behavior can differ." Eysenck's research gives a statistical base to Gold's tragic view of a species exquisitely attuned to threat. To varying degrees, he finds, all people express fear, which helps us avoid danger (Eysenck's "neuroticism," or N); aggression, which enables us to fight it ("psychoticism," or P); and extroversion (E), or an interest in the world outside ourselves, which enables us to handle it with equanimity.

Newer personality models have much in common with the venerable PEN, the acronym Eysenck uses. The "five factor" model—nicknamed "the Big Five" by psychologist L. R. Goldberg—has been advanced in several versions, notably that of psychologists Paul Costa and Robert McCrae at the National Institute on Aging, whose traits are extroversion, agreeableness, conscientiousness, neuroticism, and openness to experience. As in other models, a low score on these characteristics implies their opposites, namely introversion, antagonism, undirectedness, emotional stability, and closed-mindedness. For a more detailed description, each of the Big Five traits breaks down into six secondary ones. Neuroticism's attributes, for example, are calm versus worried; even-tempered versus temperamental; self-satisfied versus self-pitying; comfortable versus self-conscious; unemotional versus emotional; and hardy versus vulnerable.

The model for what personality psychologist and member of the celebrated University of Minnesota's Center for Twin and Adoption Research Auke Tellegen calls "human emotional temperament" consists of three supertraits. "Positive emotionality" measures what he describes as a person's "threshold for joy." Tellegen's second factor, which he calls "constraint," indicates "the proportion of the world that a person feels is off limits." An unhappy confluence of inordinate aggression, anxiety, and alienation, Tellegen's third trait of "negative emotionality" was wonderfully expressed by Evelyn Waugh and his forebears. Waugh's biographer Selina Hastings reports that the writer's paternal grandfather, known to his familiars as "the Brute," once applied his cane to a wasp that had lighted on his wife's forehead; if the creature had not been about to sting her, it changed its plans. Waugh himself lurched from blue funks to terrific tantrums during which he insulted strangers, old friends, and his own children, whom he dismissed as "defective adults."

In attempting to sort the mostly inherited aspects of personality from the mostly learned, psychiatrist and behavioral geneticist C. Robert Cloninger of the Washington University School of Medicine, has devised a model consisting of four traits rooted in temperament—the largely genetic tendencies of novelty seeking, harm avoidance, reward dependence, and persistence—and three rising mostly from acquired goals and values—the character traits of self-directedness, cooperativeness, and self-transcendence. To him, one's score in what has traditionally been called neuroticism depends on a combination of temperament—particularly being highly harm-avoidant—and character—being self-directed and otherwise mature or not. Similarly, what's usually described as extroversion is, in Cloninger's terminology, a matter of low harm avoidance and high reward dependence and novelty seeking.

To an innocent civilian on the bloody theory-of-personality battlefield, the leading models overlap quite a lot. Extroversion and neuroticism, for example, are much like positive and negative emotionality; conscientiousness resembles constraint; low scores on conscientiousness and agreeableness correspond to psychoticism. Despite such apparent grounds for consensus, however, Eysenck, expressing what seems to be a major characteristic of personality theorists, says, "There's only one useful model—mine."

Unfortunately, there's no empirical way to prove any personality theory to be right or wrong. As Hippocrates intuited, different dispositions speak of very different humors, or neurochemistries. Scientists, however, are just beginning to develop the means to eavesdrop on how the whisperings of neurotransmitters are translated into modulations of behavior and individuality. With one exception, the links between particular traits and transmitter levels remain tentative, partly because the former can involve neurochemical choruses, not just solos. Economists have the gold standard and chemists the periodic table, but psychologists, lacking similarly objective criteria, resemble the blind men who must try to identify the elephant by feeling its parts. They can document people's behavioral tendencies, arrange them on a spectrum, and estimate their heritability, but have only bits and pieces of the information about genes and other biological elements that underlie them—and a truly scientific model of personality. In 1996, an international group of scientists reported in *Nature Genetics* their discovery of the first specific link between a gene and a behavioral trait. Because of a particular genetic variation, they found, the brains of people attracted to novelty and excitement have a slightly longer receptor for the neurotransmitter dopamine, which is associated with the ability to experience pleasure and seek sensation. The finding is far from a complete explanation of the trait of novelty seeking—several other genes are also probably involved, in addition to powerful, if still undetermined, environmental influences—yet it is an important milestone in the study of temperament: the proof that clear, objective links between genes and behavior are there to be found. Even when scientists are armed with many more such pieces of data, however, the task of parsing personality will remain complex. For example, as David Lykken observes, "When they grow up, many inhibited kids will have low scores in neuroticism because they have learned how to avoid stressors. As adults, bold kids may have elevated scores because they skate on the edge and experience a lot of stress."

In many years of methodical study, Harvard developmental psychologist Jerome Kagan, whose name is closely identified with temperament research, has established some facts about the physiology, behavioral expression, and heritability of the single trait of inhibition, or aversion to novelty. According to his rigorous physiological as well as behavioral criteria, no more than 20 percent of people are "shy" because of a temperamental bias. However, about 40 percent of those who complete theorists' personality questionnaires describe themselves that way. Having spent a long time establishing a few things about one trait, Kagan insists that research must combine behavioral and physiological

tests with the paper-and-pencil sort, and compares terms such as introversion and extroversion to "saying 'heart trouble' or 'stroke,' as opposed to a cardiologist's diagnosis." Until technology and methodology
improve, the principle that who we are involves our biological as well as
social heritage mostly rests on statistical data from behavioral geneticists
and longitudinal studies of people's lives. Much of the information that
has been gleaned concerns the inhibited and bold temperaments.

Some of the most important insights into temperament come from
classical nature-nurture experiments in which generations of animals
are selectively bred for particular traits and then closely monitored in
different settings. Research psychologists Stephen Suomi, of the National Institute for Child Health and Human Development, and J. D.
Higley, of the National Institute on Alcohol Abuse, study rhesus monkeys' physiology and behavior to better understand that of their own
species. After producing strains that particularly express the anxious,
uninhibited, and aggressive temperaments, they track the animals' neurobiology through the levels of neurotransmitter metabolites, or end
products, in their cerebrospinal fluid. Discussing the two major behavioral tendencies that, with a rare and wonderful economy, he calls the
"North and South of temperament," Higley says, "within a few minutes of observing a group of primates, you identify the solitary, inhibited one who peeks at you around a corner and the bold one who leaves
the group and approaches in hopes of a treat. Our monkeys show big
differences in these traits, which tend to be the most enduring ones in
humans as well."

Like hot and cold or hard and soft, fearful and bold seem like extremes on a single spectrum. By the same light, punishment can be opposed to reward, and Eysenck's research associate Jeffrey Grey has
found that the inhibited are more responsive to the former and the uninhibited (including Higley's bold monkeys) to the latter. Long before
temperament returned to fashion, David Lykken, a principal member
of the University of Minnesota's twin research team and one of personality psychology's best bullshit detectors, was a voice crying out
from Midwestern academe's "dust bowl of empiricism" for the power

of innate traits. Not one to limit his subjects to the usual college fresh-
men, Lykken tested a group of prison inmates and gained an insight
into the neuropsychology of boldness that presaged Grey's. Unlike
other convicts, he found, the boldest of the bold, whom psychologists
call psychopaths, didn't readily learn how to escape an avoidable electric shock. They felt it all right, but they didn't fear it enough to bother
figuring out how to miss it next time.

At first glance, even animal research on the chemistry of inhibition
and boldness seems to support the idea that they're opposites. Nervous
monkeys have high levels of norepinephrine, as do their similarly fretful relatives, while bold monkeys and their kin have low levels of the
same transmitter. It makes intuitive sense that the inhibited have lots of
something the uninhibited have little of, but this explanation is too
simplistic for either Suomi or Kagan. Their experience with primates
and children has convinced them that, although other ingredients of
the formula may still elude detection, boldness includes, but is more
than, not being anxious, especially at its extremes. Although the inhibited and uninhibited (who account for about 10 and 20 percent of the
primate population, respectively, and 15 and 20 percent of the human
one) can be arranged on continua of stress responsivity and norepinephrine levels, Kagan equates the exercise and its implication with
"putting Mozart on a spectrum with your daughter who's taking piano
lessons. He's just better in music?"

Because he works with babies and small children, Kagan can't examine temperamental neurophysiology as directly as Suomi can. He infers
something of how his subjects' nervous systems operate, however, by
periodically exposing them to mild stressors—noise, sour tastes, unfamiliar objects and people, and even a mother's frown—and measuring
their behavioral and physiological responses, such as heart rate and
blood pressure. Regarding infancy, he has proved what every parent of
more than one child knows: each baby is born with a characteristic
mood, activity level, and style of responding to stimuli. By the second
and third years of life, he has found, some clearly express one of the two
great extremes that Higley calls temperament's North and South. The
children who are plainly inhibited differ from other youngsters in many
ways. Physiologically, they have greater incidences of allergies and con-

stipation, for example, and higher heart rates; even at four months old, they're highly reactive. They tend not to be firstborns and to have blue eyes and narrow faces; slightly more of them are girls. Psychologically, Kagan's so-called shy kids are constrained and fretful and have more unusual fears—say, of kidnapping. Even their monsters are unorthodox, as were those of the hypersensitive Edgar Allan Poe: "Take thy beak from out my heart, and take thy form from off my door! / Quoth the raven, 'Nevermore!' "

To the emerging portraits of childhood dispositions, University of Maryland psychologist Nathan Fox has added two important neurological details. Inhibited children show characteristic patterns of right-brain activity, as measured by electroencephalogram, while bold children show left-brain patterns. Either type of EEG, he says, is "a very good fingerprint of a particular temperament. Some children are, by and large, across many situations, very fearful. Others, no matter what you throw at them, are happy-go-lucky and approach the world with gusto." Both natures, says Kagan, are rooted in genes that bring about neurochemical differences in the functioning of the amygdala and its connections. Because this brain structure assigns emotion to experience, the same loud noise can be instantaneously interpreted as scary by one sort of child and interesting by the other.

The stimuli that jangle sensitive nerves barely stir those of the uninhibited. Most, particularly the very boldest, are boys. Their manner is energetic and spontaneous, and their physiological hallmark is their very low heart rate. In *The Right Stuff,* Tom Wolfe's account of the first NASA astronauts—really fighter pilots—this metabolic measure figured as an important gauge of machismo. At the liftoff of *Friendship 7,* the pulse rate of Lieutenant Colonel John Glenn, a Marine veteran of 149 combat missions and the first American to orbit the earth, rose only to a hypercool 110 beats per minute, in contrast to the 139- and 170-beat readings of the two other bold Americans who had preceded him in space flight. Illustrating Kagan's behavioral criterion of frisky joie de vivre, on routine squadron maneuvers Glenn liked to sneak up beside other jets in the formation going about 600 miles per hour and nudge their wings with the tip of his. In one of those planes was baseball legend Ted Williams, no shrinking violet himself, who said of Glenn, "That man is crazy."

Once as forceful a spokesman for nurture's formative power as he now is for nature's, Kagan is deeply versed in both scientific literatures, yet engagingly *haimish* in person. To the many parents in the trenches concerned by their offspring's shyness, brashness, or other untoward tendencies, he offers a few pragmatic insights gleaned from his research. First, because children are born with different temperaments, new mothers and fathers shouldn't assume they're mishandling a baby who's neither pleased nor pleasing. "Maybe they are," he says, "but not necessarily." Second, a child's disposition is malleable. "Parents shouldn't say, 'God gave me this type of kid—that's it!'" says Kagan. "They should acknowledge that some things are harder for the child to control—historically, that's not an unimportant change—but assume he can still exert *some* control." Finally, "remember that in a complex society like ours, each temperamental type can find its adaptive niche."

Like all temperaments, the reactive and bold have drawbacks and advantages that suit each better to some environmental niches than to others. In certain settings, a marked sensitivity to things not only menacing but merely novel can make life an uphill affair. At least one reactive person is known to have projected this aversion to the unfamiliar into the afterlife. During preparations for the great public celebration of her diamond jubilee, Queen Victoria heard that a statue of a predecessor, Queen Anne, was scheduled to be moved from its accustomed position. "Most certainly not!" said Her Majesty. "Why, it might some day be suggested that my statue should be moved, which I should much dislike." Few of us would wish to be *that* sensitive, yet, in an environment filled with predators or their modern equivalents, having some fussbudgets and worriers around is adaptive for the group. That's why they remain so well represented in the gene pool. Then too, those who don't live fast are less apt to die young: multitudinous trials and complaints notwithstanding, Victoria made it to eighty-two at a time when that was indeed a great age. Hans Eysenck, an iconoclast who scores zero on his own test of inhibition, says that his wife accuses him of not being afraid enough: "She is exceedingly careful, driving defensively and letting others get ahead. From the point of view of survival, her style is much better."

Survival aside, the glory of the disposition that stops to consider stimuli rather than rushing to engage with them is its long association with intellectual and artistic achievement. Neither $e = mc^2$ nor *Paradise Lost* was dashed off by a party animal. In *The Writers' Chapbook*, George Plimpton provides some amusing examples of the kinds of environmental buffering and modification required by the finely tuned sensibilities responsible for much high thinking. When the cloisters of a Trappist monastery didn't prove quiet enough, Thomas Merton moved into a hermitage on the grounds; in order to write, Erskine Caldwell sometimes took the night boat from Boston to New York; Truman Capote couldn't bear to see three cigarette butts in an ashtray or two nuns on a plane; Rebecca West couldn't "remember things" unless she held a pencil. Even among sensitive children, experience is elaborate and nuanced. Their naturally high levels of arousal incline reactive seven-year-olds to excel at what Nathan Fox calls executive functioning. When these children are asked how kids who have only one toy should share it, they offer strategies such as "Alphabetize their last names, and let the person closest to A go first." Putting theory into practice is hard for them, however, because their reflective natures and complex schemes are unsuited to the heterogeneous rigors of the schoolyard. Nonetheless, most don't end up with social and psychological problems, and the most fortunate find niches where their sensitive temperament is an advantage, becoming scientists, say, or poets.

The ranks of Nobel and Pulitzer prize winners may be filled with sensitive souls who think beautiful thoughts, but from day to day the bold have more fun. Stress that strains or even breaks high-strung spirits merely stimulates theirs. Legend has it that Jane Digby, a famous equestrian, met a dashing sheik, who may or may not have been her husband Medjuel, while trying to buy a supposedly untrainable horse from him. After she broke it, the Bedouin said his price could not be paid in coin. Jane agreed to be his if he would put away his wives; should the arrangement turn out to be satisfactory, she said, it could be renewed in three years. In the less exotic environs of Minnesota, Lykken recalls a trapper and bush pilot from the north country "whose adventures made my jaw drop. He didn't brag, but just talked about these things he did that were so *interesting*, like going to a bear den and pulling out the cubs."

The adaptive potential of steel nerves is summed up by a line of dialogue that invariably figures in action movies: "It's a tough job, but someone's got to do it." Assessing the great naval battle of Copenhagen, Lord Nelson might have been talking about his scandalous affair with Lady Emma Hamilton: "It is warm work." Ulysses S. Grant's military secretary wrote that the general "was not excited by [danger], but was simply indifferent to it, was calm when others were aroused. I have often seen him sit erect in his saddle when everyone else instinctively shrank as a shell burst in the neighborhood." A Union soldier put it thus: "Ulysses don't scare worth a damn."

Far from where literal sparks fly, in boardrooms and political arenas, the fearless can manifest sangfroid in situations fraught with other dangers. Remarking on Grant's laid-back mien in "the greatest moral emergencies," his aide recorded that at Lee's surrender the Union commander was "as impassive as on the most ordinary occasion." John F. Kennedy's biographer Richard Reeves quotes Susan Mary Alsop's comment after throwing a dinner party attended by JFK during the still-secret Cuban missile crisis: "Sitting next to Jack tonight was like sitting next to the engine of a very powerful automobile. He was enjoying himself greatly in some way that I don't understand." According to diplomat George Ball, what JFK wanted from the presidency was "never to be bored, never to be frustrated, never to be alone." The anecdotal record suggests that, marriage notwithstanding, Kennedy's credo of boldness extended to his private life.

Having a low-idling nervous system that reads "threat" as "thrill" means you live fast, but you might indeed die young—Nelson was killed at forty-seven and JKF at forty-six—and otherwise cause grief. Few of us can understand why someone would zealously compete to become a fighter pilot, considering that one in five will have to eject from a moribund plane and one in twelve will die on the job. The pedal-to-the-metal temperament has additional drawbacks, particularly where other people are concerned. The bold may be fun, but they can be insensitive. Among fighter pilots, for example, nine out of ten separations and divorces are initiated by wives. In *The Pattons,* a history of the long line of Virginia heroes who fought in the Revolutionary, Indian, and Civil wars, Robert Patton, the grandson of Old Blood and Guts, observes that George's extraordinary ability to lead was largely based on what the general called "visible personality." Dressed to the nines and trailing clouds of testosterone, Patton simply dazzled his troops into doing more than they or anyone else thought possible. Unfortunately, on the smaller stage of his home the great soldier was no less "compulsively driven to emote, dazzle, dominate—in short, to exhibit visible personality in everything he did . . . generally sucking the life out of anyone venturing too near, like a black hole inhaling a star." George Patton made it to sixty, when he broke his neck in a car accident.

Society needs some Edgar Allan Poes and U. S. Grants, but too many wouldn't serve the commonweal. "That's how biology works," says J. D. Higley. "Not too many temperaments are extreme." The one that seems most that way is the disposition Hippocrates called choleric and his modern successors call irritable, impulsive, or explosive. If inhibition and boldness are the North and South of temperament, Higley says, "irritability and equanimity are the East and West."

An offspring of Cry Havoc and One Tough Cookie, Slick Willy is the second bull terrier fortunate enough to belong to David Lykken, who takes a keen interest in temperament, particularly the go-ahead-make-my-day sort. To produce Willy's, the English bulldog was deliberately crossed with the English terrier almost two hundred years ago. The nature of the resulting fearless, tenacious fighting machine requires a different sort of nurture than that of dogs bred for complaisance. When Willy can't resist chomping his powerful jaws through a gallon jug of bleach or taking a few extra laps before responding to a summons, Lykken mostly just grumbles, reserving sterner measures for more serious infractions. Harshness would render the feisty animal vicious; permissiveness or neglect, uncontrollable. Willy's good behavior depends on an appreciation of his innate disposition and a judicious balance of carrot and stick.

A certain similarity between dogs and their masters is often remarked. Considering his own temperament, it's not surprising that Richard Burton was so fond of his bull terrier bitch, whose body bore almost as many battle scars as his own, that he took her all the way from England to India. In a postindustrial culture that claims a workaholic

Mr. Nice Guy as its temperamental ideal, the heroic spirit that animated Ruffian Dick and his swashbuckling kind has fallen from favor. Time and technology have shrunk the number of acceptable outlets for the daring, aggressive nature that conquers the unknown and welcomes the fray, to the point that it has come to be associated primarily with criminals, survivalists, and the mentally deranged. This saddens but doesn't surprise Lykken, whose work, some of it conducted behind bars, convinces him that "the psychopath and the hero are twigs on the same genetic branch."

Although irritability—the tendency to be annoyed—isn't the same as aggressiveness—the tendency to attack—the two are far from incompatible. As Richmond Lattimore observed, the tragedy of Achilleus, the supreme warrior, was that his will was "disturbed by anger." Both the dueling and diplomatic records show that the touchy Burton shared the hero's psychic heel. Just as boldness is more than the simple lack of fear, however, aggressiveness is more than just a short fuse; because of its complexity and impact on society, this inclination warrants special consideration at a later point.

The irritable temperament is the hardest to define, says psychiatrist Hagop Akiskal, but "it's the easiest to see." We pay to do so whenever we watch a movie actor who specializes in portraying restless characters who "express intense, unmodulated emotion that, seemingly out of nowhere, comes on like an avalanche, stirring everyone," he says. "That's what temperament does, and the irritable one does it most intensely." Akiskal mentions no names. In 1994, however, Jack Nicholson was charged with misdemeanor assault and vandalism for taking a golf club to a car that had allegedly cut him off in traffic. In reporting the incident, *Time* noted that the actor was "known for his onscreen volatility."

Deploring the prissy tendency to look askance at the hot-blooded nature, Akiskal says that although "civilized Western behavior assumes its relative absence, its impact is very useful in some circumstances, say, in getting a point across quickly. Many people can't express such vivid feelings because they just don't *have* them—they lack the intensity that the choleric supply." Although this disposition has the most pathological potential, it's the least studied, Akiskal says, partly because "it evokes a lot of negative feelings in people."

Despite its poor image in the modern world, Hippocrates' choleric temperament is, like all dispositions, neither good nor bad per se. General H. Norman Schwarzkopf's family may not relish playing board games with him, but in certain settings Stormin' Norman is the ideal companion. In the drawing room, too, the curled lip has adaptive potential. Of her cousin Burton, Georgiana Stisted wrote, "As he was not merely a handsome but a powerful magnetic man, women fell in love with him by the score. . . . It is certain that many of his amours were not originated by himself." Even when dealing with bureaucracy, "aggressiveness can be beneficial if it helps you pound the table and say, 'I want justice!' " says Higley. "If a society wants variability, which is what ours espouses, it needs different kinds of individuals."

From many scientific perspectives, it seems that, just as red, yellow, and blue are the primary colors from which all others are made, anxiety, irritability, and gusto are temperament's basic emotional tones. Although a few of us are so colored by a single one that we can simply be described as bold, say, or nervous, most of us cannot.

Some temperaments are shades, or permutations, of a primary one. In a person who has the obsessive variation on the reactive disposition, for example, the neural arousal system is riveted by what most of us would consider an occasional notion or pursuit. As a result, he vents his obsessions—insistent thoughts—through compulsions—actions. Reflecting on Benny Goodman's notorious lack of manners, a wise musician from his orchestra observed that the celebrated bandleader and clarinetist, who practiced his instrument eight hours a day, wasn't a bad guy; it was just that Benny didn't think about people but about fingering. The dark side of this extreme, driven nature is obvious, but the world is immeasurably richer for the work of the many geniuses, collectors, and artists impelled by it.

To promote our own and the species' adaptivity and flexibility, however, most temperaments are subtler shades of green, orange, and violet, blended from various psychobiological pigments. One of the great shortcomings of temperament research, in fact, is that, so far, it's largely a science of extremes—of reclusive Emily Dickinsons and never-alone JFKs. Much less is known about the vast population in between, whose behavior can't be labeled simply as shy or bold or explained by saying that they have half, or twice, as much of some biological juice, say, as those at the ends of the spectrum. For that matter, even an extreme disposition like Richard Burton's shimmers with many hues. The man was a walking definition of irritability and aggressiveness, as even his favorite sports, boxing and fencing, suggest. Yet his aura of rolling thunder also derived from a deep streak of melancholy that he regularly exacerbated with alcohol. Describing his haunting glance, an obituary reported that "When it [his eye] looks at you, it looks through you, and then, glazing over, seems to see something behind you. Richard Burton is the only man not a Gypsy with that peculiarity."

Just as Burton could subject his turbulent nature to his huge intellect often enough to accomplish great things, including masterpieces of sensitive scholarship, many of us balance a temperamental weakness with a strength. Some of those whose dispositions are reactive have an easier time than others, for example, because they're not socially inhibited or shy. Although fearfulness is linked to norepinephrine, what Higley calls the "nerdiness" of the loner who can't get along goes with a low level of the transmitter serotonin. An individual could have a high level of norepinephrine and so be nervous, yet also have a high level of serotonin and thus be sociable. The friendly worrywart Higley evokes is a familiar character, from Aunt Pittypat in *Gone with the Wind* to Oblomov in the eponymous Russian novel. Medical literature shows that the capacity of such people to enlist support, which Monica had even as a very frail baby but many of the anxious don't, buffers them considerably from the effects of stress. That Queen Victoria long benefited from this protective dynamic is suggested by the drawn-out reclusive depression into which she fell, much to the annoyance of her subjects, after the untimely death of her beloved Albert; he had been her partner not only in marriage but in running the family business of Empire, which they did from facing desks. Even if someone is born high-strung, says Higley, "if he's also wired to elicit and respond to social stimuli, he may get a lot of support that helps get him through that rotten, worried feeling inside." Innate emotional vulnerability notwithstanding, given enough time and support, reactive individuals can "in their quiet, introverted way, acquire the skills that allow them to be resolute and to endure anxiety and pain," says Philip Gold. "Such a person might look timid but be like a rock. If the fate of the Western world depended on someone not giving up a secret under torture, I'd rather put it in such hands than in those of a seemingly bold person who hadn't had to learn those complex skills."

As Auke Tellegen enjoys pointing out, "if our nervous systems were made of spun glass, our species would never have evolved." With extremely rare exceptions, such as psychopaths who suffer from brain abnormalities, people of any temperament, given the right experiential foundations, can succeed. Indeed, our wealth of dispositions is our species' glory, enriching the human experience with the discoveries of bold Marco Polos, the creations of sensitive Frédéric Chopins, the exploits of Alexander, and all the accomplishments in between.

CHAPTER 3

YOU HAVE TO SUFFER IF YOU WANT TO SING THE BLUES

Since antiquity, the sensitive disposition that Hippocrates called melancholic has been linked to intellectual and aesthetic achievement. Not only the pantheon of painters and poets, novelists and composers, but also the upper echelons of business and government include disproportionate numbers of two lively variations on this reactive nature. Unlike those whose temperaments are primarily depressive, individuals described as either cyclothymic or hyperthymic alternate between high and low levels of energy and mood. Because the hyperthymic, who make up somewhere between 1 and 6 percent of the population, are up far more often than down, their hard-driving, power-charged, and mostly under-control temperament confers a certain adaptive advantage in American culture.

While he was a professor of psychiatry at the University of Tennessee, innovative mood researcher Hagop Akiskal, along with psychologist Kareen Akiskal, studied an unusual group of subjects: Memphis blues musicians. Along with creativity, he found, the artists were characterized by an extremely high level of energy that literally made their days longer. "These people don't tire easily," says Akiskal. "Many sleep only two hours, and most require less than six." The inclination to burn the candle at both ends is as well represented in the halls of power as in the musical sort. Again, he mentions no names, but the slides of bluesmen that accompany Akiskal's lecture on the hyperthymic temperament include one of a certain vigorous southern politician playing his saxophone. The image conjures up other high-octane chief executives, such as Franklin Delano Roosevelt, known for his high energy level, low boredom threshold, and general appetite for life. "These people exist," says Akiskal, "and they run the world."

Certainly, having optimism, energy, charm, versatility, intellectual mobility, and overconfidence "woven into one's habitual self," as Akiskal says, is adaptive in Washington and other capitals. The fulcrum of the hyperthymic nature—a general feeling of indefatigability—is almost essential for a presidential candidate, who must eat at least two hundred rubber-chicken dinners per year. It's said that upon reading that great men never sleep for more than five hours a night, the young Bill Clinton adopted the practice immediately. As is often the way with temperamental inclinations, because sleep deprivation causes neurochemical shifts that feed hyper states—and libido—staying awake and busy only feeds an innate bias toward action. The most successful leaders not only walk the walk but talk the talk. Another hyperthymic hallmark, which Akiskal describes as a talent for "moving others to a common cause," is also a tremendous political asset. However, he adds, such eloquence can be a double-edged sword, "because the cause advanced may not always be lofty. As always, it's not the temperament that's good or bad, but what one does with it."

Like all dispositions, the get-it-on hyperthymic type has inherent drawbacks as well as strengths. Evidence suggests that the hyperthymic tend to have shorter lives, for example, less because they keep up a killing pace than because of their risk taking and accidents. "They may die younger," says Akiskal, "but in fifty years, they may live ten times more than the average person." Then too, the inclination for madder music and stronger wine can be grueling for those on the receiving end. "These people can put us in an uncomfortable state with their restlessness, excessive need for social life, provocativeness, and capricious temper," says Akiskal. "They tend to build castles in the air, squander money, and scheme. And their impulsivity and love of sex and pleasure get them into trouble. They have many affairs or marriages, and those who seek treatment are usually dragged there by fed-up spouses." Despite the literal and figurative aches and pains they cause themselves and others, he says, hyperthymic people are generally well tolerated because "they create so much opportunity for others."

Demonstrating the biological kinship between normal temperaments and disorders, gifts and symptoms, the far end of the hyperthymic spectrum shades into pathology. As the song says, "You have to suffer if you want to sing the blues," and some of those who share the Memphis musicians' generative disposition endure brief, intermittent periods of true depression and mild mania. "The significant others of some such individuals report that there are periods when they wake up wanting to kill themselves, whether for a few minutes or hours," says Akiskal. "These persons also have spells of fatigue, when they may be admitted to a hospital and given vitamins. Because such states are inconsistent with their self-image, lethargy and exhaustion are ominous developments that raise the risk of suicide." At the furthest extremes of the hyperthymic and cyclothymic temperaments lie the illnesses of manic depression and cyclothymia. The latter's short, alternating ups and downs are less marked, but both disorders respond to lithium and run in the same families prone to mood problems.

In the winter of 1993, a thousand Wall Streeters, many of them tearful top executives, gathered for the funeral of Michael Molloy, stockbroker extraordinaire, described by one mourner as "a comet of a man." Handsome, charismatic, friend of stars, and a gifted athlete, the forty-nine-year-old had been half of the Merrill Lynch team that sold the most high-yield bonds during the 1980s boom. Molloy not only did well but also did good. Along with making a fortune, he helped start a company that provides low-cost loans for needy college students; his housekeeper was a homeless woman he took off the street. More than his accomplishments, however, friends admired the valor that made them possible. When Merrill Lynch hired Molloy, it was with the understanding that the manic depression aggravated by alcoholism from which he suffered would render him unable to work for up to four months a year. The prevailing tone of his obituaries was wonderment that he had achieved so much despite myriad torments, from severe shakes to bouts of erratic behavior and delusion that required hospitalization. What happened on his final December day remains unclear, but evidently, in the thrall of mania and possibly drink, Molloy abandoned his stalled car on a dirt road in the Adirondacks. He was found dead of hypothermia in a snowbank several miles away.

"Make us nobly wild, not mad," wrote Robert Herrick in a tribute to his fellow poet Ben Jonson, alluding to what has long been understood to be a fine line at times. Although Michael Molloy was not a writer, his life, like those of many artists, was a struggle to walk the tightrope that stretches between glorious peaks and over valleys of despond. Among painters and poets, musicians and dancers, Akiskal thinks that the cyclothymic and hyperthymic dispositions may serve as "substrates for certain types of artistic ability." In studies conducted with Kareen Akiskal, he found that creativity wasn't linked to manic-depressive or any other mental illness per se, but to an underlying temperament whose "down" spells foster contemplation and reflection and "up" intervals bring the increased energy, ambition, and mental puissance that drive hard work. "Some people have more ups and others more downs—the more interesting and commoner type," says Akiskal. "Many have never seen a doctor and do quite well."

To Johns Hopkins psychologist Kay Jamison, author of *Touched with Fire* and an authority on manic depression, the most intriguing thing about the artistic temperament, which she identifies as cyclothymic, is that, "like a chameleon, it can express itself in variable ways. This temperament is to have many temperaments. A person can be mildly depressed, highly introspective, and sensitive as a Thoroughbred, and then, a few days or months later, very extroverted, outgoing, and engaged with the world. Introversion and extroversion may apply to most people, but some have both those temperaments wrapped up in one."

To those whose dispositions aren't extreme in any way, much less several, the world looks pretty much the same from day to day. To someone who has a highly variable nature, how it seems depends on whether he's seeing it plain, through the rose-colored glasses of mania, or through a gray scrim of depression. For that matter, says Jamison, who has written of her own experience of manic depression in *An Unquiet Mind,* "those three modes just convey a schematic, cartoonish sense of what are actually a hundred thousand gradations. It's not that such a person experiences two or three different 'me's,' but that, in an amphibious way, he keeps going in and out of a set of moods." Being on such intimate terms with ambiguity and complexity, inconsistency and chaos is a highly adaptive advantage in complicated, shimmering intellectual environments. "Much of what the artist, and even the great wit, is about is the reconciliation of opposite states and the coexistence of opposite thoughts," says Jamison. "To such people, someone who thinks in a very linear way is strange."

According to T. S. Eliot, "Poetry is not a turning loose of emotion, but an escape from emotion. It is not the expression of personality, but an escape from personality." Despite novels and movies like *The Agony and the Ecstasy* and *Lust for Life,* which attempt to portray the experience of Michelangelo and van Gogh, extraordinary artistic achievement needn't occur in a state of near-divine frenzy. In fact, says Jamison, ecstatic highs have their drawbacks: "Someone might come up with a lot of ideas then, but they might be terrible. And how reflective is someone who's chronically hypomanic? Is this person going to write great poetry?" Although someone who's deeply depressed doesn't do much of anything, someone who's only mildly so can experience "a drive to work, as if there were something therapeutic about it" she says. "This doesn't get talked about much, but it's very common to be creative in 'mixed' moods in which thoughts are fluent and rapid, but deeply morbid in content. Van Gogh, for example, often painted in a highly turbulent, perturbed state."

The tremendous variability of creative states means that a work of art is an unreliable gauge of the artist's mood when he made it. "You can look at his life and say he had certain affective propensities," says Jamison, "but you can't assume that Thomas Hardy, say, was severely depressed when he wrote his great dark passages. Perhaps Handel was deeply melancholic when he composed parts of *Messiah* that sound so joyous."

Scientists don't yet know exactly what transpires in such a temperamentally biased brain to effect alternately exalted and dejected mood-thought modes, but they seem to be looking in the right place. More than twenty studies of manic-depressive subjects show impairment in the brain's right hemisphere—its more emotional, aesthetic, creative half. In the foreseeable future, advances in scanning technology will allow scientists to watch a supercharged brain go through its paces during various tasks. For now, they assume that whatever happens during a burst of creativity involves a change in the associational processes in the cerebral cortex involved in learning, memory, thought, and language. Where artistry is concerned, it's interesting that electrical stimulation to this part of the brain can cause memorylike visual or auditory experiences, sometimes highly emotional ones.

Brain imagery has already illustrated one aspect of the creative process: the indivisibility of ideas and feelings. PET scans made during the highs of "rapid cyclers," who are manic for a day, then depressed for a day, show the whole brain lit up in red and yellow; during their lows, it's appropriately all blues. The vivid pictures support Jamison's conviction that it's a big mistake to exaggerate the autonomy of thought and emotion or to suggest that one necessarily precedes the other in the creative process. For that matter, she says, "whether certain states or symptoms are listed as cognitive or emotional is extremely arbitrary. Grandiosity, which is one of the most important aspects of a certain kind of creativity, is both a mood and a style of thought. Reflectiveness, recklessness, and obsessiveness in thought are clearly mood bound. When you get that postviral what's-the-point-of-life depression—and everyone has a hundred thousand reasons, from their marriage to their job, to be discontented—your enthusiasm is totally bound up with your energy. It's all in a ball together."

Although artistic temperament has sometimes excused the excesses of Byron, van Gogh, Shelley, Poe, Coleridge, and some of their kindred spirits, business and political leaders can't invoke such poetic license. They're supposed to be well-balanced nice-but-tough guys, but very often, says Jamison, "the people who get elected and run companies are very irritable, impatient sorts who may be able to control themselves a little better than artists because they've been socialized differently. People who succeed often have short fuses and a quick look in their eyes."

Whether artists or entrepreneurs, about 20 percent of those who suffer from manic depression, the illness Jamison links to a creative temperament, commit suicide. "Just as fire burns as well as lights, the thing that causes these people to be inventive, vital, and intense carries the seeds of destruction," says Jamison. "That's the paradox—a huge capacity not just for life but death. Wrapping those two things together is what makes some people unique."

From suicidal geniuses such as Ernest Hemingway and Michael Molloy to the merely moody, many creative people walk on the wild side and suffer the consequences. Yet few of them, or the legion who benefit from their heightened perceptions, would eliminate their dark clouds at the cost of the silver linings. As Akiskal says, "Not having any temperament at all is the best protection against depression." When a sensitive disposition feeds illness, sophisticated clinicians struggle to find just the right combination and potency of drugs to arrest the debilitating symptoms with minimal dampening of powers. In the course of treating and researching mood disorders, Akiskal has become increasingly "fascinated with how a patient's biography, from his aspirations to his vocation, interacts with his basic personality in producing well-being. Maximizing his ability to use his own temperamental assets can help protect him from illness."

Scientists' discussions of the artistic temperament inevitably include the upcoming completion of the Human Genome Project, when chilling debates about the paradoxical heritage of creativity and depressive illness will ensue. As soon as genes can be doctored, much artistry could be eliminated along with illness. During such a conversation, Jamison describes a cartoon. The caption reads: "What if Prozac had been available in the nineteenth century?" The illustration shows Edgar Allan Poe "looking at the raven with a sappy smile on his face and saying 'Hello, birdie.' My bias is for diversity, dark horses, and a variety of thought and experience. The whole homogenization process drives me wild. I may not want my relatives to go through manic-depressive illness, but I may want a certain percentage of other people to do things that most others don't and go through the pain. There's a real trade-off in individual cost and a societal goal that's adaptive for the species."

Tales of famous artists and leaders underscore the connection between intellectual achievement and an artistic temperament, but that's not the only link between a melancholic disposition and the life of the mind.

Prominent among postindustrial society's newest elite are grown-up versions of "Kagan kids": shy, sensitive children who, even in second grade, shine at "executive functioning." Although Microsoft's Bill Gates is the Colossus of the computer industry, some of his peers are similarly temperamentally poised to help dominate it.

After a withdrawn, friendless childhood and stint in the military as a conscientious objector, software titan and art patron Peter Norton spent several years in a Buddhist monastery in the Bay Area. In describing for an interviewer his decision to abandon that particular form of the contemplative life, he drew an important temperamental distinction: "There are two ways to leave something in bad grace. Either you leave saying 'Those rotten bastards!' or you leave by saying 'Oh, what a failure I am!' I am an internalizer, so I left there feeling that I was a failure." That perception was destined to be short-lived. As soon as Norton encountered the IBM-PC, he designed for it a program called UnErase, which restores deleted files, and became a major figure in an industry that has been called, perhaps enviously, the "triumph of the nerds." Despite his hundreds of millions of dollars, high visibility in the museum world, and solid marriage—the couple answered each other's personals ad—Norton remains reserved and perennially out of the loop. As he put it, "I have spent a lot of my life standing just outside a circle. . . . I have never felt at home anywhere. Never."

Who we are partly depends on the environments we've experienced and what we've made of them. Like Peter Norton, many of us have benefited from being in the right place at the right time. Had computers not been invented, Norton has said, he would have been either an anonymous paper shuffler like his father or "an angry cabdriver with a Ph.D." But who we are starts with our own traits, which enable some of us, even in unpropitious settings, to make our own breaks. Certain children, for example, respond to life with a depressed mother by learning to get the stimulation they need on their own, while she is simply *there.* Later in life, child psychiatrist Daniel Stern suspects, they may be especially well adapted to the solitary realms of art or academe.

Those rarefied circles also include certain individuals who from infancy seem to have a nervous system attuned to life's dark side. Their so-called negative affect is an ominous brew made up of various combinations of sad, aggressive, guilty, alienated, dissatisfied, moody, or vindictive feelings. Discussing the brilliant poet who had been hospitalized for severe depression and eventually committed suicide, Jerome Kagan says, "Sylvia Plath had a certain *tone.* That's the hardest thing to change, particularly a very dour one. There are some people who never feel good. You can see it in kids who are dysphoric but try to compensate for it. That's where temperament casts its longest shadow. If we could enter deep into Plath's limbic system, and listen, and feel what she felt . . ."

Like all temperaments, the darkly emotional one has adaptive potential; otherwise, it wouldn't be in such abundant supply. Anyone who has spent some time with a crabby infant knows that such creatures make an impression. Some evidence suggests that in harsh conditions, say, of near starvation, they're the likeliest to survive, and also to fare better developmentally in institutional settings: the squeaky wheel gets the grease, not only in terms of nourishment but also stimulation. Partly for the same reason, psychologist Mary Rothbart, who conducts research on temperament at the University of Oregon, suspects that, later on, some children who were ornery babies attract more of their teachers' attention, and thus do better than average in school.

When the critical tendency that's part of negative emotionality is turned inward in the classroom—or studio—it can inspire star performance. "Much of academic success involves realizing that you've made a mistake or that your solution to a problem doesn't exactly fit," says Rothbart. "That kind of perception is easier if you have a slightly unpleasurable feeling about what you've done that gets you to go back over it. People who don't call up negative feelings easily may be more satisfied with their product."

Seemingly unencumbered by positive emotions, baseball legend Ty Cobb focused exclusively on honing his own spectacular performance. For him, the previously genial national pastime was not just a competitive, but a contact, sport. His sprint down the glory road included techniques such as sharpening his cleats with a file, the better to stomp hapless basemen obstructing home plate. In one unconventionally appealing scene in the movie *Cobb,* the main character basks in his fellow players' loathing and proudly declares, "I was always a prick."

When crowds booed and police patrolled the stadium to protect Cobb from murder, he was delighted, even flattered, courtesy of the social insulation that's yet another layer of a difficult nature's adaptive potential. The nearly inhuman indifference to what others thought that made him so implacable suggests that, from early life, Cobb had not been accustomed to eliciting much in the way of the smiles and praise that can addict more sociable spirits. The less one depends on such pleasant feedback, the better one is equipped to attempt things that are difficult or unpopular.

Although no one wanted to buy a used car from Richard Nixon or appear on his enemies list, Tricky Dick's truculent, suspicious, baleful nature won international respect and the domestic support required to open relations with Communist China in the middle of the Cold War—the kind of feat that often eludes kinder, gentler presidents. Richard Wagner's abrasive, intolerant personality and hate-mongering racism made him the cultural hero of Adolf Hitler and his "new Germany," yet the tragic ecstasy of *The Ring,* sustained for nearly twenty hours, is a magnificent expression of the universal human mysteries of love and death. Ty Cobb is still one of the greatest baseball players who ever lived. In short, nice people may be happier, but they're perhaps not as well represented in the highest professional ranks as those who are chronically dissatisfied with average performance and not terribly concerned about others' feelings.

If a native state of not feeling nice is one factor in being ornery, the feedback such a temperament gets is the other. Not even kindly Mrs. Cratchit could look forward to a visit from the unreconstructed Scrooge, and the reaction he provoked in her only reinforced the consummate creep's own worst tendencies. It's by no means the case, however, that "difficult" individuals must be Scrooges or Cobbs. It has been said that John Lennon's appeal derived from his air of being a bad man trying to be good. Judging by the nation's misty-eyed response to Richard Nixon's death, something of the same ambivalent aura surrounds him. If Lennon had not had the Beatles and Nixon the high-minded Quaker mother whom he greatly loved and admired, the negative affect disastrously expressed in the former's drug problems and the latter's Watergate scandal might have prevented their positive achievements. An intense, moody individual has more trouble coping with upsets, separations, and jealousy. The right support, starting with skillful parents who praise his strengths and teach him how to compensate for his weaknesses, can nudge a dark disposition in a brighter direction, making many into productive citizens and some into stars. Sylvia Plath and Richard Wagner were taught how to harness some of their stormy energy and use it to create beauty. That kind of benign, skillful nurture is particularly crucial where an oppositional nature is concerned.

CHAPTER 4

EXTREME INDIVIDUAL

Who can deny the dark glamour of Lucifer, the greatest archangel, the biblical "son of the morning"? Celestial antihero in the quintessential father-son drama, prototypical bad boy with a lot of good in him, champion of the supreme lost cause, his best line, courtesy of Milton, is the ultimate definition of the oppositional nature: *"Non serviam."* Among those cloaked with something of the fallen angel's aura of glory, pathos, and whiff of sulfur was Confederate General Nathan Bedford Forrest. An unlettered slave trader turned nouveau riche Mississippi planter, he knew nothing of military life when the Civil War began. His intuitive response to that stimulus was to revise the tactics of warfare in a way practiced nearly a century later by his admirer General Erwin Rommel, the Nazi "Desert Fox." Utterly uninterested in the honorable codes of his peers, who grumbled that while he might be an officer, he was no gentleman, Forrest's most quoted remark rivals Lucifer's in its love-it-or-leave-it austerity: "War means fighting. And fighting means killing."

That Forrest was the boldest of the bold is beyond question. By all accounts, he simply knew no fear. During his impoverished youth, he adopted a code of masculine behavior that still obtains on inner-city streets where only the strong survive and disputes are settled personally with force. By the age of twenty-one, Forrest, manifesting the irritability that often underlies an aggressive temperament, had already killed a man for insulting his family. If Monica entering the pediatric ward is one textbook example of the combustion that results when a particular nature meets a certain kind of nurture, Forrest stepping onto his first battlefield is another. Despite his lack of education, military or otherwise, when the great conflict began, the forty-year-old immediately showed what historian and writer Shelby Foote—a former artillery officer himself—mildly calls "an aptitude for war."

In his first encounter, the newly minted cavalryman vanquished a superior Union force at Bowling Green by improvising a double envelopment combined with a frontal assault—classic maneuvers previously unknown to him. Not content to direct battle from behind the line, the huge horseman, bellowing "Charge!" killed two Union officers, shooting one and stabbing the other, and dislocated the shoulder of a third. In a later fight at Fallen Timbers, as he was hotly pursued by a force that outnumbered his five to one, Forrest stunned the Federals by suddenly wheeling his cavalry around and charging back into their midst, where he abruptly found himself the lone graycoat. When an enemy bullet near the spine lifted him from his saddle, it seemed that the war, at the very least, was over for Forrest. Regaining control of his horse, he plucked up a handy Union soldier to use as a human shield and escaped.

Bold minded as well, the "Wizard of the Saddle" became an artist of psychological warfare. "Shoot at everything blue and keep up the skeer," he ordered his men. "Devil them all night." In one of his most famous exploits, he conned the surrender of Union Colonel Abel Streight, whose force at Day's Gap, Tennessee, outnumbered Forrest's two to one, by repeatedly sending the same two Rebel guns over the same hill. "Name of God!" yelled Streight. "How many guns have you got? There's fifteen I've counted already." Forrest replied, "I reckon that's all that has kept up." He took 1,466 prisoners and was off the next day to raise more hell. Of Forrest, a friend of the Union commander renowned for his own nerve remarked, "He was the only Confederate cavalryman of whom Grant stood in much dread . . . if Forrest was in command he at once became apprehensive, because the latter was amenable to no known rules of procedure, was a law unto himself for all military acts, and was constantly doing the unexpected at all times and places."

Even Forrest's personal life had a martial flair. No courtly West

Pointer, he was nonetheless gallant toward the weaker sex. He met his wife, a pretty preacher's daughter, when the carriage in which she was traveling with her mother got stuck in a stream, much to the amusement of some local louts. Forrest waded in, rescued the women, throttled the boors, and was married six weeks later. Nor were his chivalrous instincts restricted to gently reared ladies. In May 1863, when a sixteen-year-old farm girl showed him where to ford a creek under fire, he took time to write her a thank-you note on the fly: "My highest regardes to miss Ema Sanson for hir Gallant conduct while my posse was skirmishing with the Federals across Black Creek near Gadesden Allabama."

Whether Forrest was a hero or a demon—aggressive or criminal—depended in no little measure on which side one's sympathies lay. But the same disdain for rules that allowed him to outwit the enemy fueled the scandal of the Fort Pillow Massacre, in which his troops, enraged at the sight of southern-born Union sympathizers known as "homemade Yankees" and ex-slaves in blue uniforms, proceded to shoot some of them even as they tried to surrender. That after the war Grant went to the White House and Robert E. Lee to virtual apotheosis, while Forrest returned to a tainted near obscurity, speaks of a difference less in nature than in nurture.

The superficially odd similarity between the guys in the white and black hats, vividly portrayed in Clint Eastwood's film *Unforgiven,* illustrates Freud's observation that while a particular instinct always has the same aim, it may have different objects. As personality psychologist and student of the bold David Lykken says, the difference between the psychopath and hero is not a matter of temperament but of "their experience and their parents." As America reels from a wave of violent crime, this distinction has a special importance. After being quietly conducted for twenty years, research on the temperamental elements of aggressive behavior—in particular, criminal violence—has suddenly been caught in political cross fire. Certainly it raises many disturbing issues. Are murderers and rapists "mad" or "bad"? Should they be treated or punished? Should the children who used to be called "bad boys" and are now said to suffer from "conduct disorder" be put on drugs or into some sort of therapeutic setting? These questions become even more complicated when race is considered.

Nationally, black men make up an eighth of the general male population but half of the imprisoned one. In a story on corruption and civil chaos in Washington, D.C., *The New York Times* reported that "on any given day 42 percent of black men ages eighteen to thirty-five in the city were either in jail, on probation or parole, awaiting trial, or being sought on arrest warrants." No one denies the desperate situation. The Reverend Jesse Jackson has sadly confessed to feeling relief one night on a city street when, hearing footsteps behind him, he turned to see a white man. Indeed, black males are at terrible risk of being crime victims: one in twenty will be murdered before reaching the age of twenty-one—a truly astounding statistic.

The reasons advanced to explain the explosion of violent behavior run the nurture-nature gamut, from poverty, drugs, and lack of training and employment to overtly racist "born bad" hypotheses. As more jails are built and even more violence is predicted, discussions of the roots of crime have become potentially incendiary. Political protest in 1992 eventually led psychiatrist Frederick Goodwin, the world's authority on manic depression and then director of the federal Alcohol, Drug Abuse, and Mental Health Administration, to leave the government for academe; the furor ensued after he drew a parallel between inner-city crime and research showing that young male primates in the wild who compete for scarce resources are more violent and sexually active. That same year, protesters also successfully lobbied the National Institutes of Health to withdraw money for a conference, to be held at the University of Maryland, on possible biological components of violent behavior; in 1995, scientists convened there for a similar symposium. Despite the apprehension that such research could stigmatize individuals or groups as "bad seed," what the data actually show is that, particularly where natures like Bedford Forrest's and Richard Burton's are concerned, nurture is the best predictor of good or bad behavior.

That aggressiveness is not only partly biological but heritable is a venerable concept. Throughout history, mankind has deliberately bred animals for the fighting spirit. David Lykken's pet Slick Willy and the bulls of the corrida are obvious examples of an effort not exclusively limited to animals. From the time of Atreus and his son Agamemnon, the aristocracy has traditionally taken more pride in producing warriors than scholars. Even the present hapless Windsor scion pilots military aircraft and wheels steeds on polo fields, if not the battlefields of his ancestors. In Shakespeare's *Henry V,* the French King Charles VI cautions his overconfident nobles: despite the erstwhile Prince Hal's reputation as a wastrel, the young invader "is bred out of that bloody strain / That haunted us in our familiar paths. . . . This is a stem / Of that victorious stock; and let us fear / The native mightiness and fate of him."

Bloody strains there may well be. A Danish study comparing twins revealed that if one identical male twin had been convicted of committing a crime, the other twin was five times likelier than the average Danish man to be a criminal, too; a fraternal twin in the same situation was also more apt to be a criminal, but only three times so. In a Swedish study of adopted children, the incidence of criminality among those whose adoptive parents were lawbreakers was a little more than twice as high as the 3 percent rate among youngsters from crime-free families; among those whose biological parents were criminals, the incidence was nearly double that figure; among the children who had four troubled parents (both adoptive and birth), 40 percent were criminals, too.

Despite statistics that suggest that heritability can play a role in bad behavior, the only bit of evidence for the sort of simple "crime gene" touted in newspaper headlines concerns a rare mutation that affects violence-prone males from a single Dutch family. If nature conspires in the breeding of bloody stock, it seems that she does so in more diffuse ways. That 90 percent of violent crime is committed by men implicates the genetics of masculinity itself. As a group, men score almost twice as high as women on Hans Eysenck's trait of psychoticism—a combination of aggressiveness and impulsivity. Masculinity's most volatile ingredient seems to be the reproductive hormone testosterone. Men have about ten times more than women, and there's some evidence that male criminals generally have somewhat higher levels than average. For that matter, in one study of female prisoners and controls, testosterone levels in saliva were highest in convicts who had engaged in unprovoked as opposed to defensive violence.

In earlier days, attempts were made to associate a tough guy's disposition with his constitution, from a supposedly criminal cranium to a brawny build. A tall, powerful man whose bullhorn voice scared his own troops, Bedford Forrest was as well suited to a highwayman's life as an officer's. Just as professional dancers and athletes, soldiers and policemen need certain physical attributes to succeed at their work, so do many criminals. Someone whose livelihood depends on fighting, robbing, running, and scaring others must be strong and agile to prosper. Although prisons and reform schools house a higher proportion of the muscular, broad-shouldered, narrow-hipped athletic type known as the mesomorph, modern researchers have found no evidence for the age-old pseudoscience of matching psychological and physical types. More significant than mere muscle is an early pattern of rough-and-tumble play that becomes second nature to the mesomorphic child. The Duke of Wellington observed that "the battle of Waterloo was won on the playing fields of Eton," and Lykken agrees. "The mesomorphic kid will do better in boys' dominance games, which makes him a better fighter who's confident about taking on the opposition. It's not that some evil mental state goes with the body construction, but mesomorphs are probably a little more adventurous."

Advancing beyond particular physiques or odd bumps on the skull, modern biological inquiries into aggressiveness center on the neurophysiology of traits: not just one of that name, but several that in different combinations produce the same effect. Boldness is often mentioned as a prime ingredient. To Jerome Kagan, for example, aggressive children are primarily characterized by fearlessness: badly brought up, they become bullies instead of heroes. As Lykken observed in his prison studies, the toughest tough guys—the type psychologists call the primary psychopath—are relatively indifferent to and unapprehensive about painful consequences, to a degree that makes them nearly strangers to anxiety. In a complementary study, the levels of stress-related chemicals of garden-variety criminals increased as their trial dates loomed, but not those of the fearless psychopaths. In experiments in which such subjects have been primed with an arousal-producing chemical such as adrenaline, they learn to escape the electric shock that they would normally not bother to avoid because the artificially induced "anxiety" makes them react as the rest of us do.

That a person who isn't fazed by an electric shock or the prospect of a guilty verdict probably needs quite a bit of stimulation to feel jazzed up at all doesn't excuse the mad, wild excesses of some of the very bold but makes them somewhat more understandable. "I think these people are born with a weak innate fear reaction," says Lykken. "Others have a strong one, and most of us are in between." Intuiting that principle, Forrest knew that the "skeer" to which he himself was impervious was one of his most powerful weapons.

Primate research, which allows direct neurochemical testing as well as intense behavioral monitoring, adds another dimension to the emerging portrait of aggressive dispositions. In early life, the defining quality of J. D. Higley's specially bred strain of aggressive rhesus monkeys is irritability. Later on, it's the unsociability that correlates with the low balance of serotonin they've inherited. Nor is a troop's most aggressive member usually its leader. That popular figure is apt to be a pacific, high-serotonin backslapper who knows how to work the crowd. "In stable settings, a monkey who tries to run things with force gets kicked out," says Higley. "If the females don't like a male, for example, he's gone." The monkeys who acquire the most wounds over a lifetime—a pragmatic gauge of a belligerent temperament—are hotheaded loners who both attract and instigate attacks. Richard Burton was a higher primate of this type; his spectacular gifts brought him comparatively little advancement largely because of his flair for provoking the lesser mortals who were his bureaucratic superiors.

While people convicted of violent crime are by no means a homogeneous group, many have a few sad biographical features in common, including a history of inappropriate aggressiveness from early childhood and a personality described as angry and impulsive. Interesting support for the idea that aggressiveness is closely bound up with the tendency to react without reflection comes from data concerning individuals who are belligerent but not fearless. While the majority of one group of unruly young subjects headed toward what psychologists call conduct disorder were indeed bold, Nathan Fox was surprised to discover some anxious ones, too. Higley also numbers some inhibited individuals among his scarred-up bad boys. Despite the fearfulness associated with these fretful monkeys' high levels of norepinephrine, the impulsivity that correlates with their low serotonin levels means "they don't think way ahead," he says. "They end up in encounters that might have been avoided." Like all temperamental tendencies, this "act first, think later" inclination can be influenced in either direction by a person's other traits and intellect. If the imprisoned population is in better physical shape than the general one, for example, it doesn't measure up as well where IQ is concerned: the average score behind bars is 10 points lower than the national average of 100.

Far from America's crowded prisons and troubled inner cities, research conducted in Scandinavia, where social influences such as poverty figure less in crime and governments keep careful public health records, suggests a link between aggression's impulsive component and the low levels of serotonin that run in certain families. Although it's suddenly getting a lot of attention, this hypothesis is not new. In 1976, Yale psychiatrist Michael Sheard studied prison inmates who had been given lithium, which seems to maximize serotonin activity; after three months on the drug, the men's impulsively aggressive behavior had almost disappeared, only to return when they were given a placebo.

Recent complementary evidence suggests that people involved in violent crimes that are "hot," or impulsive, rather than "cold," or premeditated, tend to have a low serotonin level. Rather than using aggression as a tool to get something they want, as thieves do, the hot types simply lose their heads. The ultimate example is violent suicide. Many depressed people have low serotonin levels, and those who attempt to kill themselves have the lowest. According to research conducted at the NIMH by psychiatrist Markku Linnoila, violent male criminals who had impulsive or antisocial personalities had lower serotonin levels than other offenders did. Interestingly, in a study of men and women who had personality disorders, low serotonin was linked to assaultive behavior in the men—and verbal aggression in the women.

The idea that a biochemical imbalance can underlie aggressive behavior has received far more attention than another, equally important and interesting association. "Guess what?" says developmental psychologist John Richters, who directs the NIMH's research on conduct disorder. "Those connections can also work the other way round."

On June 17, 1994, in Philadelphia, a sixteen-year-old boy robbed and shot Mohammad Jaberipour, an Iranian immigrant and father of three, who was working in an ice cream truck. It was his first week on the job.

As the driver lay dying, a crowd of teenagers, attracted by the gunfire and the tinkling Mr. Softee music, gathered to laugh and mock him, asking for ice cream. Describing the scene, one of Jaberipour's colleagues said, "It wasn't human."

Even if the science of how genes and neurochemicals influence traits such as aggressiveness were far advanced, the number of people who could be helped by such knowledge would be dwarfed by that of temperamentally normal children whose characters are primed for violence by poor nurture. While Richters allows that "a very, very small proportion of antisocial kids who are extremely aggressive and hostile—those we think of when we say 'bad seed'—may have some important biological and genetic influences on their behavior, the vast majority of violence, including things like drive-by shootings, probably has nothing to do with biological or inborn characteristics. These kids are products of their environments."

Although the demise of the nineteenth-century bourgeois conscience doesn't matter for some types of people, Freud said, it makes a big difference for others. Gene-environment correlation almost guarantees that bold, impulsive children raised without social limits will create mayhem, and the number of such homes has proliferated since the 1950s. Harvard psychiatrist Alvin Poussaint has long been concerned about the impact of violence on the black community in general and on black men in particular. Commenting on research that closely relates crime rates to unemployment rates, he says, "When you push aside all the social factors, such as whether a child has been abused or repeatedly witnessed violence, and say, 'We're looking for a crime gene,' people are going to think it's a little odd. Scientists can do any kind of research they want, but in terms of biological influences on aggressive behavior, I wouldn't pursue genes but other factors. Alcohol is involved in fifty percent of homicides, for example, and alcohol has a biological effect." While not disputing the fact that children are born with different temperaments, Poussaint says, "I really think a lot of violence is learned behavior."

Research that challenges the traditional distinction between nature and nurture suggests that such learning can be more than skin-deep. On the surface, the fact that kids who get hit are in turn likelier to hit others looks like mere imitation. Sophisticated studies by University of

Indiana psychologist John Bates, in collaboration with psychologists Kenneth Dodge, at Vanderbilt, and Gregory Pettit, at Auburn, suggests that this mimicry has more complicated roots. Regardless of a child's temperament, as measured by the team, they found that the experience of hard punishment actually skews the whole way a child processes social information. He's likelier to pay less attention to social cues, to interpret neutral ones as hostile, and to favor aggressive solutions to problems. What may look like innate cussedness or simple copycat behavior can spring from an inaccurate, maladaptive worldview that guarantees someone will see provocation all around him, whether it's really there or not. His reactions to his misperceptions ensure the negative responses from others that keep the vicious circle spinning.

The idea that what looks like a philosophical worldview can be rooted in biochemistry as well as experience is supported by animal research. Scientists have known for some time that when male monkeys who have low levels of testosterone are put into a new social group in which they have a better place in the pecking order, that experience raises their level of the hormone, which in turn changes their behavior. Similarly, a male's testosterone level—and spirits—dip after being defeated by another male but rise again if the vanquished is quartered with a female. Neurotransmitter systems, too, may respond to as well as help shape experience. J. D. Higley and Stephen Suomi find that when a normal infant monkey is raised with inept juveniles rather than competent adults, it will eventually resemble, both behaviorally and physiologically, a troubled monkey selectively bred for a low serotonin balance. Such provocative data mean that the search for biological substrates of antisocial behavior shouldn't be limited to genes or exclude environment. Even when a trait is genetically modified, "that doesn't mean that you're *programmed*," says Higley. "Someone could be disposed to respond to certain stimuli with, say, inappropriate aggression, but learn early in life that if he does, he'll get into trouble. He may also learn to like the reinforcement he gets from positive interactions."

Considering his conviction that most traits have a strong genetic basis, David Lykken's position on the etiology of criminal aggressiveness is notable. "Where socialization is concerned, the environment is very important—it's the main exception to the general principle," he says. "How you're raised is far likelier to change your impulsivity than your extroversion. All across the land, urban and rural, black and white, but mainly in the inner cities, thousands of illegitimate children aren't brought up by, but only domiciled with, parents who are too indifferent, incompetent, or unsocialized themselves to socialize their offspring—the primary function of parenting. That's the big thing, which can be changed. We're running a crime factory that's turning out little sociopaths." He concedes that "there's not a prayer in the world" that his solution—the licensing of biological parenthood according to the same criteria that apply to adoption—will be tested in the near future: "My purpose in making an extravagant suggestion is to start a discussion. The problem is so real, and nobody is talking about the solution."

Where young Bedford Forrests or Richard Burtons are concerned, providing the right kind of nurture can be challenging. When individuals who are nearly indifferent to punishment, whether by innate temperament or habituation, meet a society intent on deterring them with it, the result is a lot of expensive, ineffective "correction." Something of the same dynamic prevails in many homes. The development of conscience involves a child's need to anticipate parental reaction to his behavior and avoid doing something he'd be punished for, says Lykken: "Because the child thinks, 'I don't want Father to be mad at me,' he ends up not liking what Father doesn't like. Good behavior depends on the desire to reduce fear, but if fear doesn't play a big role in your life, you're less likely to pay attention to what Father doesn't like or to be affected next time by the punishment you got last time. Our society depends so on punishment, but that's based on the assumption that later on it will elicit fear in the punished." At least in some cases, better results might be achieved by exploiting a principle that military officers and coaches have long employed and that Lykken has noticed even in prison populations. A tough young Lucifer can sometimes be socialized by appealing to, or even instilling, a sense of pride, because, says Lykken, "he may care if people stop admiring him."

Labor and skill intensive, child rearing was easier in the tribal, extended-family settings in which our species evolved, especially where frisky boys who can go in either the heroic or demonic direction are concerned. "It's hard to be a persistent rule breaker in a community in which many people put an arm around you," says Lykken. "In modern culture, we think the right kind of family is a pair of inexperienced young people, but at least there are supposed to be two of them."

Single parenting is rough even for a well-balanced, well-meaning adult blessed with an easygoing baby. When a hard-to-handle child is paired with an inept single parent, the result can be disastrous, particularly for sons—and their communities. Observing that boys raised without their fathers are seven times likelier to end up as delinquents and later as prisoners, Lykken says, "Many little boys are potential criminals who find it perfectly natural to take things, break things, and beat up on people. It's their parents' responsibility to stomp some of that out—to inhibit antisocial behavior, instill prosocial values, and cultivate the work ethic. Because the father is bigger and stronger than his boys, they grow up with a sense of a greater power that would be foolish to resist."

By observing his father participate in the responsibilities and rewards of family life and orderly competition, a boy learns how to secure Freud's Big Two elements of a healthy life: love and work. Deprived of the experience or something approaching it, he can remain uncertain about his own manhood. Hiding his insecurity behind an angry, aggressive machismo, he shies away from the challenge of real achievement in the world. On the social plane, male neediness and rage, multiplied thousands of times in the nation's ghettos, exact a grave toll, even from strangers like Mohammad Jaberipour. Heinous as they are, such crimes are indeed "a cry for help" that comes too late, but for the commonweal must be addressed in the generations of boys still young enough to be reached.

"What shall become of us without the barbarians?" wrote Constantine Cavafy. "Those people were a kind of solution." In many parts of an increasingly cerebral, sit-down, service-oriented, electronic world, the live-free-or-die temperament seems anachronistic—suited only to survivalist compounds. Yet traits that wreak havoc when undisciplined win trophies on playing fields and corner offices in corporate headquarters. Aggressive sorts are not unknown even in the groves of academe. Lykken grouses that the scientific texts on sociopaths and psychopaths "are always getting stolen from the library." One of the most important authors of these works, H. M. Cleckley, noted that his subjects voluntarily came to see him only when they needed his help—to dodge a criminal charge in court, say, or raise some money; his staff knew when he had had such a visit because, despite his expertise in the field of psychopathy and previous bitter experience, he usually ended up writing a check.

Sometimes what society regards as deviancy has less to do with innate psychology than with "some of the weird environments we've created," says Richters. "Humans didn't evolve, for example, to sit in tightly structured classrooms reading small print. Children in that setting diagnosed as having attention deficit disorder may actually have some selected advantages over the ones who just sit still. There isn't a clinician in the world who wouldn't be concerned about the kid who toes the line all the time."

His own history partly explains Richters's skepticism about what's considered a normal or abnormal trait. "I never went to high school, was in and out of jail right on up to young adulthood, and am statistically deviant on tests of ability to sustain attention," he says. "Now I'm an honest citizen who publishes scientific literature on this stuff. I still have many of the same basic traits, but I channel them differently, say, into ferreting out crude academic thinking and pushing a good idea as far as I can, even if some people tell me it won't float. The intolerance for boundaries that got me into trouble as a kid serves me extraordinarily well now that I get paid to be oppositional. We've got this notion of pathology as all things bad and normalcy as all things good turned around. Show me the top achievers in any field, and I'll show you loads of psychopathology. Show me someone who doesn't have any sharp edges, and I'll show you a boring person who hasn't made a mark."

An iconoclastic study suggests that a certain amount of testing the limits is a sign of good emotional health. First researchers gave a group of youngsters personality tests at the age of five and also collected data on their mothers' style of parenting. When the kids were tested again at age eighteen, it turned out that the best-adjusted ones had tried marijuana; the most anxious and constricted just said no, and the alienated and impulsive abused it. In short, one of the perks of a sound, flexible personality is the occasional walk on the wild side. Even among the obstreperous children identified as having conduct disorder, says Richters, only a third will meet the criteria for antisocial personality disorder as adults. "That doesn't mean you'd want them to baby-sit for your children," he says, "but I bet many of them filter into very interesting occupations. If I could have environmental control over some of the kids who work the streets pretty successfully, a lot of them could function exceptionally well in mainstream society. But they wouldn't be the worker bees."

Dennis Rodman, the giant, tattooed, nose-ringed, bleached-blond African-American rebounding machine of the Chicago Bulls, is no worker bee. He has a colorful history of ignoring his own team's rules and penalties and even its other members, continuing to ride the Harley that trashed his shoulder, showing up when he pleases before games, and not infrequently getting thrown out of them for rough stuff. His previous team, the San Antonio Spurs, put up with such bad-boy histrionics not only because Rodman is a great player but because, as assistant coach Dave Cowens, an old biker himself, told *The New York Times,* "You need hardened criminals out there." The Spurs got more cooperation out of their ornery star after they started channeling communication through Jack Haley, the only fellow player Rodman really talked to and even partied with. Haley's technique might have been dictated by Richters or Lykken. Regarding "the way to deal with Dennis," he says, "under no circumstances threaten him. Because if you threaten him, he'll seize the opportunity to go the other way. If you want him to do something, you have to ask him. Say, 'Hey, Dennis. We need you to do this. Can you come do this?' And he'll say, 'Sure, no problem.' It's funny, because for a guy who's an extreme individual and who's so into standing alone, he loves to be needed. And he loves the fact that the team needs him."

Writing about the *Odyssey,* Ezra Pound observed that "the news is still news," and the same is true of the ancient Greek concept of why we are the way we are. Over the past two decades, research on temperament has slowly become intellectually acceptable again—even trendy—but in certain circles it's still regarded as a right-wing theory of predestina-tion. Formed in a gentler social and intellectual climate, many of those who study temperament can be defensive or even vaguely apologetic about their findings. David Lykken rolls his eyes over his reputation as a "biological fascist." Jerome Kagan admits that, "because of my train-ing, politics, and values, in my work I once muted the power of biology and maximized the environment's." Twenty years ago, when he ob-served a shy toddler, Kagan saw a child influenced by unpleasant social experience; today, he sees one who has a certain type of neurochemistry. "I have been dragged, kicking and screaming, by my data to acknowl-edge that temperament is more powerful than I thought and wish to be-lieve," says Kagan. "That's where I am, not out of prejudice but realism."

To get a sense of temperament's role in making us who we are, Kagan suggests that we each think of ourselves as "an onion, a series of layers. First, there are our superficial traits—our attitudes, whether we're lib-eral or conservative—and here a lot of change is possible. Then we come down a layer to our basic identity—issues of love, work, gender—and those things are a little harder to change. Finally, we come down to the emotional *tone*—how we feel just walking around—and that's the hardest to change. Two people could have the same tone, yet look very different on the surface. The traits we see are very malleable, but the stuff that's invisible . . ." Much of that invisible stuff that makes us who we are has been inherited.

PART II

HOW WE BEGAN

CHAPTER 5

THE GENETIC LEGACY

Watching scenes of little Monica with her parents makes plain just where she got her star quality. Of all the early childhood films, she herself is most dazzling in a sequence in which she perches on her father's knee, sunny Shirley Temple to his darkly attractive, macho Robert Mitchum. When that redoubtable ladies' man wandered off for good, however, Monica's jilted single mother of five showed that she had grit as well as style. While running a bustling, spit-and-polish home back in the 1950s, when few women, especially from her blue-collar background, had careers, she worked her way up to a position as manager of a major company's mail-order department. Her success surely depended in part on her flair, apparent on film, for social engagement. As Daniel Stern puts it, Monica's mother could "really turn on the gas." These handsome, vital parents provided Monica not only with what he calls "good models of how to be special" but also with their sparkle-plenty genes.

The idea that heredity influences behavior, from star quality to snarling aggression, is hardly new. Many of the familiar European dogs who do man's work, from hunting to herding, have been deliberately bred for their innate abilities since the sixteenth century or earlier; the origins of the sled-pulling Alaskan malamute and the gazelle-hunting Iranian saluki go back as far as 3000 B.C. Among humans, the upper classes have historically mated their offspring as selectively as their dogs and horses, incorporating into the family ranks those suited to advancing the Plantagenet puissance or the Rothschild acumen. Attempting to promote such dynastic impulses among the masses, Francis Galton, Charles Darwin's cousin and the father of eugenics (from the Greek for "good birth"), observed that "nature prevails enormously over nurture" and preached that "better breeding" would mean a better society. Earlier in the twentieth century, the many efforts to augment this theory ranged from the tragic to the comic. In the United States, where a number of states allowed the sterilization of "defective" prisoners and mental patients, biologist Charles Davenport evaluated thousands of families and claimed that criminality, "pauperism," and "thalassophilia," or the purportedly masculine love of the sea that accounted for the abundance of men afloat, were heritable traits. At state fairs, people entered "Fitter Families" contests to be judged like cattle or hogs. After the rise of Nazism, however, the pseudoscience of eugenics acquired a stench that by association still taints the discipline of behavioral genetics.

Medical advances in finding the genetic origins of certain physical traits and illnesses such as Huntington's disease have restored credibility to the idea that heredity also influences behavioral ones. After all, the brain is part of the body, too. However, behavioral genetics retains its political charge. The new, simplistic "gene for" explanations of old problems such as addiction, crime, and the "permanent underclass"—pauperism—are welcomed more enthusiastically in circles that prefer hard-edged conservative perspectives on such complex matters. Even at the individual level, someone might invoke heritability when discussing the "neurochemical imbalances" linked to depression, say, yet dismiss it out of hand where aggression, intelligence, or homosexuality is concerned. In just the past thirty years, for example, the last has been definitively declared to be a disease, a choice, or, most recently, a biological predisposition; in the absence of a single clear explanation—the norm when human behavior is concerned—which etiology is invoked depends largely on ideology.

Regarding genes and politics, from the remove of Europe Hans Eysenck says, "*Of course* most people believed that behavior and personality are influenced by genetic factors, until this recent American insanity of rejecting them for a total tabula rasa. In the past, people had a much more realistic conception of such matters, and we must have a fairly good system of insight or our species wouldn't have survived. In fact, how anyone who has more than one child can deny genetic influences on personality is quite incredible to me. We didn't need Newton to discover that if you drop an apple, it will fall to the ground. What we need to do now is to make behavioral genetics into a science, just as we did with physics."

The sturdiest pillar of that effort so far has been research that contrasts the behavior of twins. As other scientists with a taxonomic bent document rare birds or butterflies, psychologist Thomas Bouchard, director of the University of Minnesota's Center for Twin and Adoption Research, together with David Lykken, Auke Tellegen, and their colleagues, gathers stories of uncanny family resemblances. Tony Milasi and his identical twin, Roger Brooks, were separated shortly after birth. Tony was quickly adopted and raised in New York by well-off Italian Catholics. Roger spent his first three years in an orphanage, however, before being adopted by a single Jewish mother of modest means who brought him up in Florida. At the age of twenty-five, the two brothers met after one was mistaken for the other while dining out. Despite their very different pasts, the men were almost creepily alike: not only were their voices indistinguishable, but they both drank coffee without touching the cup handle and used the same cologne, hair cream, and imported toothpaste. In the photos of research subjects that decorate Lykken's office, the identical twins look identical, of course. More striking than their matching eyes and noses, however, are their matching postures and smiles. "What makes you stand a certain way to have your picture taken?" asks Lykken. "A whole bunch of things, both physiological and psychological, and identical twins share them all."

Like other siblings, fraternal twins, each made from a separate egg and sperm, have only half their genes in common. But identical twins, who are made from a single fertilized egg that splits, are equivalent to genetic clones. By comparing the characteristics of pairs of identical and fraternal twins who have been reared together or adopted separately in infancy and raised apart, scientists can establish which traits are strongly rooted in heredity and which aren't. When identicals express a certain characteristic more similarly than fraternal twins do, that trait is assumed to have a genetic basis. Because identicals have the same genes, differences between them must have environmental causes, from the biological, such as the intrauterine milieu, to the social, such as upbringing.

For most of the twentieth century, psychologists have maintained in thousands of studies that the imprint of early experience on our basic human clay pretty much determines who we are. From this perspective, identical twins who are raised apart from infancy should be quite different. However, research from large twin studies in the United States and Scandinavia shows that the personalities of identical twins, even those reared apart from birth, are about twice as similar as those of fraternal twins—to date, the best argument for a strong genetic influence on behavior.

Monica's star quality is one dimension of the personality trait that seems to be the most heritable of all: what theorists since Carl Jung have called extroversion. When behavioral geneticist and psychologist Robert Plomin, who conducts his research at Penn State and the Institute of Psychiatry in London, reviewed four studies of more than 23,000 pairs of twins, evaluated according to their responses to personality questionnaires, he found that half the identicals had very similar scores on extroversion, while fewer than a third of fraternals did—a suggestion of strong genetic grounding. As far as the Minnesota team is concerned, genes account for about half of a population's total variation in personality. The Swedish Adoption/Twin Study on Aging, involving 25,000 pairs of same-sex twins, including 99 sets of identical adults reared apart, puts the average figure at about 40 percent. What such statistics *don't* mean is that someone's personality, or even one trait, is 40 or 50 percent genetic, as is often reported by the media. Scientists have no way to determine that a certain percentage of Jane's extroversion, say, is due to her genes and the rest to her upbringing. They can only show that a proportion of the difference between shy Dick and outgoing Jane can be attributed to their heredity.

After much analysis, Plomin estimates the amount of personality variance within a group that can be explained by genes to be "forty percent, plus or minus twenty percent." To illuminate the roles of genes and environment in making us who we are, Plomin turns to the physiological realm. For some characteristics, such as height, heredity accounts for most of the variance in a population; for other traits, such as those linked to various cancers, environmental influences explain most such differences. For personality traits, however, he says, "both genetic and environmental factors are important."

Considering how little the huge body of traditional environmentally focused studies has explained about personality and that, in general, "psychology is a mountain of statistically significant results but a molehill of important, powerful findings that explain something," Plomin considers the correlations between heredity and behavior gleaned from twin studies to be "unbelievably high. In behavioral science, it's rare to explain more than five percent of variance, so to explain forty percent is important. Not only is genetic influence on personality significant, but, unlike anything [else] we ever see, it's substantial."

Statistics from twin studies—usually, mangled interpretations of them, such as "shyness is half genetic"—have become symbols of heredity's importance to who we are. To Jerome Kagan, they're no more than that. Fully accounting for a particular person's ways would require measuring not just nature's and nurture's separate impacts, he says, but their interaction, "which can't be done easily unless you can control who grows up with whom, which you can't." Nor can scientists measure epistasis, the process by which one gene suppresses the expression of another. Because one's degree of inhibition, say, depends not only on the genes directly involved in that trait and one's environment but on one's other "background" genes, they would also have to be measured; the born-reactive person who's also sociable, for example, will be very different from one who's reclusive or aggressive. Rather than asking how much of shyness is due to genes and how much to environment, Kagan would pose a different question: "What is the combination of experience and inherited physiology that makes a person fearful?" By way of analogy, he asks, "What has to come together to make a blizzard? Both cold temperature and humidity. If you ask a meteorologist what proportion of a blizzard is due to each factor, he would laugh and say, 'I can't answer that question.' That's the way I view this issue of what proportion of personality is genetic."

Where the individual is concerned, trying to sort nature's work from nurture's may be a futile and meaningless effort, but not when it comes to explaining why one person is different from another. Offering his own analogy, Lykken says that "asking whether Isaac Newton's genius was due more to genes or environment is as senseless as asking whether a rectangle's area depends more on its length or its width." However, he says, if a certain *group* of rectangles varies in width between one and ten inches and in length between one and a hundred inches, the variation in area within that group depends more on the variation in length than on the lesser one in width. Similarly, says Lykken, regarding genius, "it *is* meaningful to ask whether a population's genetic differences are more or less important than their experiential ones in producing the variations in the traits involved in that quality."

In the effort to understand the origins of behavior, the million-dollar question is not how much, but how, a person's genes influence who he is. Charles Darwin's wife, Emma, once mentioned to her mother-in-law that, while stirring in his sleep, Charles habitually abraded his nose with a button on the sleeve of his nightshirt. The elder Mrs. Darwin replied that Charles's father had done the same thing. How could such a bizarre predilection pass from father to son? "The short answer," says Lykken, "is that we don't know." Despite formidable efforts, geneticists have found only one hard link between genes and behavioral traits—that of novelty seeking—and none for disorders such as alcoholism, schizophrenia, and manic depression. This lack of elegant simplicity doesn't mean that behavior doesn't have a genetic basis, only that it's vastly complicated.

Right from conception, we each have a genome, or some hundred thousand genes, half of which have been contributed by each parent, arrayed on forty-six chromosomes on every one of the body's cells. Half are common to all people and differentiate us from chimps and worms. The other half, which varies from person to person except for identical twins, is the uniqueness copyright held by each individual, whose genetic potential is so vast that the number of environments he can experience in a lifetime can only begin to tap it. That the genetic variations on the theme of Homo sapiens are so plentiful guarantees that our species can adapt to wildly different settings, from the North Pole to the tropical rain forest, that most temperaments will not be extreme, and that none of us will turn out just like Mom, Dad, or Uncle Scrooge.

A list of the activities involved in a simple conversation suggests something of behavior's complexity. That's why it requires the workings of multiple genes, which in turn means that uncovering its genetic basis is far more difficult than determining that of, say, eye or hair color. For that matter, even where "mere" physiology is concerned, there are many genetically influenced characteristics, from height and weight to blood pressure and cholesterol levels, in which the relation between gene and expression is byzantine. To produce atherosclerosis, for example, dozens of genes influence lots of things from lipids to platelets. In this respect, says psychiatrist and behavioral geneticist Kenneth Kendler, who conducts his studies at Virginia Commonwealth University, the geneses of intelligence and personality as well as psychiatric illnesses resemble that of coronary heart disease, "but they're played out in the brain—an organ we understand much less well than the heart." But an organ, nonetheless. Kendler allows that "when you ask someone if he's depressed, that's not the same as taking his blood pressure. Despite this idea that they're not physiological, however, psychological functions are a function of central nervous system activity."

Given behavior's complexity, the question isn't "What is the gene for this or that trait or disorder?" but "How do multiple genes collaboratively influence the neurochemistry that underlies behavior?" Mere nucleotides, genes themselves don't produce thoughts, feelings, or actions. Whatever it is that they do to help behavior along takes place at the molecular level, amid the neurotransmitters, enzymes, and hormones that regulate autonomic nervous system activity, sensory thresholds, homeostasis, reflexes, and other such things. A glance at current scientific literature would seem to hook up particular kinds of behavior to serotonin, dopamine, and norepinephrine, much as ancient texts attributed them to bile or phlegm. These three transmitters are surely important, but some of the several hundred less well studied others must also be, so trumpeting a new theory of humors seems premature.

Although the particulars of how genes affect behavior remain to be discovered, what is clear is that the shy child of shy parents has not inherited that social quality per se. He has been born with a tendency, dependent on a number of genes, to react to new stimuli strongly in many physiological and behavioral ways that, taken together, make up an approach to the environment that scientists call inhibition. One stimulus that's likely to set off this complex reaction is a stranger, who triggers the particular kind of inhibition known as shyness. Because behavior is stochastic, however, a biological push toward shyness doesn't mean that such a person *must* be reserved, or is so twenty-four hours a day and in all situations, only that he's likelier than others to be. Just as positive learning can help him overcome it, profound negative experience can inhibit even a naturally outgoing child, as was the case with Monica.

In short, genes can't *make* a person do anything, such as avoid or take risks. They can only help create a nervous system that's so chronically over- or underaroused that its owner may try to compensate by lining his bedroom with cork, as Marcel Proust did, or by testing jet fighters. A less industrious soul, whether sensitive or bold, might simply spend a lot of time feeling respectively anxious or bored.

As far as Julius Caesar was concerned, "The fault . . . lies in ourselves, not in our stars, that we are underlings." To most psychologists, however, the slings and arrows of outrageous fortune, which they prosaically call "life events," such as divorce, bereavement, and job loss, have been the classic examples of how the outside world can impose itself willy-nilly on an individual's destiny, regardless of his plans or genes. A particularly iconoclastic twin study conducted by Kenneth Kendler, however, supports Caesar's insight. Upon analyzing his data, he found that what predicted who would suffer a bout of depression over the course of two years wasn't what the stars had in store but a genetic inclination to react to disturbing events in that way. In other words, what actually happened to his subjects didn't affect whether they got depressed or not. Given enough stress, everyone gets upset, and intensely traumatic events, such as severe child abuse, produce psychic scars. According to Kendler, however, despite traditional theories, for most people in his general—not clinical—population, who have not inherited a tendency toward depression, the effects of bad experiences are short-lived: "The suggestion," he says, "is that terribly traumatic life events that scar you for the rest of your life are relatively rare."

Good fortune as well as bad seems to involve a certain innate quality. When Auke Tellegen and David Lykken analyzed twin data for clues to the genesis of happiness, defined as "subjective well-being," they found it varied unsystematically around a set point characteristic of the individual, and that whether that set point is high or low—happy or dysphoric—is very substantially determined by genetic factors. Some of Kendler's research implies that the people who cope best with stressful events are those who claim, before the upset occurs, to have good social support—which they turn out not to need. In other words, those we call "lucky" are more accurately described as the kind of resilient, competent individuals who can take care of business and attract others' interest and affection. Twin research also shows that identicals, even those reared apart, experience many of the same life events, from financial to family problems. Thinking of such things only as results of the ill winds of chance is "a naïve view of how a person impacts on an environment," says Kendler. "All clinicians see people who trail disaster behind them, and in many cases, it's not simply bad luck."

Early in the twentieth century, the temperament-minded psychiatrists Ernst Kretschmer and Emil Kraepelin threw up a bridge between Hippocrates' dispositions and the behavior problems that modern clinicians call personality disorders by remarking on particular sorts of people whose characteristics, when taken to extremes, became illnesses. His thin "aesthenic" patients tended to be retiring, serious, and more prone to schizophrenia, said Kretschmer, while short, fleshy, "pyknic," or neurasthenic, types were sociable, impulsive, moody, and more vulnerable to cyclical manic-depressive problems. Further anticipating psychology's dimensional perspective on personality by putting the sick onto a spectrum with the well, Kraepelin, the patron saint of modern biological psychiatry, observed that schizophrenics and their relatives were shyer and more paranoid and eccentric than others. On the other hand, he observed, a collection of manic-depressives and their kin would include disproportionate numbers of individuals who were gloomy, worried, and sexually inhibited—the depressives—and arrogant, grandiose, and ambitious—the manics. In between their virulent ups and downs, Kraepelin said, the patients seemed much like their normal relatives.

Equipped with better tools, modern psychiatrists can look for more specific connections between traits and disorders. While something as fuzzy as neuroticism could not be a genetic characteristic, says Kenneth Kendler, it *is* influenced by genes; twin studies show that 40 to 50 percent of its variation among a population can be explained by heredity. A high level of the trait is also a strong predictor for depression, suggesting that common genes are involved in proclivity and illness. "It's not necessarily that neuroticism causes the risk," says Kendler, "but that the same set of genetic, or temperamental, factors [is] reflected in the trait and in vulnerability to depression." That persistent feeling of nameless dread that psychiatrists classify as "generalized anxiety disorder" also has a close genetic relationship to depression, Kendler finds. On the other hand, panic disorder, which is another form of anxiety, is much less closely linked to depression and more closely to phobias.

The stunning implication of research on the connections among genes, traits, and America's two commonest emotional illnesses is this: people affected by either depression or generalized anxiety share the same, or a very similar, genetic vulnerability and that who gets what depends on the differences in their experience. Depression is more closely linked to loss, for example, particularly the death of a close relative, than generalized anxiety is. While bereavement means an eighteenfold increase in risk for the latter illness, it produces none for the former. On the other hand, when a relative suffers from a major illness, an individual's risk of anxiety increases five times, while his chances of having a depression increase only threefold. Thus it seems that, given an affective vulnerability, loss produces depression, and threat, anxiety. While this theory, says Kendler, "isn't perfect—financial difficulties, which would seem like a threat, turn out to be depressogenic—it has an intuitive appeal."

Adding a sociobiological perspective on the relationship between anxiety and depression to Kendler's biogenetic one, clinical psychologist Thomas Widiger, who researches personality disorders at the University of Kentucky, connects both emotions to loss. Anxiety is the affect that accompanies its anticipation, he says, and depression, the experience itself: "You are afraid of what might happen—anxiety—and become depressed when it does." From the point of view of adaptivity, just as anxiety is a signal to protect oneself against the impending loss, says Widiger, depression tells others that one's attempt failed and their help is needed. "Given that both affects are associated with loss," he says, "it's hardly surprising that that they're closely related neurochemically."

The fact that inherited influences on personality can no longer be denied has had a tonic effect on warm-and-fuzzy, platitudinous psychological theorizing. Even when assessing what have long been considered archetypal environmental influences, such as parenting and peer interactions, says Robert Plomin, "we've yet to find an area that doesn't show genetic influence." Unfortunately, however, the most eloquent point made by the usual "gene for" explanations of behavior trumpeted from headlines and sound bites is their expression of the human desire for complicated things to be made simple. The reductionist way in which genetic influence is usually presented dismays thoughtful scientists, who know it must always be partial and diffuse. Even certain highly heritable illnesses have powerful environmental components. The severe retardation caused by a genetic disorder called phenylketonuria, for example, can be prevented if the amino acid phenylalanine is eliminated from a vulnerable person's diet. Schizophrenia is the most "biological" and "genetic" of mental disorders, yet the correlation among identical twins is still only 50 percent. "We don't know exactly what else is involved," says Plomin, "but we do know the problem isn't all genetic."

The mountain of studies of how environment influences behavior largely concerns the social environment, particularly the micromilieu of parent and child. Yet even in that area, disappointingly little has been established. In *No One Ever Asked Us . . . A Postscript to Foster Care,* the author reports on the lives of many of 277 adults who had been reared from early childhood in New York City's foster care system. When compared with a control group, they hadn't done quite as well in school but were otherwise similar in terms of employment, health, positive outlook, satisfaction, and dependence on public support. Despite having had the kind of upbringing that sends shivers up middle-class spines, only a few of the orphans were "failures."

After nearly a hundred years of research on the subject, "we don't know much more about how nurture operates than we do about genes," says Auke Tellegen. "It must be important, though. In the Middle Ages, no one could do calculus, but now significant numbers learn it. More puzzlingly, IQ has also gone up substantially just over the past few decades. We don't know why, but the reasons for these things must be environmental."

To date, the most important insight into the effects of both nurture and nature on personality is that heredity's influence, which is limited and indirect, shapes us primarily by inclining us to "select" certain experiences and environments: a small child's preference for playing alone or with others, say, or an adult's vocational choice of writing poetry or selling cars. According to this more sophisticated modern understanding of gene-environment correlations, heredity may be the beginning of personality, but it's certainly not the end of it. From this perspective, nature and nurture aren't autonomous, much less opposing, forces; rather, each person's experience is shaped by the biology he inherits— and to some extent vice versa. Here is psychologist and temperament researcher Mary Rothbart's revision of the old nature-or-nurture question: "Given his genetic material, what are temperament's influences on the kinds of experiences that a person has, which then help him become one or another sort of person?" Not only will different kinds of people seek out different kinds of environments, she says, "but different temperaments will not perceive the same setting in the same way."

Scientists who study the intricacies of a person's perceptions of his inner and outer worlds work on a very different frequency from those who conduct twin studies and other probes of genetic influences on behavior. Based not on thousands of statistics but on extensive observations of single individuals, their work illuminates how we become the creatures of our experiential history no less than of our genetic one.

CHAPTER 6

THE HISTORICAL LEGACY

In the Monica films, the most electrifying scenes are those in which she bottle-feeds her dolls and, later, her own daughters. At first, it's difficult for someone who has fed a baby in the conventional cradling way to watch this devoted young mother lay the tiny infant, arms windmilling, vertically on her lap and stick in the bottle, barely supporting the wobbly head with her knees. Even during burping, Monica doesn't cuddle but perches the infant stiffly on her arm. Her explanation for her unusual behavior is that the baby "feels like a ton of bricks" and "makes my arms ache." When questioned about her style of giving a bottle, she looks mildly exasperated. She plainly doesn't see why everyone, not just the doctors but her husband and other relatives, makes such a big thing about it. As she patiently explains that her way is also more comfortable for the infant, who would feel constrained by the conventional position, too, an image suddenly flares in the viewer's mind: a solitary baby lying in a hospital crib, both uninvolved in her remote feedings and dependent on her arms and legs to speak for her.

Partly for historical reasons, the feeding of babies, from Monica herself to her dolls to her infants to theirs is the study's major preoccupation. Scientists now understand that different aspects of a child's maturation proceed simultaneously, in so-called parallel development. From Freud until quite recently, however, the process was thought to be "sequential," or occurring in predictable phases, each of which proceeds from the one before. Because problems in what Freud called the first, or "oral," stage would skew all the subsequent ones, feeding was considered of great moment in the 1950s, when psychoanalytical theory, including its views on personality, still dominated psychosomatic medicine and psychiatry.

When the Monica study began, psychiatrists no longer talked about Hippocrates' personality types but Freud's. He hooked his patients' characteristic troubles to one of five developmental phases, during which, he said, libidinal energy gradually shifted from the mouth—the "oral" phase—to the genitals. The wrong amount or kind of attention from parents caused a "fixation" at a particular stage and a rigid personality that was too passive or demanding, say, or too stingy or lavish. "If you were deprived of something important, such as your mother, during early development, then you'd have an oral personality and be dependent," says psychiatrist and personality researcher John Gunderson, clinical director of Harvard's MacLean Hospital. "If you had terrible toilet training, you'd be anal and grow up to be obsessive-compulsive. If you had a highly conflicted Oedipal period, you'd be hysterical."

Although subsequent research has shown that Freud's personalities weren't anchored in development or hierarchical in terms of pathology, says Gunderson, "the dependent, obsessive-compulsive, and hysterical ones live on as viable types." Freud would have said that Monica's early maternal deprivation and feeding difficulties gave her an oral personality of a dependent cast. What is sure is that were it not for psychiatry's fixation on that phase of development during the 1950s, the study might not have existed, and certainly wouldn't have had such an emphasis on feeding.

Forty years later, Monica's orality is less interesting than what her special approach to feeding babies suggests about the way in which we're shaped by memories of past experience. Even as a very small girl, despite others' example, she fed her dolls *her* way. In a usually compliant child who tries very hard to please, such assertiveness in doing what comes naturally is striking, and despite criticism, Monica has maintained it through grandmotherhood. Somehow, the mantle of maternity empowers her to shed her usual concern about what others think and to act from her own deep, hands-on sense of how the thing should be done. Her behavior may spring from experience, but it's no less an innate part of Monica than her smiling charisma is. As Harvard psychiatrist George Vaillant says, "Monica feeds the baby the way she does *because that's who she is.*" Like her unique history, ours have profoundly shaped who we are, but often in different, subtler ways than have been generally assumed.

As babies, we didn't have a personality, but only a characteristic bunch of discrete states—simultaneous physiological and psychological conditions—whose tone and duration depended largely on our temperaments. Over time, these modes, which included our styles of sleeping or being alert or distressed, were repeatedly triggered by environmental cues, such as being put to bed, talked to, or left. With experience, we became adept at slipping into certain states at certain times, thus fashioning our first schemas, or concepts of what the world is like and how we should behave in it. One of the most valuable dimensions of the Monica study's early films is their depiction of how our preverbal experience influences who we are.

During Monica's early isolation, she learned to cope with that dismal situation by going into a state of profound withdrawal: an adaptive, energy-conserving reaction to a cold, cruel world. Later, safe in the hospital, she responded to a newly benign environment with a charming state of active engagement. As a baby develops, such simple responsive conditions evolve into emotions—joy, fear, anger, sadness, interest, disgust. In time Monica not only withdrew from or engaged with certain stimuli but also looked as though she felt sad or happy. Moreover, each of these emotional states become tied to a self, such as an anxious, infantile one or a contented, sociable one. Formed largely by our temperamentally mediated responses to the repeated positive and negative events of early life, such states and selves are the core of our personality, which lies mostly submerged, like a psychic iceberg, in the depths of memory.

The science of memory is complex and evolving, and someday the many questions for which researchers now have only theoretical answers will have empirical ones. What is clear, however, is that there are more than one kind: different sorts of information get handled and stored in different ways by different parts of the brain. The process by which subjects in traditional experiments learn lists of words, for example, is not the same as the one that allows them to remember emotional experiences, particularly highly charged ones. When we speak of memory, we often mean the so-called episodic sort that concerns the recollection of events, from what we had for lunch today to what we got for our birthday last year. Yet all the learning and knowledge we've acquired, from the shortcut to the beach to Shakespeare's sonnets, is memory, too, of the semantic sort. Episodic and semantic recollections, based in the brain's amygdala and hippocampus, are both forms of well-lit conscious, or representational, memory: we're aware that we're aware of what's stored there and with minor lapses, particularly after the age of forty, can access it.

Sunk in the brain's striatum and caudate nucleus lies a deeper kind of memory, variously termed habit, emotional, or procedural. Much harder to call up at will than representational memory, it's involved in much more of our behavior. In many respects, procedural memory resembles what Freud, working before the days of modern neuroanatomy, called the unconscious. We remember what happens to us, he said, but, depending on how well we do so, the memory is either available to consciousness or, particularly if it's upsetting, cut off from awareness and repressed in the unconscious. Neuroscience has updated Freud's brain model, turning his terms into adjectives. By way of modern analogy, the brain's conscious awareness is the computer's screen and its unconscious processes are the circuits hidden in the box of the CPU.

Generally, it's a very good thing to have these two memory systems rather than just one to expedite behavior. If we had to pay simultaneous, deliberate attention to talking, thinking, listening, and gesturing, we couldn't even manage a simple chat. Fortunately, most of our standard operating procedures are handled by unconscious processes usually activated by subliminal cues. Our far more limited, focused, specialized conscious capacity is thus free to deal with matters that require deliberation. Where routines are concerned, we can function on automatic pilot, acting first and thinking later, if at all. We don't have to ruminate over how to ride a bike or whether we should cover our noses on sneezing or, if we're lucky, go to the gym; that information has been stored in a way that enables us to "just do it." As we drive home, we can shift and brake without thinking, focused on what to make for dinner or pack for vacation; if a traffic jam interrupts the flow, we can snap to and deliberate about a detour.

In making us so efficient, however, nature has considered the forest rather than the trees. Conducting business as usual may generally be cost-effective, but not all unconscious schemas based on the past serve us well in the present, or at least in certain situations. Unfortunately, the same brain function that enables us instantly to apologize for stomping on someone's foot or to hold out a hand when meeting a stranger can automatically swamp our adult ambitions with childhood's fear of failure or spoil yet another promising relationship with that same old jealousy or stinginess.

Examples of the inappropriate behavioral generalization inspired by procedural memory crop up in Monica's life as in ours. Her early experience taught her to be very careful about taking risks, which was a good strategy in a dangerous situation. In adult life, however, this habitual caution can needlessly limit her, as it has in her reluctance to drive. She learned how, but several shaky initial forays behind the wheel caused her to give it up.

In short, the way in which the promptings of procedural memory cue knee-jerk behavior is awfully convenient when it comes to unloading the dishwasher or saying please and thank you. The same form of remote control, however, can turn any boss or spouse into a facsimile of a troubling parent or cause us to crave a snack or a shot whenever we pass a kitchen or a bar. The ways in which we've encoded our experience—good and bad, adaptive and destructive—not only direct our behavior and shape who we are as surely as genes do but often seem no less mysterious or resistant to change.

In *Through the Looking Glass,* the Queen remarks, "It's a poor sort of memory that only works backwards." In supporting her insight, recent research shows that not only is there more than one kind of memory, it involves more than one tense. Rather than being just a simple melody about past events, memory is increasingly revealed as a harmony in which the present sings an important part. Despite our fond prejudices, our experiences aren't tidily sealed up and stored in some cranial filing cabinet. With his demotic flair for making ponderous scientific theories accessible, Daniel Stern says, "There's nothing in the memory but fragments, sitting around in a not very elaborated form." At the moment of remembering, we reassemble certain bits of this experiential flotsam and jetsam into a collage whose background is our current state. That's why the memory of being twenty-one is different at forty-two than at twenty-two and why a wedding day is recalled differently years later by a happy couple and a divorced one. When memory is understood in this dynamic way, says Stern, "what's procedural or representational or whatever, isn't interesting, even if true. You remember in the present, not the past. How you put together the historical fragments and come up with a particular memory depends on how you experience yourself as you do so—your 'remembering context.' "

Memory may even be multidimensional in a social as well as a temporal and a functional sense. In *Wuthering Heights,* when Catherine Earnshaw tries to explain her bond with a seemingly unsuitable man, she says simply, "I *am* Heathcliff." Her perception is reinforced by painstaking studies in which Stern investigated several difficult questions: When one person is with another, what really goes on in his mind? How does the past color his experience of the present? To what extent does the event activate his memory? How much does his sense of what that experience is all about actually influence what he does? To find some answers, Stern intensively interviewed mothers of preschoolers about a "moment" that involved their children.

In one moment study, a woman watched her son be enthusiatically greeted by a good friend at nursery school. As she observed her child's happiness and sense of acceptance, she shifted around in her seat. Then, as she was barraged with memories and thoughts triggered by the seemingly inconsequential event, her attention turned inward and she withdrew into her chair. What was going on inside her at that point concerned her own childhood in a troubled family and a consequent feeling that she had never "belonged." Because of the woman's own experience, says Stern, "she hadn't thought that feeling part of something could be experienced by anything that was part of her. But she felt that with her son. Along with the rush of identification with and happiness for him, however, she also felt sad for that little girl of the past."

In another moment study, a mother watched her son examine a shelf of dolls and then choose the daddy. "When she started talking about how he really preferred to be with his father," says Stern, "I first thought she was going in a jealousy or competition direction concerning who was the better parent. Had I been asking her the usual clinician-type questions, that's what I would have gone after. But she wasn't into that at all. She felt very comfortable with her son's choice, and it turned out that her own father had mostly taken care of her as a child."

The striking implication of the moment studies is that when we have a significant interaction with someone else, we register the event in two parts: what happened to us and our take on what happened to the other person—so-called empathic capture. When Stern asks a mother who's paying attention to her child, "Whose skin are you in right now?" she often says, "I can't tell—about in the middle." This kind of reaction inclines him to think that, "at least as a memorial fragment, you experience both sides of an important relationship."

If we are haunted in such a way by our pasts, Monica's style of feeding her baby derives not only from her own experience of being fed *but also from her sense of her mother as nurturer.* Inadvertently tipping his hat to the mother-in-law jokes that are one of the small banes of wifely existence, Stern says, "So often, without the foggiest idea of why, a mother suddenly starts acting like her own mother. That's not regression or even memory in the usual sense but rather the way that the woman reconstructs her past life, given her present situation. When you find yourself in a situation that you haven't been in since you were little, a memory will get worked into your present experience." It's often unremarked, even among scientists, but we spend much of the present listening to the background hum of the past and feeling both sides of whatever story is unfolding. Stern can plot on paper the way one of our reactions to an event triggers and retriggers another, back and forth and almost simultaneously. His charts notwithstanding, "these moments are not objective thoughts," he says, "but very subtle, highly nuanced subjective landscapes."

Although Stern can't interview babies as he can their mothers, he is a pioneer in exploring the infant's inner landscapes and their formative effects. In *Diary of a Baby,* he writes about year-old Joey's experience of the separation response—the distress felt by all mammalian infants on being parted from their mothers: after wandering off from his mother—his "psychological oxygen"—Joey's ensuing panic involves "a feeling of becoming fragmented, of losing boundaries, of disappearing into a lonely, empty infinity." Without her presence, the world becomes "boundless," he feels: "Nothing holds me." Later in life, writes Stern, this sensation particularly torments victims of agoraphobia—a fear of open spaces—and panic disorder, which many psychiatrists view as an acute adult separation reaction. But none of us is immune to such feelings, which Stern compares to those that would be elicited by "finding oneself swimming in the ocean, out of sight of land and the boat drifting away."

Throughout life, the threat of losing our most important partner— whether spouse or parent—has similar, if less dramatic effects. "The separation reaction is basic to us all and may not change much from the age of twelve months till death," writes Stern. "Certainly, we become better at avoiding it, coping with it, and, perhaps most commonly, at designing our lives so that crucial separations are less of a potential threat. But they are always with us." Recovery for this little boy, as "for all primates," comes in the form of ventral contact with his loved one— chest to chest, his head upon her shoulder and neck. With the sensation of his mother's touch, "the ultimate magic of attachment," Joey's "quieting starts at the surface and flows inward." His anxious state subsides as "the pull of her presence helps him to reconstitute and integrate himself after feeling dissolved." Restored to his relationship and himself, Joey will soon be ready to set forth again.

We have all been in Joey's small shoes. If we learned, as he did, that our cries would usually be answered and our needs mostly met, many of us concluded that the world was a pretty good place and behaved accordingly. For some of us, however, temperament made the lesson harder to absorb; still others, such as Monica, were taught something different. If her innate star quality is the bright theme of the film study, just how profoundly Monica has been shaped by her early experience of separation and deprivation is the dark one. In one scene, Monica, a young mother, explains that at feeding time, she usually puts the baby into an infant seat with a propped-up bottle. "I don't hold her," she says. "She seems to eat better lying down by herself." Not only has Monica re-created her mother's remote behavior during her infancy, but her own.

Even during her early life, however, Monica had other teachers who taught other lessons, and their legacy, too, is apparent in the films. Particularly when her baby is lying down while Monica hovers above, as during a diaper change, she's warm and involved, playing, talking, and smiling—the proverbial "different person" from the bored woman who watches TV or smokes through feedings. Monica's attunement with her children in these moments is so heartening that one can't help but think that, as Lynne Hofer says, "maybe feeding isn't as important as they thought back then." No longer the dybbuk of her own depressed young mother, left alone to feed a seemingly doomed baby, this other Monica is a reincarnation of Dr. Reichsman or kindly Nurse Dailey doting on the darling of the pediatric ward lying in her crib. In demonstrating Stern's belief that "mothers repeat actively what they learned passively as infants," these eerie scenes—both the chilling and the heartwarming—underscore as no words can our past's inextricability from who we are. If personality is our distinctive suite of temperamentally mediated states, selves, and schemas hooked to recollected experience, we are creatures not just of our genes but of our histories, and we shift our psychic shapes in the flickering light of things past. Without memory, we would have no personality at all.

"Who can say what events formed his own character?" writes sociobiologist E. O. Wilson. "Too many occur in the twilight of early childhood. The mind lives in half-remembered experiences of uncertain valence, where self-deception twists memory further from truth with every passing year." The question of exactly what Monica, or any of us, recalls of life's first few years is intriguing. Like the films of her giving a bottle to her babies, earlier scenes of Monica playing with dolls, along with the study's written records of her behavior and remarks, allude to her own unusual early feedings. Although there were never any photographs that showed her gastric defect to prod such recollections, little Monica talked about babies who don't have mouths or who leak from the neck or have an "open tum." Nor is Monica the only person in the films who seems to remember feedings in infancy. In one particularly spine-tingling sequence, her eldest daughter, recorded at the ages of nineteen and twenty-six months, gives her doll a bottle in the same idiosyncratic manner in which she and her sisters had been fed in their own first months. Only later in childhood do the girls play at feeding in the conventional way favored by their father.

Pioneering personality theorist Henry Murray observed that "children perceive inaccurately, are very little conscious of their inner states, and retain fallacious recollections of occurrences. Many adults are hardly better." Many scientists agree, considering real self-awareness—consciousness of an "I" who acts—and the ability to use language to be prerequisites for the meaningful storage of events. Then too, that parts of the brain involved in the physiology of memory don't mature till the age of two casts doubt on recollections before that point. While Stern thinks that there's "no question" that very young children have some procedural memory of certain emotional experiences—Monica's of her early feedings is one example—he finds that their ability to record history in the conventional sense is harder to gauge. To him, the accuracy of such memories "depends a lot on how much recalling and reminding go on in the interim between the event and the recollection. Remembering depends an awful lot on how much gets retriggered, and that's something we don't ask or know much about."

One reason that the words of "The Star-spangled Banner" spring to mind more readily than those of the "Liebestod" aria in *Tristan und Isolde* is that our recall of the national anthem is stimulated at every baseball game. Something of the same phenomenon seems to be involved in our more personal memories as well, even early in life. Experiments show that a three-month-old baby usually forgets an isolated experience after three to five days. If during that interval he gets little reminders of what happened, however, he remembers the event for several weeks. As Stern observes, each memory has lots of different elements—whatever you felt, saw, heard, or otherwise perceived at the time. "Presumably, any one of those cues can be a reminder, especially if the memory is functional—that is, doing something for you." By this light, Monica and her daughters needn't remember being fed as infants because of some mental videotape of the event that's stored in their heads. They remember because *they kept their own experience alive* in their behavior with their dolls or babies. Their reenactment of the past illustrates the "phenotypic cloning" by which families can transmit learned behavioral tendencies to children for generations. Thus, we—and our ancestors—live on not only through our genes but through our memories, states, schemas, and selves, empathically captured, modified, and handed down throughout time.

When we talk about our memories, we usually aren't referring to the deep, gut-level form of living recollection but to the so-called autobiographical sort: what happened on the first day of school or during vacation. While most children's accounts of such events "aren't bad," says Stern, "there are troubles with them." He finds that when children try to remember on their own, they "lose pieces." Moreover, most of what they come up with involves "coconstructions that they make with someone else. Kids remember much better that way, but the input of the other person starts to get very important."

Where highly stressful events are concerned, questions regarding children's recollections become particularly complicated. When a small child experiences something that's upsetting, say, a fight between his parents, he may say to himself, "I don't want to know what's happening here." The situation has activated a coping mechanism that allows him to protect himself by partially turning off. Later, however, he really *doesn't* know what happened. If the child is asked if he remembers the incident, what he recalls may not be the fight but his coping mechanism: not the historical event but his emotional reaction to it. "What most determines what a kid says about something that happened," says Stern, "is how he dealt with it at the time."

The most contentious issues regarding early memory and how it shapes us concern recollections of trauma, particularly child abuse. Despite the impression often given by pop psych and media accounts, while some people who were so tormented have trouble recalling what happened, the vast majority don't. Part of the reason for that may be physiological. Although most memories are mere fragments, certain very vivid events seem to be stored whole. Psychologist James McGaugh found that subjects who took a common antihypertensive drug that blocks certain stress hormones that are involved in storing emotionally charged information had poorer recall of emotional experiences than those who didn't. In unmedicated subjects, the affective jolts set off by an arousing event activate the hormones that sharpen the memory of such experiences. Painful as they are, from an evolutionary perspective the vivid flashbacks that plague some combat veterans and other trauma victims have an adaptive aspect: they promote survival by ensuring that that particular danger will never be forgotten. Along with the possibility that abuse generates such neurochemically heightened recall, the fact that it usually takes place in the everyday world of home and family, where the context cues abound, also decreases the chances that it will be forgotten. As Stern says, "There's always a reminder, not necessarily of the abuse but of 'something.' "

Partly because the psychic membranes between memories, selves, and states are so permeable, the life stories that we reflect on and recount are not objective newsreels but allegories. That's why, particularly in the collaborative process of psychotherapy, some people innocently "remember" things that never occurred, especially where early life is concerned. Certain incidents of child abuse suddenly recalled by adults vividly demonstrate that a memory is a construct rather than a record. At first, on listening to his patients, Freud believed that, as children, most had really been molested. He later concluded that, in many cases, what he was hearing were the remembered imaginings of someone too young to distinguish fantasy from reality.

Particularly when returning to a troubled past, a person may vividly recall not only certain stressful events but also "traumatic material that's based on a combination of events and nonevents, which can be hard to differentiate," says psychiatrist and psychoanalyst Mardi Horowitz, who conducts research on conscious and unconscious states and personality at the University of California in San Francisco. "We've all experienced something similar when we say, 'Did I dream that or did it happen?' It can be very difficult to tell." Not even the fact that some people confess to crimes of abuse that they didn't commit surprises him. "A fundamental human question of great evolutionary significance is 'Who or what is to blame?' One source of what Freud called the unconscious sense of guilt is certain bad, evil, degraded representations of the self. When they're activated, even if they're unconscious, they can organize consciousness into a whole story according to this script."

His exploration of the nuanced, highly subjective landscapes between our ears inclines Stern to regard scenes of Monica feeding her dolls or babies as reflections less of stimulus deprivation than of a skewed experience of what relationships are. To him, her predicament was "not about what's lacking, but about how a child—in this case, one who has a depressed mother—constructs reality in terms of her situation." The way in which all of us, not just Monica, handle this developmental task of conceptualizing the world in our own unique way has, as Stern says, "huge implications for future continuity."

One of the most interesting but least heralded insights from twin studies is this: even identicals reared apart, whose temperaments are so uncannily alike, can be quite different in terms of their educations, beliefs, and other parameters of private experience. One of them—a special type of memory—particularly fascinates psychiatrist George Vaillant. His tenure as the director of Harvard's Study of Adult Development, which incorporates three major longitudinal surveys of people's lives, has convinced him that the ways in which people important to us have influenced how we construct reality not only are vital to who we are but are the "wild cards in scientists' game of trying to predict behavior." Standard personality questionnaires and evaluations don't measure what psychologists call coping strategies and Vaillant and his fellow psychoanalysts call defense mechanisms: the characteristic ways in which an individual frames stressful phenomena in order to limit anxiety. The "assimilational" personality model that Vaillant favors centers on a form of highly emotional memory by which we incorporate certain values—good or bad—of special people: a process he calls "taking another inside." Depending on whom we've absorbed in this way, we hear an internal message telling us that we should deal with a difficult situation by getting drunk or going for a run, by calling in sick or going in early to catch up. Like other children who've had a depressed mother, Monica has "taken inside" that sad persona, whose voice prompts her to give up and withdraw. But she has also assimilated her doting grandmother and the doctors and nurses of the pediatric ward, whose voices call up the lovable, smiling star.

To Vaillant, Monica's story is a testimonial to a healthy personality's adaptive defenses. Heeding the lessons of early deprivation, she skillfully employs anticipation, or reducing stress by avoiding, or at least preparing for, difficult situations. She also continues to shepherd her resources carefully, for example, rising early to sit alone on her porch and gather herself for the day. When pressed to the limit, Monica uses denial to soften life's vicissitudes. When this same defense mechanism is employed to excess by, say, an alcoholic who insists that his drinking is under control, it can be disastrous, but Monica uses it judiciously. The most poignant example is her filmed reaction to watching movies of herself as a depressed, nearly moribund baby: "Oh, she was tired," says the woman of that pitiful long-ago self. "She doesn't look too good. Maybe it was the medication or the tubes that made her sad." Years before just as she and her husband made a wrenching move south, Monica tells her interviewer that she is dealing with this frightening prospect by not believing that it will really happen. In a later sequence, she attributes her muted reaction to her mother's death to her inability to believe that the woman with whom she had such a complex relationship is really, truly gone. To Vaillant, the insulation provided by her mature deployment of ego defenses largely accounts for Monica's triumph over adversity that would have leveled most others.

Among the Harvard men whose lives have been tracked for decades by the famous Grant study of physical and emotional health, a few elements stand out as profound influences on well-being. The beneficial effects of the love of a good woman and the destructive ones of alcoholism and untreated depression are prominent examples. But, says

Vaillant, "if you looked at who had, between the ages of twenty-one and seventy, spun straw into gold or gold into straw, you'd find that there were so many unpredictable transformations that it was almost random. Any formula you'd come up with would be closer to chaos theory than how-to advice."

To illustrate his conviction that wild-card defense mechanisms are the major obstacles to pat personality theories, Vaillant cites some compelling anecdotes. In response to vicious death threats against him and his family, Martin Luther King "got up and talked about bringing out the love in our brothers," he says. "How did he do that? He 'took inside' his minister father, a principled, consistent man who had a strong worldview. He also took inside a grandmother, who, because she wept whenever his stern, old-fashioned father beat him, let Martin know that he was special and lovable. But can you *really* explain someone who reacts to threat by telling people to be loving? No book can tell a person how to turn disadvantage into advantage or how to make his central nervous system instantly transform stress into compassion or humor. Whether a personality researcher looks for nature or nurture, defenses are an enormous confound."

All defenses serve the same purpose—reducing anxiety—yet they are not created equal. Their adaptivity can be arranged according to the degree to which they permit a true consciousness of what's really going on—say, a painful divorce. Least helpful are the "psychotic" defenses, such as delusion: "She's only leaving me because aliens are controlling her mind." Next come the "immature," such as hypochondria: "I'm not upset that she left, but I think I have cancer." Then there are the "neurotic" defenses, such as intellectualization: "She wasn't good enough for me, anyway." Of the best, or "mature" ones, humor is the most lovable and altruism the most nearly divine. Martin Luther King was not the only great leader who mastered the latter. A shy child whose cold mother died, leaving her to an alcoholic father, Eleanor Roosevelt grew up to spend her life with a demanding cripple who was not only an unfaithful husband but allowed his tyrannical mother to bully her. In response, says Vaillant, "Eleanor looked out for all the other poor people who were shortchanged by life and got for them some of the good things she wanted for herself." Many great artists have tapped the power of another mature defense, which enables them to use their stormy affect to create rather than destroy. By way of illustration, Vaillant brings up an enormously talented young boy whose alcoholic father beat him and tried to crush his spirit: "What were the chances that he'd end up as Beethoven did? The Ninth Symphony wouldn't have been written if he hadn't inherited the musical genius of a hated father whom, with the help of Schiller's 'Ode to Joy,' he turned into an idealized one. You can't predict a Beethoven, who could have been just another man filled with rage. To get at defenses, you first have to see where nature and nurture predict that someone would fit and then see where he gets and how he got there."

Defense mechanisms can be observed and their etiologies speculated about, says Vaillant, but such theories only go so far. "How did van Gogh, only modestly talented as a draftsman, use his brain disease to make those pictures? To ask why some people have good defenses and others poor ones is like asking why everyone can't paint like van Gogh. When someone finds his Christmas stocking full of horseshit, what makes him able to say, 'Isn't Santa great? He knows I'm going to need this to grow those strawberries I love!' It's a gift. Some people are psychological klutzes, and some, like Monica, are psychological artists."

No simple solo plainsong, memory's rich harmony has many parts. Its notes aren't just a record of the past but a sketchy score for the present and future. In the most recent film, the Monica who gives her little grandchild a bottle is far easier and more animated than the serious young mother in the earlier sequences—but the baby still reclines at a remove on her cocked knee. Like Monica, we do much of what we do because a memory of some sort produces a certain state or a state evokes a memory. Either one elicits a self and a schema of what's going on in the world and what we should do about it. The selves that get evoked most frequently become what we and others recognize as who we are.

Borrowing from neuroscientist Gerald Edelman's model of how the brain works, Daniel Stern regards this *process* of personality as a continuous Darwinian selection that goes on within each individual. "In the course of evolving itself," he says, "the mind develops schemas for similar situations—sometimes several for the same one—that compete with each other not for neural space but functional time and control over the executive machinery." When Monica feeds a doll or baby, for example, the familiar robotic schema evoked by that situation usually wins the competition. Occasionally, however, she picks up her toys or daughters in a less rigid, more conventionally cradling fashion: the triumph of another schema that she "owns" but that usually loses the battle to determine her behavior.

Unlike more abstract, static personality models, a Darwinian perspective on why an individual is the way he is accommodates both personal continuity and growth. "Such a system can change," says Stern, "but isn't likely to change very much—it's both a conservative and radical solution. History is against change, but the system is dynamic, so that things can happen that will throw it off and permit something new."

CHAPTER 7

BEING YOURSELF

When Monica marries her Prince Charming, the proud Rochester doctors are naturally there to record the great event. At the reception, everything is just so. The elaborately gowned, veiled, and coiffed teenage bride ceremonially pecks her new husband on the cheek and cuts the cake with almost surgical care. The sight of such a young person on the brink of adult life, much less one with Monica's history, inspires empathy. No matter how intuitive, however, no one else could discern all the gossamer threads that connect this day to those of her past, weaving the intricate pattern, unique as a snowflake, that is Monica's experience of her wedding.

Just as who we are is shaped by the external world, so it is by our internal one. Perhaps because it's so difficult to describe how a personality *feels*, it has been more art's province than science's. "How queer to have so many selves," wrote Virginia Woolf, one of the stream-of-consciousness authors Daniel Stern admires for attempting to express what private experience is really like. Because they pursue an aesthetic goal, however, even these writers must "cheat on reality," says Stern. "Their writing feels correct, but it's actually not." Another group of keen professional observers is distracted from the moment by a different, scientific aim. "You'd think psychoanalysts would know everything about personal experience, but they don't, either," says Stern, "because they use it as a springboard to associations. They know a lot about people's lives but not about what really happens in the moment.

It's not that one kind of knowledge is truer than another but that they're different."

In one of his research efforts to capture a person's experience, Stern asks subjects to think back to their breakfast that morning, zero in on a particular interval of up to thirty seconds, and spend an hour telling him everything they thought, felt, and did. Helped by certain cognitive techniques, such as pretending to be a cameraman who's filming the proceedings, the volunteers recall "a huge amount," he says. "So many things happen at the same time, in parallel layers and with many discontinuities, that the data almost have to be scored like music."

By way of illustration, Stern describes the breakfast moment of a little girl who has just moved to a new town. Sitting at the table while wondering whether she should get a place mat, she listens to music that reminds her of a friend back home. She "sort of" feels she ought to set the mat, because she doesn't want to annoy her stepmother. On the other hand, the woman is still in bed with the girl's father. As she thinks almost simultaneously about herself, her stepmother, her father, and her friend, "where is the child's center of gravity as an experiencer?" asks Stern. "That's a very hard thing for her, or anyone, to tell you, because it floats back and forth from dining room to bedroom, new town and old one, this person and that. It's extremely difficult to describe and score, yet it's how life *really* is. Very, very complicated."

Not only a life's current themes but also a personality's most salient features shine through particular moments. In one such, a woman who's both dieting and trying to get pregnant stands in the kitchen, preparing to make a low-cal shake. First she turns on the radio, hears a preacher talking, and thinks, "Oh damn, I wanted music." Opening the refrigerator to get an egg, she hesitates over which one to pick but finally takes the last in the row. When she puts a little too much milk into the blender, she wonders if she should pour it out, so as not to cheat on her diet. An impulse impels her to turn off the preacher—she doesn't want to be lectured to—but the phone rings. As she says hello to her brother, she worries that the noise has awakened her husband. Her mind travels to the bedroom and, from a diagonal vantage point near the ceiling, watches him sleep. Then, as her brother tells her where to meet him later, she's back in the kitchen. As the moment ends, she's holding the phone in one hand and the blender in the other. While contemplating the patterns in the tile floor, she's also seeing herself in the future, waiting for her brother, who's always late. Stern observes that the woman who's trying to conceive is about to dine on eggs and milk, has a somewhat obsessive, impulsive personality, and is troubled by her brother. But he's mostly interested in the fact that "she's never just where she is. Because what happens in the chosen interval is important, you pick up very central things about a person. This moment is her world."

Asked by the awestruck Moses for some identification, God answers from the burning bush, "I am who I am." Such cool must be a divine prerogative. For the rest of us, personality and the insider's view of it called self aren't eternal absolutes but characteristic repertoires of behavioral patterns that allow us to react flexibly to the environment. Despite evidence to the contrary, from moment research to our own experience, both comfort and convenience incline us to shy away from our multiplicity. We speak as if we really harbor in our heads what psychologist Theodore Millon calls the "the host": a central mental agency that transcends our different ways of being. No one has such a handy psychic Jeeves. Some personalities, however, look and function like a bunch of odd beads rattling around in a box, while others are like a beautifully matched strand of pearls. Much of the difference depends on our ability to recall information about one state and self when in another. Memory is the thread that strings together all our modes into a personality.

In choosing breakfast as a setting in which to study what people and their inner lives are really like, Stern deliberately selected a time when the brain, somewhat fuzzy and occupied only with pedestrian activities, "idles a bit." The popularity of hobbies and sports, crossword puzzles and meetings, TV and talk radio attests to the fact that many of us try to avoid quiet, inward-looking states. At such times, we're more open to what Carl Jung called shadow—or negative, private—experiences, from complex feelings about a parent's remarriage to the conflict between getting slim and getting pregnant. There can be "fun" in reflective self-awareness, says psychiatrist Mardi Horowitz, "Yet some people don't think so, because in that state they experience self-loathing. Most of us carry on an interior monologue, based on our previous associations, that's a gloss on ongoing events. Because this stream of thought is mostly made up of unfinished business of long standing—little chats with mental caricatures of parents, for example—tuning into it is often mildly aversive, provoking emotions of fear, guilt, and anger."

This history- and affect-laden stream of consciousness has to do with memory but is something more, too. When the brain is idling a bit, or daydreaming, we're likelier to tap into the stuff of night dreams, or what Freud called the unconscious. Freud thought that, like behavior generally, personality arises from the struggle between our powerful, largely unconscious sexual and aggressive instincts and our conscious awareness of society's demands, which are nearly as hardwired because we absorb them from our earliest days. Personality is revealed not only by what we do, but *why*. Although Freud's is not the only theory of motivation, it is the most magisterial.

Cigarette advertisements that show gorgeous young people radiant with health and perfumes called Opium and Obsession illustrate the ongoing war between unconscious and conscious motivations that Freud called "psychodynamics." Anyone who has ever broken up with one loser only to take on another, dieted by day and snacked by night, or slept through the alarm on the morning of an important meeting has had firsthand experience of Freud's great insight: things that we wish for or fear without being conscious of the fact can nonetheless shape personality and behavior. In the eighteenth century, a hundred years before psychoanalysis, hypnotists demonstrated that we have two mental systems that don't always send complementary messages. By successfully ordering subjects not to see objects in plain view and even to forget being "mesmerized," they demonstrated the existence of unconscious processes.

In a modern film exploration of the phenomenon, the protagonist-volunteer in a documentary called *The Honest Liar* is hypnotized by a memory researcher, then told that there's a Communist plot to infiltrate American media. The subject has no conscious awareness of learning that some people he knows are involved and that only he can sound the alarm. But in a later scene, when he meets with two men he thinks are major television executives, he passionately tries to persuade them to defend the United States against this ideological menace. Eagerly, he denounces old friends as Commie traitors, embroidering his false assertions with many particulars. When he's finally told about the nature of the experiment, the honest liar is stunned by the realization that who he is and what he does depend on two internal systems, one of which operates without his awareness.

Even in Freud's day, other scientists acknowledged the importance of the unconscious activity that constitutes most of what's going on upstairs at any moment. Freud's rival Pierre Janet decided that, other than being relatively inaccessible, material from what he called the subconscious wasn't necessarily irrational, sexual, aggressive, or otherwise different from the conscious sort. As an alternative to Freud's theories of the unconscious and repression, Janet proposed the principle of dissociation, or the separation of normally related psychological processes into independent units. A traumatic event could generate an "automatism"—a behavioral entity incorporating thought, emotion, and action—that was cut off from a person's conscious awareness and control. Like the monkey wrench in the works, this idée fixe would then proceed to interfere with the smooth functioning of a person's behavioral machinery.

To illustrate how motives we don't even know we have can shape who we are and what we do, psychoanalytically oriented Harvard psychologist and personality theorist Drew Westen conjures up a husband and wife committed to avoiding sexual stereotypes in their home life. Despite their good intentions, gross disparities in the amounts of domestic labor they do are almost inevitable until the woman finally says, "Honey, you haven't been taking care of the baby much lately." The husband says, "Gee, that's right," and pitches in, but over the course of time his efforts drop off again. "As research now documents, we have two motive systems," says Westen. "When we purposely focus on our conscious aspirations, they're activated. When we don't, which is most of the time, our unconscious ones are in charge." As the well-meaning couple's cycle shows, the way to handle problematic unconscious motives is to haul them into the light of awareness, where they can be inspected, evaluated, and modified. "In a nutshell, that's what psychoanalysis is about," says Westen. "Anyone who doesn't appreciate that we can have conflicting motives has missed much of the twentieth century's understanding of the human condition."

Psychoanalysis is often disparaged as unscientific or as a narcissistic luxury for "the healthy and wealthy," but its take on how we experience ourselves and why we do what we do has extremely practical applications. Racism is one example. If research subjects are primed with certain words, such as "black" and "Hispanic," that are flashed at them too quickly to be consciously perceived, their subsequent responses reveal their unconscious prejudices; compared to unprimed subjects, for example, they're quicker to recognize "bad" as a word. Given that it's not a perfect world, even people who are determined not to be prejudiced get caught between their conscious values, says Westen, "and unconscious ones that are based partly on irrational stereotypes and partly on reality. One reality, for example, is that there's a disproportionate number of people of color behind the weapons that terrorize the cities. Another is that black male professionals report that, in their presence, white people may shrink back or check their wallets. Yet if you said to the same person who reacted that way, 'What's your impression of that young man over there in the suit and tie?' he might be unaware that he had patted his pocket and give a totally different response based on his conscious values."

As the example of racism suggests, the conflicts between our conscious and unconscious mental processes shape and misshape not only our own personalities but our society. As a college professor and clinician, Westen is particularly aware of one example. If a minority student is failing a course, he can consciously decide to compensate by working harder and getting extra help. Or he can unconsciously fall back on the attitude of "It's not me, it's the system"—a rationalization that worsens his situation. Teachers, too, can get caught in the same internal crossfire, either attributing such a student's poor performance to race or overlooking it because of misplaced feelings about social injustice. Unable to discuss, much less resolve, their individual conflicts, students and professors can become polarized or settle for an awkward, unsatisfactory status quo.

When an issue pits buried feelings against deliberate goals, said Freud, we may unknowingly attempt to reduce the resulting conflict by taking an extreme position. "Until we understand our tendency to defend ourselves against conflict by moving toward an extreme position, we'll have incoherent public policy and trial verdicts," says Westen. As examples, he cites the initial acquittal of the policemen who beat Rodney King and the minimal sentence given to the man who, during the ensuing riots, damaged Reginald Denny's brain with a slab of concrete. In such situations, he says, "if jurists aren't aware of both their conscious and unconscious motives, they can either condemn a person for the color of his skin or fail to condemn someone who deserves that judgment for the content of his character."

Hardly restricted to matters of race, unconscious conflicts undermine many social institutions—even the field of psychology. Although research shows that girls who have been sexually abused are often drawn in adulthood to situations in which they're vulnerable to more abuse, for example, researchers and clinicians are unwilling to recognize and discuss the problem openly. "Today we have two dialogues about gender, affirmative action, and anything else related to political correctness," says Westen. "One is public, and one is private. That's what happens when we're not honest about our conflicts. Denying things doesn't make them go away. The solution, Freud said, was to make unconscious things conscious, so that then you can reflect on them and act accordingly."

At a time when drives are as out of fashion as original sin, Freud is the genius we love to hate, with some reason. He mirrored his culture's male biases regarding women, and even his contemporaries objected to his grisly emphasis on mankind's base motivations. Carl Jung said that his former mentor treated the brain as "an appendage to the genital glands." Neo-Freudians have turned away from the instincts of the funky id to a sunnier "ego psychology" in which more volitional "wishes" replace deterministic drives, and development, whose particulars Freud got wrong, continues beyond reproductive maturity. By the time Erik Erikson devised his full-fledged developmental theory of personality, the individual's goal had become "ego identity" rather than genital sexuality. Then too, psychoanalytic theory can seem anachronistic in the age of "chemical imbalances." Many of Freud's constructs, such as repression and the id, ego, and superego, can be neither proved nor disproved and must therefore be regarded as metaphorical rather than scientific.

After thousands of years during which the origins of behavior were often regarded as supernatural, Freud offered a coherent explanation that was as systematic and scientific as the tools at his disposal allowed. Although he's often cast in the antithetical role, Freud was a biologist who put behavior into a developmental context and would have delighted in Paul MacLean's discovery of the structures of the limbic system, the site of sexual and aggressive instincts. Freud realized the influence of the past, particularly childhood, on the present, and the important differences between child and adult. He probed the unconscious a century before it was empirically proved, discovered our defensive tendency to "remember" à la *Rashomon,* and saw that only the tip of a personality's iceberg bobs at the surface of the conscious mind. The psychoanalytic technique of talking about oneself, which he developed not as a treatment but as a research tool, has generated a uniquely sophisticated body of knowledge about personality and remains the therapy of choice for those with the time, money, and inclination to restructure character. In the future, some brilliant person will reconcile modern neuroscience with the deepest views of what people are really like, which continue to be mined from the psychic vein discovered by Freud.

As surely as innate traits, all the things stored in our heads that can figure in our conscious experience, from unconscious motivations to carefully chosen goals, from what happened when we were three to what happened yesterday, shape who we are. Many of our formative memories date from early childhood, but not all. Very stressful events, such as combat, an assault, or a serious illness, can recast the world as a less benign, predictable place and the self as more vulnerable.

In studies of the long walk down memory lane that is an integral part of bereavement, Mardi Horowitz tracks the transitions of an individual's states and selves not from moment to moment, as Daniel Stern does, but over longer periods of time. "Merely thinking through the loss and what it means, which one could do quickly, doesn't accomplish mourning," says Horowitz. "Unless it's stifled, something occurs on an unconscious time schedule. Months of denial, for example, may be followed by a period of intrusive thinking. The person doesn't deliberately intend any of this, so the unconscious must be doing something." Because mourning offers a glimpse into an individual's hidden as well as deliberate processes, Horowitz considers it an ideal venue for the assessment of a personality: "the psychological equivalent of the cardiovascular stress test" that reveals not just traits, but characteristic ways of regulating emotion and coping with the world.

Because bereavement involves what amounts to a grand tour of a person's memories, it throws into high relief a person's whole collection of states, selves, and schemas. Whether someone is grieving or not, good memories engender benign states and comfortable selves, and bad ones, anxious states and distasteful selves. If, for example, our earliest winter holidays were happy, those memories stir each December, put us in a merry mood, and enable us—and others—to enjoy ourselves. If our memories are of family feuds, drunken relatives, and coal in the stocking, however, December plunges us into a dark pit in which we partly become that unhappy child, who may strike our familiars as "a different person." Cued by various recollections of his lost relationship, the bereaved reviews not only the death, but all the facts and fantasies of his life with the deceased. On one occasion he idealizes their experience, and on the next is unable to think of anything good about it. With these memorial fluctuations come selves that are "good, kind, and loving," says Horowitz, "and weak, rotten, and so evil that he wanted the person to die."

Albeit less dramatically, the same solid and shaky, ridiculous and divine selves populate our day-to-day lives. When upset, for example, "you recognize your unstable state," says Horowitz, "and so does your spouse, who says, 'There you go again.' " Because we have multiple selves, when the situation demands it we can usually tap, say, a cool, collected, professional one that blocks, at least briefly, an anxious one: you may be chewing your nails at breakfast yet "pull yourself together" at the office threshold. These shifts also explain a lot of our behavioral inconsistencies. When a friend tells you about a problem he's having, for example, you can react in one of a number of stereotypical ways. Most of the time, you say something like "Oh golly, that's so painful." But on certain occasions, you might say, "You think you've got a problem? I've got a problem." Or "Why did you get into a situation like that in the first place?" As Horowitz says, "Your memories of your friend haven't changed, but you react to them according to your different selves, or styles, *all of which are you.*"

Some of the contexts that elicit our selves and styles are internal, such as memories. One interesting illustration of the connections between what LSD researchers during the 1960s called "[mind-]set and setting," however, involves a swimming pool. In this experiment on so-called state-dependent learning, some members of a university swim club learned a list of words while in the water, while others learned them while on land; later the subjects who were tested in the setting in which they had learned the words recalled them better than those quizzed in a different milieu.

Substituting a chemically induced state for the swimming pool, NIMH psychiatrist Frank Putnam, who studies the effects of trauma on an individual's states and selves, first gave one group of subjects a placebo and another group either the sedative Halcion or alcohol. Then he and his colleagues asked the volunteers to describe themselves. When the researchers compared these descriptions to accounts given later, when no placebos or drugs had been administered, they found that the consistency of a person's autobiographical memory depended considerably on the context. The various self-reports of subjects who hadn't been drugged corresponded much better than those of volunteers who had been tested while influenced by a psychoactive substance. Moreover, the people who varied most in how they described themselves had a more compartmentalized sense of self. Less adept at transferring information from one state to another, these subjects gave very different answers to the same word association test given at different times and had trouble distinguishing their own previous responses from someone else's.

Taking a drug or jumping into a pool is just a more dramatic form of the state changing we do all day long, often triggered by shifts in our roles. "The fluidity with which we can move among our different context-dependent selves and integrate them is critical to a healthy personality," says Putnam. "It's the ability to remember your own history and incorporate your various context-dependent senses of self that enables you to say, 'Oh yes, I might have behaved quite differently in that situation, but it was still me, and I remember what I did and said.' Such a person is different in different contexts but has a metacognitive ability to track his behavior and recognize it as his own."

Those who have the most difficulty with integrating their states and selves, such as combat veterans afflicted with post-traumatic stress syndrome and abused children vulnerable to multiple personality disorder, are clustered toward one end of a vast spectrum. Most of us have had experience with less extreme forms of "amnesia." Anyone who has confronted a friend or colleague about a hurtful remark, only to hear "I never said that!" has encountered an individual who can become so captured by the state he's in that he can't remember his others or circulate information among them. "When their relationship feels sour," says Horowitz, "some people don't recall the good times, so they get a divorce or have an affair. When their child is acting obnoxious, he's evil, and they smack him. Some literally don't know the 'other side' of people."

Unlike the personalities of those who alternately idealize or devalue themselves and others and look at life through good-or-bad, black-or-white lenses, those of the mature are healthily ambivalent. Rather than charging from one state to another and slamming the door behind them, they incorporate an awareness that no matter how life looks at present, says Horowitz, "things are sometimes good and sometimes bad. Even in the idealizing state of romantic love, for example, they remember that no man or woman is perfect. More important, they can remember another person's past kindness even when they currently hate that same person."

By the lights of what Horowitz calls the "state-of-mind approach," a healthy personality is a "repertoire of contradictory traits and states of mind" that's neither a drifting cloud nor a granite pillar but, he says, "kind of unstably stable." This conception of personality and the private experience of it as the changeable creature of one's characteristic yet shifting states, selves, and schemas, all profoundly related to memories, differs from more traditional static "types" or models. The complex, shimmering portraits drawn by Daniel Stern and Mardi Horowitz, like those of Henry James and Virginia Woolf, have the particularity of art.

Notwithstanding the enormous impact of experience on making us who we are, "there's a big role here for temperament," says Stern. "Biological tendencies to react in certain ways are also cues that keep coming up. With your first baby, you don't believe in temperament, but by the second baby . . ."

CHAPTER 8

THE ADAPTIVE NICHE

The way in which a fabulous dancer or track star experiences life is shaped by her awareness of her innate ability. An athlete of a different kind—a psychological one—Monica knows that she "can make people want to look at her and possess her in a fairly exclusive fashion, as those who have cared for her did," says Daniel Stern. "That schema, which she keeps all the time, does a lot for her identity." Since he and child psychiatrist Nadia Stern-Bruschweiler worked with "warehoused" Romanian orphans in the 1980s, he has been particularly interested in that "special something about Monica as a baby that sparks that reaction in people of wanting to adopt her," says Stern. "I've come to see that as one of the more vital temperamental differences among individuals. Most of those traumatized, institutionalized kids deteriorate mentally and physically pretty fast. After three years, eighty percent of those who haven't died are sent off to mental hospitals for the rest of their lives, which might have been Monica's prognosis. But in all these situations, you notice that there are always one or two children who get 'adopted' by a member of the staff. Because those kids are in a special relationship, they get more input and do the best. From the point of view of species survival, their particular star quality is a very important attribute."

Scenes of little Monica turning the hospital into a home, complete with loving parental surrogates, vividly illustrate how, given a chance, nature tends to evoke the kind of nurture that in turn reinforces it. As her rebirth in the pediatric ward demonstrates, the response a smiling baby evokes in all but the hardest heart helps ensure the survival of the young and helpless. An impassive, much less scowling or howling, infant doesn't get the kind of reception Monica does. The innate program to smile is so strong that even after a year of almost no socializing or playing, the Romanian orphans indulged with the least encouragement, says Stern, "as if they'd been hanging around waiting for a stimulus." Although nature gives all babies this genetic weapon with which to disarm adults, Monica's well-modulated model is double-barreled: not only contagious but selective. Unlike many "affectively promiscuous" orphans and other emotionally starved children, Monica doesn't beam desperately at just anyone. Because she makes them feel special, the recipients of her limbic largesse are even likelier to put themselves out for her. Laden with the temperamental supertrait that Auke Tellegen calls positive emotionality, particularly its social attributes of engaging others and generating intimacy, such delicious babies get positive feedback that dour or shy ones don't and become even more the way they are.

Who we become depends not so much on the tendencies we've inherited per se as on the way in which they both orient us toward and away from, and attract and repel, certain stimuli. Even someone as innately appealing and engaging as Monica can't blossom in a vacuum. To flower, her personality required the hospital's nurturing milieu. Despite Western culture's fondest prejudices about individuality and independence, much of who we are depends on how others respond to us.

Social experience is so important to shaping our identity that the pioneering psychologist Harry Stack Sullivan declared that "personality is made manifest in interpersonal situations, and not otherwise." Even an individual's private sense of self, he said, is a set of beliefs based on perceptions of others' reactions to him; depending on his guesstimates of their judgments, a person either feels content—the "good me"—or anxious—the "bad me" or even "not me"—and behaves accordingly. According to Tellegen, when we evaluate ourselves or others, we not only use the broad descriptive criterion he calls "evil," but also another called "excellence." "All of us locate ourselves somewhere on the social spectrum of having high standing, or not, or being a bad person, or not," he says. "That's how we think. Am I important or not? Good or evil? As Jung said, we find it easy to imagine the Devil. The reason is that he's so important and bad."

That who we are is so closely tied to our social milieu is no accident. From an evolutionary perspective, personality answers our species' need to demonstrate and assess who's who and what's what—basic survival skills. As Tellegen says, "Even a duckling can tell if a predator is flying overhead," and our Pleistocene progenitors were no less dependent on their ability to portray themselves as, and identify and react appropriately to, friends and enemies. Homo sapiens was also profoundly shaped by the press of life in a group within which the individual must simultaneously cooperate and compete. Getting along while getting ahead requires a powerful consciousness (or the sense of an "I" who acts) that allows us to run through an action mentally before we actually attempt it and to consider how others are likely to react. Our consciousness is absorbed not only with questions of "What shall I do?" and "How will others respond to that?" however, but also with personality: "Who should I be?" Thus, the most adaptive person is not simply one way or the other but flexible: able to rise to any occasion and do what needs to be done. In short, considering evolutionary history, it's not surprising that we developed such fine powers of social discrimination nor that the vast majority of the words that describe personality refer to interpersonal attributes. Who we are is largely a matter of how our individual traits play out in the social field.

In her examination of the lives of Franklin and Eleanor Roosevelt during World War II, biographer Doris Kearns Goodwin draws, as accurately as any psychologist, the portraits of two very different temperaments, the ways in which they experienced the same environment, and their legendary effects on the nation and the world. Extroversion and boldness personified, the heat-seeking, tough-minded FDR craved stimulation and worked best when excited, in bursts that he compared to a cat's way of pouncing, then resting. When FDR steadied a nation panicked by the Great Depression by saying, "The only thing we have to fear is fear itself," he wasn't mouthing a platitude culled from a focus group. Because of who he was, that was how he saw life and behaved in the world. Many of FDR's other traits also commonly travel with extroversion, from aggressiveness to a sense of being in control to a higher threshold for pain and lower one for sedation. That he accomplished what he did from a wheelchair almost pales beside another fact. After their initial shock at realizing that the president was crippled, most of the people who saw him *forgot all about it*. As if describing his friend's hallmark positive affect, Winston Churchill said that meeting Roosevelt was like opening your first bottle of champagne.

Although she eventually learned to conquer the nearly paralyzing shyness that plagued her well into adulthood, Eleanor retained the introvert's greater sensitivity to stimuli and lower pain threshold. She noticed more things in the world, and more of them upset her. Of the idylls in the South that so rejuvenated and delighted Franklin, for example, Eleanor observed that they required blinding oneself to social injustice. Because she focused inward and considered the perceptions and principles she saw there to be reality, she also wore the introvert's mantle of stubborn righteousness. The combination of her vigilance and zeal greatly benefited the oppressed and made Eleanor Roosevelt's name a synonym for compassion, yet she was an awkward mother and a chilly wife who, despite her extroverted spouse's entreaties, couldn't forgive his dalliances. As Goodwin puts it, "Indeed had she [Eleanor] been given the choice between supplying the relaxation for her husband that Lucy [Mercer, his mistress] was providing or summoning her powers to effect a change in the lives of Negro Americans, she would have undoubtedly chosen the latter."

In their public as well as personal lives, the Roosevelts show how, even under the same roof, different natures dwell in different worlds. Goodwin again: "While Eleanor thought in terms of what *should* be done, Franklin thought in terms of what *could* be done. She was more earnest, less devious, less patient, less fun, more uncompromisingly moral; he possessed the more trustworthy political talent, the more finely tuned sense of timing, the better feel for the citizenry, the smarter understanding of how to get things done." It's not that one extraordinary Roosevelt was "better," only that they were different, and good at different things. How we regard each of them depends in no small part on our own dispositions.

From FDR on the stump to ER in the sweatshop, our innate traits not only help frame our view of the world but attract us to the parts of it that reinforce them. To illustrate the way genetic tendencies can shine through the clouds of even an unpropitious environment, twin researcher David Lykken tells the story of a man who has served as president of all three of the world's important ornithological societies. In the hardworking Midwestern agricultural community in which he was raised, he was a strange duck. There were no books in his home, but he was always at the library. His family had no interest in sports, but he was a gifted athlete who played baseball and basketball and later won tennis tournaments. When he discovered by accident at the age of eleven that he had been adopted by his farming family, he was relieved, because he finally understood why he was so different. Later in life, when he had become a successful businessman as well as an ornithologist, he was able to track down his biological mother. He learned that he had been born out of wedlock and given up for adoption, his parents had later married and had several more children, whom he was also able to meet. Moreover, he discovered that his father, long dead, had been the younger brother of a former dean of the University of Minnesota and a member of what Lykken describes as a "high-falutin' intellectual family. Because his adoptive family didn't interfere with his inclinations, his genes pushed him here and there. If he had had an identical twin who had been adopted by another similarly laissez-faire family in different circumstances—an urban one, say—they still would have been very similar."

While the nascent scholar was drawn to the library that in turn lured him closer to academe, another of Lykken's favorite real-life characters expressed his very different genetic potential in less tranquil settings: Chuck Yeager, the test-pilot hero of *The Right Stuff* and the first flier to break the sound barrier. "He could step down from the belly of the bomber into the rocket ship and push the button not because he was born with *that* difference between him and me," says Lykken, "but because for the previous thirty years his temperament impelled him to work his way up from climbing trees through increasing degrees of danger and excitement." From the cradle, the naturally fearless live in the fast lane. As soon as they can crawl, they're everywhere at once, exploring, falling, pushing themselves and likely their parents, who may react with a disciplinarian mien that a shy, reactive sibling may never see. When they're older and stronger, "they climb a few fences, become desensitized, and climb up on the roof," says Lykken. "They'll have all sorts of experiences that other kids won't. Genes affect the mind indirectly, creating formative experiences."

For the past century, the idea that the ultimate formative experience is our first relationship—the so-called attachment bond between mother and baby—has been accepted almost as divine revelation. If a child or, for that matter, an adult is timid or reckless, friendly or cold, not to mention "good" or "bad," Western society has long known where to look and whom to blame. The conviction that the home is the anvil on which personality is forged, with Mother doing most of the hammering, has been so powerful that only a few finicky scientists have been bothered by lingering questions. One was unavoidable: If nurture was so important, why couldn't it more consistently predict how children would turn out? Why, for example, despite severe early trauma, did Monica develop her smiling personality and rich life, while another child seemingly born with "every advantage" might become a miserable misanthrope, unable to find satisfaction in love and work?

Only her experience with her own children's different reactions to family life caused psychologist Mary Rothbart to switch from strictly environmental to more temperamentally oriented research in mid-career—an ordeal also undergone by many of her "born-again" colleagues. (In fact, she recalls with some amusement a long-ago professional meeting at which Jerome Kagan, at the time an eloquent voice for the power of nurture, "being critical" of her research on innate dispositions.) "Before I had my sons," she says, "I had studied differences linked to gender and birth order, and I had really strong ideas on how my boys would differ because of the latter. They turned out to be the opposite of what I predicted. Had one been a girl, I would have tried to chalk up their differences to gender. Because they started out and stayed different in major ways—one was a math and computer science major at MIT, for example, and the other studied sculpture at the

Rhode Island School of Design—they forced me in the direction of studying temperament."

What is surprising about the voluminous literature on how nurture affects children is how little has been truly established, at least as far as positive influences are concerned. Regarding the effects of our early relationships on personality per se, Rothbart has "some hunches" concerning the trait called agreeableness in Big Five parlance, "which really has to do with the degree to which we care for people. Attachment experiences are probably important to the development of our motivation to want to be good to others." A strong voice for such benign environmental influences, Purdue University psychologist Theodore Wachs offers another example—authoritative—firm but kind—parenting correlates with competence in offspring. Children at high risk of developing behavioral problems, such as those of addicted or otherwise troubled parents, can benefit from various supports outside the family, from a good school to the attention of a kindly neighbor or relative. Although scientists still know little about how either environment or heredity actually works, cautions Wachs, it's increasingly clear that, rather than operating in a simple, direct, cause-and-effect fashion, "nurture operates interactively with nature in much more complex ways than originally thought."

Where hard data on how the family affects children are concerned, however, more concern what's bad than good. According to behavioral geneticist Robert Plomin, what's worst is chronic discord caused by parents who, over the long term, don't agree and aren't steady at the helm. "Conflict and lack of support—the nasty side of parenting—make a difference," he says. "The kid who takes the brunt of that does quite a bit worse than the one who doesn't in terms of depression, antisocial behavior, self-esteem, and other measures of adjustment. As long as he isn't neglected or abused, the child who just gets less affection than a sibling doesn't do worse. The action seems to be on the negative side— the dark force." Although he agrees that "a pretty run-of-the-mill family probably doesn't affect you much," psychologist Thomas Widiger, a personality theorist at the University of Kentucky, says that "one that puts you through a lot will. I don't care what your genes are, if throughout childhood your father had sex with you, it's going to affect your personality, perhaps making it more anxious, inhibited, and submissive."

That research hasn't demonstrated more connections between parents' behavior and children's personalities doesn't mean that they don't exist. Part of the problem is methodological. Proving such an effect means ruling out genetic influences. In traditional studies, however, says Hans Eysenck, a researcher simply finds a correlation between, say, aggressive children and parents who use corporal punishment. "It could be that the children are aggressive because their parents beat them," he says. "But it could also be that the parents beat them because the children are aggressive and they didn't know what else to do. You can't look for environmental factors without simultaneously considering genetic ones, so you have to investigate this kind of question with twin studies and so on." Most research on personality's environmental influences hasn't ruled out genetic ones, so that, regarding questions of how the family affects personality, says Eysenck, "the truth is that we just don't know."

It's hard to imagine that how upbringing shapes personality can ever be reduced to a few general principles. First off, each attachment bond is unique: a complex, two-way, back-and-forth affair in which the offspring's disposition evokes certain parental responses that in turn trigger others in the child. Because parents are adults and babies are babies, the burden of building the bond rests on the former, but right from day one, it's hardly a one-sided project. In sorting babies' dispositions into broad, sheep-or-goats categories, pediatrician Stella Chess observed long ago that "easy" ones are regular in their ways, outgoing, adaptable, and inclined to positive responses—the Monica type that features in prospective parents' dreams and fantasies. The obliging mite who takes a nice long nap at the same time each day, coos winningly at strangers, eats anything, and giggles when he falls down is a very different companion from the one who sleeps in brief, irregular snatches, flinches from Grandma, eats only hot dogs and Cheerios, and reacts immoderately to life's little ups and downs.

Many things apart from temperament, from the child's intelligence to the parents' social and financial status to their previous experience with children and expectations for them, affect the chemistry between them. Nonetheless, as Daniel Stern saw writ large in the Romanian orphanages, smiling babies who make their caretakers feel cheerful and competent are better equipped to attract the hugs and other good things that reinforce their "don't worry, be happy" inclinations. Much of the damage caused by Monica's early environment was later repaired by the nurture that her innate appeal was finally able to attract.

The expression of a very different sort of temperament can excite a very different sort of response, even in a kindly parental breast. In *The Tempest*, Prospero describes Caliban: "A devil, a born devil, on whose nature / Nurture can never stick; on whom my pains / Humanely taken, all, all lost, quite lost . . ." In this seminal reference to the venerable opposition of heredity and environment, Shakespeare acknowledges not only the relationship between a temperament and its milieu but also the Teflon effect that often shields the extreme disposition from external influence. Many parents who have thrown up their hands along with Prospero have offspring who have traditionally been described in the literature as "difficult babies." Definitions vary and can include more than one characteristic, but the common denominator in most is "negative affect": a fretful, irritable, hypersensitive temperamental disinclination to go along or get along.

Monica's effect on the doctors and nurses of the pediatric ward illustrates one sort of dynamic between temperament and environment. The higher abuse rate suffered by premature babies, whose immaturity means that they generally fuss and cry a lot and are more difficult to comfort, tragically testifies to another. An infant's wails usually motivate a parent to soothe him, if only to gain some peace and quiet. Repeatedly ministering to a demanding infant who's hard to console can, however, incline some adults to feel incompetent and unloved; to varying degrees, they may be tempted to save their energy, leaving the baby to formulate his worldview accordingly. When an infant who would challenge the patience of Mother Teresa is born to a stressed-out, inept, immature, or emotionally ill parent, a domino effect of disastrous reactions can endanger the child's ability to modulate his emotions and behavior, and increase his risk of developing a disordered personality.

Not even Monica could penetrate her mother's depression; conversely, even a hair-raising baby can prosper in the right home. Then too, parents' attitudes about what's "difficult" or "easy" don't always jibe with psychologists'. "Some people prefer very active, lively babies, and others quiet, 'good' ones," says Rothbart. "Should a doctor tell parents their child is 'difficult' according to some research standard if they don't think so?" Because that label is simplistic, subjective, and somewhat pejorative, she prefers to describe a child by a number of his qualities. Like Hagop Akiskal, Rothbart feels that an irritable temperament is particularly apt to be misunderstood. Although there's nothing inherently bad about the tendency to be easily aroused—indeed, it can be an advantage—American culture idealizes the easygoing, regular-guy personality and too readily lumps irritability with hostility and other unpleasant things. Nonetheless, we've all silently cheered the person who interrupts an interminable meeting to ask "Can we get to the point?" History is full of people, from Moses to Rosa Parks, who got irritated and became heroes. "Choleric characteristics are seen as problematic and are not even much discussed in our society," says Rothbart, "but in others, such as Israel, they're encouraged and allowed to shine."

Monica's early experience with her family confirms that, to a significant degree, the "difficult child" exists in the eye of the beholder. Before the disastrous move to the desolate farmhouse, she had spent a lot of time in the lap of her loving grandmother, who, despite Monica's handicap, considered her a "good" baby. Perhaps the older woman had even favored the delicate, pretty little girl over her frisky toddler brother. Later, during the long months of their mother's depression, this older, mobile sibling was able to wrest enough attention from his lethargic parent, who may have felt guilty every time she looked at "difficult" Monica, to enable him to develop normally. Traditionally, that two very young children living in the same home with the same parent should have such very different experiences and outcomes would have been considered an exception. Research increasingly shows that it's closer to the rule. A home may shape the children within it, but it does so in very different ways.

Over the past few years, behavioral geneticists have confirmed the experience of Mary Rothbart and many another mother by statistically demonstrating that siblings' personalities are about as various as those

of unrelated children, to the point that their differences can far outnumber their similarities. These data are supported by evidence that
siblings raised apart are no less similar than those reared together, and
that the personalities of unrelated children adopted into the same family are very little alike—about 5 percent.

At first it seems contradictory to say that genes are a strong influence
on personality and behavior but that siblings, who have half their genes
in common, aren't any more alike than they are to the children down
the street. So antithetical is the idea that some scientists reject it as a
false conclusion drawn from inadequate questionnaire data. Given
enough videotape and time, says Jerome Kagan, he could prove sibling
similarity: "I guarantee it." Others resolve the apparent contradiction
by concluding that members of a family don't have the same experience
just because they share the same home. Except where identical twins are
concerned, nature plays a role in intrafamilial variations, but nurture
isn't evenhanded, either. As the stories of Jacob and Esau and the Prodi-
gal Son illustrate, even conscientious parents don't treat their offspring
alike. Mothers and fathers claim that they love and treat all their children "the same," but videotapes show otherwise, as literature has long
done. In *War and Peace,* for example, the filial devotion of gentle, self-
effacing, emotional Princess Marya Bolkonsky only irritates her blunt,
bold, cerebral father. How differently the old prince treats Andrei, her
brother, like him the soldierly epitome of sangfroid. Even across gender
lines, says Kenneth Kendler, "I think parents find it easier to raise kids
whose temperaments are similar to theirs. I'm introverted and very
much like my daughter but quite different from my son, who's more
extroverted. He likes to do different things than I do, which is just a little bit harder for me—it takes more of an effort."

Parental temperament and affection aren't the only influences in the
home that affect siblings in different ways. A second or third child, for
example, lives in a different world than the firstborn, simply because
he's not an only child. His parents are also older, more experienced, and
perhaps more affluent. Indeed, the similarities in personality that tend
to show up among siblings, such as the highly heritable difficulty in regulating emotion, seem to depend more on genes than on the experiences siblings share. To Daniel Stern, it makes sense that environment
emphasizes rather than minimizes their differences "because of the way

traits and attributes get partitioned in a home. When you talk about the 'family environment,' you have to talk about the imaginary child in the parents' minds."

The hoopla over a firstborn son is just an example of a much broader phenomenon. In many homes, for example, one child is unofficially designated the smart one, or the pretty or athletic or bad one. Gender, rank by age, physical appearance, which parent a child identifies with, and countless other variables also create different microenvironments at the same address. Stern describes one of his first studies, which concerned a set of three-and-a-half-month-old male fraternal twins: "Every day I would watch the mother play with them, and after five minutes one was crying and one was happy. What became clear was not only that she was treating them very differently at a moment-by-moment level but also that she had very different imaginary babies—and fantasies about them—in her mind. It turned out that, even during her pregnancy, she had assigned one to herself and one to her husband, and things snowballed from there. Unless you know the imaginary situation for the parent, you can't make any coherent story about environmental influence on the child."

Robert Plomin observes, twin studies suggest that certain infants are more, or less, likely than others to feel loved—Monica must be in the former group. If something as seemingly "psychological" as a child's perception of parental affection shows a strong genetic influence, "even environmental influences on personality can't be assumed to be environmental in origin," he says. "That you treat your two kids differently relates to their differences in adjustment, but none of that might be causal. If relationships with parents account for how children's personalities turn out, that would be very big news."

Taking a sanguine approach to a vast and difficult problem, Plomin says, "we don't know what the important environmental influences on personality are, but we know that they're not what we thought. Contrary to what every socialization theorist from Freud onward has said, we now know that two kids growing up in the same family don't share the same environment. It's a very big step forward to say that the reasonable assumption that environmental influence is doled out on a family-by-family basis is nonetheless wrong." That said, scientists must now work on the problem on an individual-by-individual basis, asking not why kids in the same family are similar but why they're different. Like many ideas about why we are the way we are, this one is not new. Early in the twentieth century, Freud's disciple Alfred Adler noted that competition for power, dominance, and affection would differentiate siblings precisely *because* they were from the same family.

An answer to the ultimate question of how genes and environment *together* produce personality requires the kind of painstaking, complicated studies that are seldom done. After decades of the modern nature-versus-nurture wars, behavioral geneticists still rarely talk to environmentalists and vice versa, much less build the others' part of the equation into their research. Ideally, both groups of scientists would track how different kinds of people deal with different environments over the course of, say, twenty years. To do that would require an initial evaluation of the characteristics of each subject, who would then be repeatedly monitored in a variety of natural settings—a huge, costly undertaking. Over the course of this dream experiment, says Theodore Wachs, "I'd look for whether children with certain characteristics do better under certain conditions. Clusters of children and clusters of environments. It's too deterministic to say that genes 'drive' environments. Genes drive amino acid sequences. Where it's all going is that the impact of the setting is moderated by the characteristics of the individual. An environmental factor that's relevant for one type of child won't be for another."

The earliest scientific attempt to explain why we are the way we are grew out of a physician's intuition that certain temperaments are linked to certain diseases. More than two thousand years later, Hippocrates' successors are unable to demonstrate just how personality impacts on health in either the short or long term. The key element, however, seems to involve an individual's characteristic way of dealing with the environment, particularly its stressful aspects: not a mere trait but a personality process. Although it hasn't come up with any simple prescriptions, research on personality and health is an important demonstration of the need to put a person's traits into the perspective of his way of life. In short, it's an interesting and instructive effort to integrate the effects of nature and nurture.

The usual analogy for the connections between the brain's function-ing and that of other organs has been an electronic communication net-work. Recent research suggests something much squishier that's more like an aquatic ecosystem than a computer: tides of neurochemicals seeping from many sites and eddying through the body, sending mes-sages via receptors on immune, nerve, and organ cells. This highly re-sponsive web affects and is affected by the individual's characteristic style of self-regulation and handling challenge. Both of these behavioral patterns are major subjects of research on the connections between who we are and our health—particularly the two illnesses that kill most Americans.

The constructs of the so-called Type A personality and coronary heart disease and the Type C personality and cancer are contentious, not least because they can smack of blaming the victim. It's bad enough to have breast cancer without having to hear that Galen connected it to the melancholic temperament nearly two thousand years ago, so why weren't you more cheerful? Nonetheless, having long researched the ties between traits and health, Hans Eysenck boldly summarizes the re-search: "We have now firmly established that there are a large number of risk factors for cancer and coronary heart disease, and that stress and personality reactions to it are important ones. The difference between the heart disease people and the cancer people is that the risk factor for the former is the anger-hostility-aggression constellation; for the latter, the opposite." Many other behavioral scientists feel that while the evidence for the Type A and C personalities isn't the greatest, it can't be dismissed, either—particularly for the former.

Among the many risk factors for coronary heart disease are smoking, cholesterol, high blood pressure, age, weight, diet, maleness, and a sedentary lifestyle. All these, however, account for only about half the cases. In exploring what else could be involved, researchers have looked at stress, social support, and personality, particularly those traits associ-ated with Type A, first identified by cardiologists Meyer Friedman and Ray Rosenman in 1974. After assessing 3,500 healthy men, they found that, eight and a half years later, those who had been identified as Type A were twice as likely as laid-back Type Bs to have suffered from angina, a heart attack, or sudden cardiac death.

The original Type A profile sounds much like someone who has a high level of what personality psychologists call neuroticism or negative emotionality and is also preoccupied with time and getting lots of things done at once: aggressive, obsessive, ambitious, competitive, impatient, vigilant, and task oriented. More sophisticated probing now suggests that this whole familiar boss-man package—the Type A construct doesn't translate very well to women—is not the problem as much as specific potential components, particularly what's variously called "cynical" or "antagonistic" hostility: this attitude, expressed by up to 20 percent of American men, paints life as a free-for-all in which it's every mean, selfish bastard for himself. Such a philosophy guarantees them—and their associates—not only much unpleasantness but also a chronic state of psychobiological stress. In a world perceived to be bristling with threats and enemies, they must remain on guard, constantly scanning for and reacting to trouble.

A personality trait can't "cause" a heart attack. In someone who has primed the pump with years of eating too much and moving too little, however, it can help produce a response to challenge that sets loose a fatal flood of catecholamines, or stress-related hormones. As Eysenck says, "Risk factors don't just act by themselves but synergistically. They multiply. Our group found that smoking by itself, without any other risk factor, has no effect at all on health. Once it's combined with air pollution or certain personality traits, however, a person's vulnerability rises steeply. It's the combinations that have the effects." According to one scenario of how personality can contribute to disease, someone who has difficulty calming down or cheering up may avail himself of nicotine's psychoactive effects and smoke a lot. (There's a high correlation between smoking and depression and a very high incidence of the former among psychiatric inpatients, who now are often the only people in a hospital who are allowed to smoke.) "Although it has been oversold," says Eysenck, "Type A has been an important development. Most of it doesn't have anything to do with coronary heart disease, but the anger-hostility-aggression combination certainly does and is predictive." Amused by Americans' keen interest in mortality, he observes that "everyone has to die of something. You can't possibly follow all the health measures that are recommended."

Regarding the shakier construct of the Type C personality, the suggestion is that, under stress, a pleasant but inexpressive individual may tend both to neglect his own emotions and to fail to reach out for support, thus jeopardizing his health. Some sort of suppression of the immune system may be involved, but, more obviously, people who are inclined to ignore their needs, fail to take good care of themselves, and shrink from getting help when they need it are likelier to get sick for any number of reasons. In an impressive study, Stanford psychiatrist David Spiegel unexpectedly found that of eighty-six women who had advanced breast cancer, those who attended group therapy focused on how to deal with the practical and emotional aspects of their predicament lived almost twice as long—thirty-seven months—as those who didn't participate.

The complex connections between traits and states, coping strategies and well-being, aren't readily picked up on written personality tests. Drew Westen brings up a type of person who rigidly defends himself against angst, described by Freud as "repressive" and more recently as having "illusory mental health." Asked on a questionnaire if he has trouble expressing his feelings, he says, "such a man, who has gone through the typical American training course in insensitivity and has a problem acknowledging his affects, marks 'no.' He reports having few psychological problems, but he has many and is also more vulnerable to certain diseases." Although such individuals report little anxiety when confronted with a stressful stimulus in lab experiments, physiological measurements show a strong reaction. Even though "repressers" may not consciously suffer the psychological symptoms of stress, they're more physically reactive to it—the kind of complex personality dynamic that's easily overlooked. "Understanding someone doesn't just mean knowing his scores from a questionnaire," says Westen, "but about his past, his normal ways of coping, why he's upset now, and to what extent he's aware of those things."

To illustrate simplistic thinking about genes, environment, and behavioral tendencies, many thoughtful scientists offer the same current example: the latest version of the etiology of homosexuality. Other surveys have given higher estimates, but data from 1,265 middle-aged twins from the respected Minnesota Twin Registry suggest that the prevalence of homosexuality in the population is between 1 and 2 percent for both sexes, while that of bisexuality is between 2 and 3 percent. Although some gay people have gay relatives, even parents, and homosexuality is now often described as "genetic," says David Lykken, if it were strongly so—that is, transmitted exclusively through sexual reproduction—"how on earth could you explain it?" The interesting question to him is to what extent the inclination is biological, perhaps involving the prenatal hormonal environment, rather than heritable. Among the fifty pairs of twins in the Minnesota study that include a gay sibling, "there seems to be a familial tendency," he says, "but it's not a simple story." There's a higher frequency of homosexuality among the nontwin siblings of the gay twins, but most of the co-twins of the gay and heterosexual ones describe themselves as heterosexual, and there's no difference in the rates among identical and fraternal twins. Considering all this evidence, says Lykken, "homosexuality certainly isn't very strongly genetic." Although there may be environmental influences on homosexuality, from the uterine milieu to political philosophy, in his opinion, "they're not the psychoanalytical bullshit."

According to Freud, homosexuality is an immature behavior caused by a young person's failure to transfer incestuous feelings for the opposite-sex parent to an opposite-sex peer: a girl or boy just like the one who married dear old Dad or Mom. In a letter to the mother of a gay man, Freud wrote that homosexuality is "assuredly no advantage, but it is nothing to be ashamed of, no vice, no degradation, it cannot be classified as an illness." An outspoken anti-Freudian, Eysenck nonetheless agrees on this last point. Regarding personality per se, he says that "homosexuals are not a unified group. They score higher in psychoticism"—largely a combination of impulsivity and aggressiveness—"but then, many males do. There's nothing to distinguish them from others of their social class except that they earn three times as much." Drawing a typically colorful analogy, he brings up prostitutes, whom he has also studied: "Some like sex, and some don't. Many are driven to it because of drugs or children they can't support, and others are high-class call girls. Prostitutes are like any other women, and being one has nothing to do with personality. You can't generalize about prostitutes, and it's the same with homosexuals."

Headlines and sound bites notwithstanding, it increasingly seems that, as is the case with other complex forms of behavior, homosexuality can't be pinned down to one cause. "Sometimes, as in the higher incidence among men and women in prison, it's a matter of being better than nothing," says Lykken. "We also know that from puberty many male homosexuals had no doubt about their orientation at all. Some of those are effeminate, and some aren't. In the three pairs of female identical twins in our study that include a homosexual, that twin is physically different—larger, for example—in a way that suggests a different biological origin for homosexuality in women and men." Like many researchers and clinicians, however, Lykken suspects that, for women, gayness is often largely a socially mediated choice based on a combination of greater cultural toleration of female intimacy and annoyance at men.

In short, while genes, the uterine milieu, or some other piece of biology may orient some individuals toward homosexuality, social influences of various kinds or a combination of both nature and nurture may so incline others. Discussing the influence of nature and nurture on homosexuality, George Vaillant could be talking about personality itself: "While your extroversion score depends a lot on your genes and what language you speak entirely depends on what your parents taught you, whether you're homosexual or not is like whether or not you play the violin or shortstop for the Yankees. Surely temperament and character are both involved."

At the end of the twentieth century, the most important insights into why we are the way we are concern the process by which our genetically influenced temperamental traits help "select" the environments and experiences that further shape us. At the beginning of the twenty-first, the most exciting research will expand on pioneering studies of how environment can change biology in a way that's indistinguishable from the work of genes.

CHAPTER 9

SECOND NATURE

Once caught up in Monica's saga, one soon forgets that the original point of the study was to test a psychoanalytical speculation about an interplay between physiological and behavioral processes. Not even Freud, a neurologist who was as much of a biological psychiatrist as it was possible to be at the time, could have hoped for a clearer link between the baby's activity and her stomach's. When she was happily engaged with the attentive Dr. Reichsman, Monica's gastric juices flowed vigorously, and even more so when she got angry. When she became withdrawn upon being separated from someone she liked or approached by a stranger, however, the secretions ceased completely. On encountering loss or novelty, life's two great sources of stress, not only Monica's psyche but also her stomach simply shut down. This impressive empirical support of a psychoanalytic theory was, however, just the first of the study's illustrations of the futility of trying to separate nurture's influence on who we are from nature's.

Monica was not in the hospital to be experimented on but to be fixed. Although pediatricians, gastroenterologists, and other specialists treated her various problems, the root cause of her predicament evaded detection. Neurologists couldn't even find an organic source of her most obvious symptom: the large-motor deficit that kept her from sitting up, rolling over, and walking. The debate over exactly what was wrong with Monica still continues. The most obvious place to look remains her birth defect.

For adults, the basic point of eating is getting adequate nutrition. For babies, however, the mouth is the major sense organ and gateway to the external world, and feedings are a perceptual and social as well as gustatory feast. Mealtimes provide them not only with calories but with an opportunity to engage with their mothers, fathers, and other affectionate parties in delicious emotional and sensory exchanges—visual, tactile, olfactory, auditory, and vestibular. This complex physiological, psychological, and social experience, which Lynne Hofer calls a "dance of attunement," is a cornerstone of a baby's physical, emotional, and cognitive development.

In his illuminating animal studies of the "hidden regulation" built into apparently pedestrian functions of mothering, psychobiologist Myron Hofer has found that, for the infant, the postnatal maternal environment is nearly as "biological" as the prenatal one, robbing the traditional distinction between nature and nurture of any real meaning. When he analyzes the overwhelming distress an infant rat experiences on separation from its mother, he finds that her temperature, movements, touch, sounds, and smells each control certain aspects of the baby's physiology and behavior, from heart rate to growth hormones. Thus, the infant doesn't simply psychologically "miss" his mother, as so-called social attachment theory would have it. Not unlike an addict deprived of his drug, the offspring suffers simultaneous withdrawal from the physical cues that stabilize his metabolism. Monica's esophageal defect meant that she lost out not only on the obvious social, psychological, and physical pleasures of hands-on feedings but on their regulation of her metabolism. By the developmental lights of either Sigmund Freud or Myron Hofer, for Monica infancy's central experience was drastically perturbed.

The human drama of Monica's story sometimes obscures what Hofer considers its most important scientific contribution: telling researchers where to look for more clues to the developmental process. "Monica's experience defines the next questions we must ask," he says. "What components of the maternal environment act so powerfully to shape the early emergence of each of the baby's functional systems? And how do they do this?"

While Hofer investigates these questions through his study of individual hidden regulators, child psychiatrist Scott Dowling, a supervising analyst at the Cleveland Psychoanalytic Institute, focuses on the synchrony of such sensory stimuli. Having more recently treated a number of children born with gastric deformities similar to Monica's, he believes that their main behavioral problem is what he calls "a defect in going forth to meet the environment." Their predictable slowness in sitting, walking, and the like are "motor expressions of a pervasive passivity" that derives, he thinks, from an unforged connection between assertiveness and early feeding experience that normal infants make. For a baby, the maternal environment is as much stage, schoolroom, and jungle gym as snack bar. One of the crucial lessons he learns in this complex setting is that he'll be rewarded—or not—when he vigorously pursues his needs and desires, not just for food but for smiles, caresses, conversation, and other good things. During feedings, as Dowling puts it, "a baby's reaching out to his mother is an extension of his oral activity, and his drinking in of his mother an oral activity of the eyes." Deprived of what he calls these "I'm-going-for-it" experiences, Dowling thinks, babies fed as Monica was fail to develop the basic drive, or "intentionality," that fuels normal development and behavior. Their experience not only retards their motor skills but deprives their personalities of oomph.

Having sensed that this indissoluble blend of early physiological and psychological experience profoundly affects who we are, Dowling experimented with various ways to compensate for the magic missing from his young patients' feedings. Eventually, he devised a way to give them a bottle in the conventional fashion simultaneously with a fistula feeding modified to enable cradling. The babies aren't bothered by the milk that pours out of the opening in their necks, although their parents sometimes don rain gear for the event. By the age of twelve weeks, one boy was so enamored of his bottle that if his tired parents occasionally tried to cheat and do just the fistula feeding, his convulsive howls of protest forced the formula back up his gastric tube; this determined young man proceeded to mature normally.

Even before Dowling came up with his inventive scheme to supply the sensory dimension of feedings, however, he had observed that the bottom line of his patients' recovery from nature's low blow is "skilled, loving parenting. The children I've seen who lacked this suport didn't become normal, or nearly normal, adults." Although afflicted with severe motor, affective, and social deficiencies, one of his early patients, who, like Monica, had had no oral feedings until after the surgical repair of the defect, received tremendous support from his family; he gradually recovered to the point that he ran track and took a graduate degree in science. Like Monica's, this man's achievements vividly illustrate human resilience, in the form of what Dowling calls our "capacity for the gradual acquisition of skills that haven't been achieved in the usual manner": if we can't get what we need in one way, we try to get it in another.

The most successful of Dowling's handicapped patients, however, benefited from an artfully crafted combination of nurture and nature, of emotion and sensation, simultaneously delivered in a single physical and psychological experience. Although the cherished boy who hadn't had the sensorily rich feedings went on to became an athlete, a respected professional, and "a very nice man," says Dowling, he continues to have one big personality problem: an inability to maintain the interest of the opposite sex. Faint heart never won fair lady, and Dowling thinks the man's lack of forcefulness is rooted in the boy's going-forth-to-meet-the-environment problem. Despite lots of support from devoted parents, some hidden regulator or other component of the ability to "go for it," concealed within the seemingly pedestrian business of feeding, failed to engage. Of such children who missed out on some of the richness of early experience, Dowling says, "Their drive expression is very much attenuated. They're pleasant, but that's it."

If social appeal is one trait often cited as characteristic of young Monica, a kind of passivity is the other. The study repeatedly describes her as easily discouraged. Lack of gumption is a serious problem for a child, because basic learning, whether to walk or to read, requires persistence in the face of challenge and frustration. Illustrating the point from animal research, Myron Hofer observes that one reason the rat excels in learning experiments may be that the peculiarities of the mother's abrupt "letdown" lactation response mean that an infant attempting to nurse sometimes gets milk and sometimes doesn't. To survive, the baby must learn to try and try again.

Because Monica's attempts to get attention—even her cries for help—were for a long time not even randomly rewarded, she, even more than other babies born with the gastric defect, couldn't forge the connection between the effort of going for it and the pleasure of getting it. Repeated social and physiological experience during a crucial period of development had taught her that there was no point in pursuing what she wanted, so she failed to develop persistence and a sense of efficacy. Later in childhood, for example, despite normal intelligence, she neglected her schoolwork to the point that she had to repeat a grade. Despite her great appeal, even Monica's social life was pervaded with a certain inertia. People liked and helped her, but some also took advantage of her. Rather than driving her circumstances, she was often carried along by them. The dynamic style of her kin suggests that Monica certainly wasn't born lacking drive. Yet the peculiar air of being becalmed that she acquired in the crib became just as much a part of her temperament as her smiling star quality.

An organism's phenotype—the way it is, from behavior to physical appearance—depends largely on the way its genotype—genetic constitution—has been expressed in a series of environments. Despite our penchant for equating environmental influences with social settings such as home or school, they needn't involve other people. "Early exposure to lead paint is one example, and my guess is that we vastly underestimate the number of such things," says psychologist William Greenough; his research at the University of Illinois at Champaign-Urbana is at the cutting edge of demonstrating how, at the microscopic level, environment can change biology. Nor does the environment necessarily even sit outside our skin. Our individual cells are profoundly affected by the electrochemical doings of their neighbors. Animal experiments show that, even before birth, maternal and fetal hormones, for example, affect the developing nervous system, playing an important role in later sexual orientation. Such factors are nonexperiential in a sense, says Greenough, "but not totally so, because events can cause an organism to release adrenocortical steroids that impact on development. There are all these blurred, nonspecific things that are very real, and temperament is the big integrator that averages them."

The inextricability of an organism's biology and experience has been rendered crystal clear by experiments with animals raised in various kinds of places. Compared to those of rats housed in standard cages, for example, the brains of rats reared in stimulating, toy-filled quarters are not only bigger but better: their visual-cortex neurons have about 25 percent more synapses, which are involved in storing the information that affects behavior. Moreover, the rat's neurological development is profoundly affected not only by the quality of its environment but also by the degree of the animal's engagement with it. Rats confined in a smaller cage inside a large, complex one can see and hear everything that goes on, but their brains are little affected. Passive spectators, they're deprived of the kind of interaction with their world that can best change the brain.

Outside of the lab, there are plenty of examples of this two-way process by which experience affects both biology and behavior. If an astigmatic child isn't diagnosed till he's ten years old, says Greenough, some of that visual tendency endures even after he gets eyeglasses: "It's not in his eye but in his brain, which never got the information that's necessary to develop the ability to see patterns properly." Any middle-aged person who has tried to learn to ski, play the piano, or develop some other such complex skill has experienced the same phenomenon. As Greenough says, along with his genetic legacy, "an individual's history is encoded in the wiring of his nervous system."

If temperament is an individual's deeply ingrained, characteristic response to the world, particularly its stressful parts, many biographies offer clues to how history helps to forge it. *Leading with My Heart,* the memoir of Virginia Kelley, President Bill Clinton's late mother, paints a vivid picture of another exemplar of star quality whose hard early life inspired a particular way of handling stress that became part of who she was. "I'm friendly, I'm outgoing, and I like men," wrote the classic extrovert, who spent about a third of her time gambling at the track and, like her many friends, loved "to eat and laugh and go and do." No flower born to blush unseen, Virginia favored bright clothes and elaborate coifs and could spend over an hour on her makeup. She enjoyed talking to strangers, hated going unnoticed, and thought her sons were the same way.

Innate joie de vivre notwithstanding, Virginia had never had it easy. When her volatile mother, who was addicted to morphine, got angry, she whipped the little girl's legs till they bled. After her first husband died while she was pregnant with Bill, Virginia trained as a nurse and raised her two boys while working. By the age of fifty-one, she had been battered by one husband and widowed three times. All this she weathered with the combination of a resilient temperament and an acquired state that she described as "living in the present," which she achieved through a mental process she called "brainwashing." She wrote, "Inside my head I construct an airtight box. I keep inside it what I want to think about, and everything else stays beyond the walls. Inside is white, outside is black. . . . Inside is love and friends and optimism. Outside is negativity, can't-do-ism and any criticism of me and mine. Most of the time this box is strong as steel." When it wasn't, experiencing the different state—and self—that called up such defenses must have been painful indeed. Practiced over a lifetime, the psychobiological mode of "living in the present" became as much a part of who Virginia Kelley was as leading with the heart.

As poll after poll shows that most Americans consider crime to be the nation's number one problem and prison construction becomes a boom industry, research on criminals is increasingly important and controversial. It's sometimes said that the cop and the robber are the same person, working different sides of the street. Psychologist John Richters, the NIMH's bad-boys specialist, agrees that law enforcement and lawbreaking can attract the same bold, aggressive personality, but he doubts that a magnetic reaction between a certain temperament and environment explains all such career decisions. To an underappreciated degree, he believes, the tough-guy temperament can be made as well as born. "More attention should be paid to the remarkable story of what happens to cops physiologically, as well as emotionally and socially, from the time they're rookies to the time they've become seasoned officers," he says. "Their nervous systems adaptively adjust to the job's environmental demands."

When a young male who's neither particularly inhibited nor bold first dabbles in either cop- or robber-type activities, the novelty and danger are very arousing, both psychologically and physically. After the first few times, however, his physiological as well as psychological excitation dampens, settling more into the thrill, rather than fear, range. That this "habituation" to once-stressful stimuli also boosts performance in turn enhances the odds that he'll repeat the experience and perhaps even turn professional. As Richters says, "If you show the classic signs of anxiety, you can't make a criminal living even as a con artist." The neurobiological changes produced by repeatedly engaging in events the average person would find wildly exciting, if not downright terrifying, "in some meaningful sense help cause subsequent aggressive behavior," says Richters. "Certain kinds of experience physiologically free up a person to do things that he otherwise might not."

Cops and robbers are hardly the only people whose professionalism increases with exposure to experiences that most of us are poorly equipped to cope with. Marriage into the world of car racing has enabled Frank Putnam, who studies how trauma affects a person's ability to integrate his states and selves, to observe a group of world-class professionals whose lives as well as incomes depend on their skill in coping with intensely stressful situations. It's hard to exceed a race car in that regard, he says: "It can be a hundred and thirty degrees in summer. The noise is unbelievable. Because it's operated just on the edge of control, it shakes like crazy. Conditions change constantly, yet all that can be seen is a wall." That's on a good day. Many drivers have near-fatal crashes, yet they're back on the track "as soon as they can get casted up enough," says Putnam. "A week later, they still can't move their fingers, but they're racing with big Velcro gloves stuck to the steering wheel or shift stick. The cars are hell, but when the drivers get back in, all the pain goes away."

Part of what keeps the drivers—and the cops and robbers—coming back for more is no mystery: an addiction to the high that results when a certain personality encounters an environment that pushes all the buttons needed to evoke an optimum state of well-being. The essence of this experience, which psychologist Mihaly Csikszentmihalyi calls "flow," or peak experience, is total absorption in what one is doing. So powerful is the craving for this involvement, says Putnam, that "the drivers suffer withdrawal when they can't race." They exert incredible powers of concentration. "They follow certain rules in a kind of gentlemanly code, but they're intensely *there,* pushing as hard as they can. The question of whether they're athletes or not is a sore point for them, because, in terms of being in the moment, they argue that they're as athletic as anyone." Like David Lykken, Putnam finds that where drawing the line between heroic and sick behavior is concerned, "sometimes it's hard to know."

It's not particularly surprising to learn that athletes are distinguished by their ability to "flow." But even what strikes most people as hell can seem like heaven when it offers an opportunity for peak experience. Among professionals, Csikszentmihalyi has found that surgeons, whose grisly work would make most people queasy, enjoy the most of these on-the-job highs. Like race drivers, these be-here-now doctors are suited for settings that most of us aren't. "A lot of surgeons work in altered states," says Putnam, "often ones of irritability and extraordinary sensitivity. Some get very high and like to sing or listen to loud music. Like nobody else in the hospital, they have permission to be as zany as they want, and can be lots of fun to be with."

Like some cat burglars, ace detectives, and race car drivers, some doctors, nurses, and firemen are naturally cool and collected when their training begins—bold and naturally inclined to focus. Others whose temperaments are in the average range must acquire their sangfroid. As Richters observes, each episode of the venerable medical detective show *Quincy,* now in perennial reruns, starts with the pathologist-hero introducing a group of new medical students to their first cadaver, with predictable results. Nonetheless, says Richters, "three weeks later, they'd be so desensitized that they'd be eating lunch next to the corpse." An experiment by psychologist Seymour Epstein supports his contention. When he compared the physiology of novice and seasoned parachutists as the day of their jump approached, Epstein found that the novices grew more anxious as their first leap loomed. Veterans became less so, however, because their bodies were physiologically anticipating an event that they had become accustomed to and even learned to find psychologically pleasurable.

Just as many doctors come from a long line of sawbones, today's racing stars mostly come from second- or third-generation driving families. Although genes could contribute to such vocational orientations, these professionals also share a special environmental history. Along with the seductive formative experience of racing itself, for example, most of the drivers Putnam observes have had "kind of rough childhoods," he says, and only two have finished college.

Like the hell on wheels that's a racing car, the stress of a rough childhood is more easily handled by someone who can employ what psychologists call compartmentalization, or the ability to shut off and turn on certain states and selves at will. "Even on TV, you can see the drivers do it," says Putnam. "I position myself where they're making transitions, like getting out of the car after a race or being pulled from a wreck. Some blink their eyes, become inarticulate, and reorient, just as multiple personality patients do when they switch alter egos. I think the drivers switch from garage to track personalities." Although they choose to have these hair-raising experiences, the fact that racing pros react in a way that's not so different from the pathologically traumatized doesn't particularly surprise Putnam. As to whether the ability to brainwash, compartmentalize, or flow with ease is inherited or acquired, Putnam says, "My money is on divergent causality."

Because a personality depends not on a single trait but on the interaction of many, two children who compartmentalize will develop very differently if one is outgoing, like fighter pilot and senator John Glenn, and the other introverted, like the legendary late virtuoso pianist and eccentric Glenn Gould. "The introverted kid might become very much lost in his own fantasy world and have trouble with reality testing," says Putnam, "while the extroverted kid becomes a hero." Experience, too, can push two children who have the same tendency in different directions. One who grows up in a healthy environment might become an athlete or surgeon, but another, reared in an abusive home, say, can end up with a fractured, dysfunctional personality.

The temperaments of surgeons and criminals, cops and race car drivers are reinforced—even altered—by highly arousing events in ways that better suit them to their worlds. Sometimes, however, stressful experiences are simply painful and destructive rather than adaptive. Facing a dread event, such as a harsh medical procedure, we may have an eerie feeling of detachment, as if this awful thing were "happening to someone else." If we couldn't at least briefly step out of ourselves in this way, and later "forget" our pain or grief, we couldn't keep functioning. As the Bible observes, the recollection of childbirth dims when mothers see their newborns; if it didn't, the species might have died out long ago. Where victims of severe, repeated child abuse or other grave traumas are concerned, however, a reaction that's meant to offer short-term protection from occasional stress becomes chronic. The amnesia and depersonalization that shut out awareness of the hell at home while a child is, say, in school, can no longer be turned on and off at will, but spin out of control, slicing experience and identity into bits and pieces and preventing states and selves from forming a coherent personality. To wall off their misery, some victims pretend that the abuse is happening to "some other little girl," and eventually suffer from multiple personality disorder.

Having long studied how experience alters the physiology as well as psychology of children who have been repeatedly and severely abused, Frank Putnam stresses that "biology isn't necessarily all genetic, inborn, permanent, fixed—that's one of the pieces of the nature-nurture argument that seems to get lost." As a result of the overwhelming environmental insult his young subjects have suffered, their cortisol and catecholamine systems, which play a major role in regulating mood and stress reactions, and perhaps thyroid and immune functioning too, undergo what Putnam calls "biological derangement." In complementary studies, psychiatrists J. Douglas Bremner, Dennis Charney, and colleagues have reported that some trauma victims, including Vietnam combat vets and victims of child abuse, may experience physiological brain changes—specifically, a shrinkage in the size of the hippocampus, a structure important to memory and learning—as a result of the "toxic" levels of stress they've endured. Because Putnam didn't see his young subjects as infants, he can't make cause-effect statements about how trauma has affected their innate dispositions and constitutions. His research suggests, however, that their experience could have rendered them temperamentally indistinguishable from those born highly reactive. "We have a case," he says, "for the alteration of biology as a result of stress."

Because teasing apart the work of nature and nurture in a single person is so problematic, Richters is dubious about facile explanations for the etiology of behavior, particularly the criminal sort. He points out that both Tom Sawyer and Huck Finn, for example, meet the criteria for so-called conduct disorder, which he considers to be a label for "a heterogeneous group of kids who do things we don't want them to do. In the past, masturbation disorder and runaway slave disorder were also official mental illnesses. Psychiatrists may claim that such diagnostic excesses are behind us, but that's probably what their predecessors thought." For purposes of argument, Richters offers to assume that a significant number of the adolescents diagnosed as having conduct disorder actually have a dampened autonomic nervous system reaction to anxiety-producing stimuli. But, he says, "There isn't a shred of evidence that they behave antisocially because of those differences, which may be the *consequences* rather than causes of the behavior."

The people who are the least seduced by simplistic biological explanations for behavior are the ones who understand biology best. If the effects of good parenting are more than skin-deep, to the point that they can alter a reactive physiology, J. D. Higley reasons that they could affect a belligerent one, too. He plans to rear impulsive, ornery young monkeys with adults "who demand they behave appropriately and punish them when they don't" and monitor their neurochemical as well as behavioral changes. He suspects that he'll find that their low serotonin levels rise along with their bonhomie.

The clearest picture to date of just *how* experience can change the neurobiology of temperament concerns animal research on a phenomenon called learned helplessness. The first time a rat is given a shock or a single dose of a chemical that produces arousal, it shows no reaction. If subjected to such insults for five consecutive days, it exhibits signs of the stress response. If exposed for seven or eight days, the rat has a seizure, and thereafter this "kindled" animal will do so with little or no provocation. A cascade of chemical reactions initially set off by stressful experience has changed the way genes within the rat's brain cells function, permanently altering these neurons' biology. Thereafter, the response meant to ready the organism for external danger can be triggered by its own perturbed internal chemistry.

Even normal neurobiology and behavior can be perturbed by overwhelming external stress, from child abuse to warfare. Some people, however, are so innately sensitive that they behave as if they too had been kindled. Because they require a particular type of input to turn on or off, only some of a neuron's thousands of genes, each of which is involved in some aspect of cellular structure or communication, are activated at any given moment. According to research psychiatrist Philip Gold, when a temperamentally vulnerable individual is constantly bombarded with upsetting stimuli, the genes that keep getting turned on are those involved in the cellular components of the stress response. Over time, this person's nervous system is configured accordingly, becoming a kind of two-way radio that specializes in receiving and transmitting unhappy signals. The concluding chapters in what Gold calls "the natural history of an affective disorder" chronicle such an individual's repeated struggles with anxiety or its chronic form, depression.

In the search for what really ailed Monica, rather than focusing on early problems concerning sensory stimuli and their synchrony, as Hofer and Dowling do, Daniel Stern looks to her relationship with a depressed mother: the ultimate experience of learned helplessness. From a baby or small child's uncomprehending point of view, it's hard to imagine something worse than a mother who is, as Stern says, "physically present but psychically absent." Little is known about the particulars of this dark time in Monica's life, because once she recovered, her mother could hardly bear to talk about it. Research shows that babies tend to respond to a depressed mother in one of two basic ways: by becoming Mommy's cheerleader or by copying her. The latter reaction is the sadder. Even a young infant may imitate melancholy's stony expression and drooping posture to a degree that can stunt motor as well as psychological development. A baby who makes a leap toward such an "absent" mother twenty or thirty times a day without reward undergoes that many microdepressions, which undermine his sense of efficacy and persistence.

Although Monica developed the withdrawal response typical of such children, the films suggest that, primed by her first five benign months at her grandmother's, she also made some effort at trying to be what Stern calls a "human antidepressant." Experiments show that to coax a smile from his parent, the baby of a healthy mother tries all his wiles till he has failed many times. The challenge of summoning some sparks from a melancholic mother, especially one who responds at least occasionally, can cause a child to become very charming, says Stern, "and one is struck by this quality in the adult Monica." Had she not also been saddled with her birth defect, it seems likely that Monica would have taken the Miss Firecracker approach to getting what she needed from her mother. Instead, she apparently steered a middle course: depending on the circumstances, she turned on or off, mostly the latter.

Aside from any influence it may have on the nervous system, perhaps the most chilling effect of being on the receiving end of maternal depression is the lesson it teaches the child about how *to be,* particularly in relationships. Stern sums up the worldview that Monica seemingly developed in early childhood: "Nothing happens unless someone brings it to me. If they do, I'll be charming. If they don't, I'll deflate." The films repeatedly show how this theme permeated her youthful behavior and shaped her personality. Monica relies on her star quality to handle most situations, and often that's enough. When it's not, she responds to stress much as very reactive, inhibited children's genes have primed them to do, and not even Jerome Kagan could tell nurture's work from nature's.

Just as nervous systems and personalities can be deformed by experience under certain conditions, they can also be, in scientific slang, "toughened up" by it. To investigate how the environment, particularly a traumatic one, might modify neurobiology as well as behavior, NIMH research psychiatrist Alan Breier put an ad in *The Washington Post* asking for the help of adults who had, between the ages of two and seventeen, been permanently separated from a parent through death or divorce. Of the experiences that can color even a rosy temperament blue, doctors since Freud have singled out the childhood loss of a parent. Breier was not surprised to find that about two thirds of his currently emotionally healthy volunteers had previously suffered from depression. The rest, however, had not. One potential explanation for the difference is that their genes made some subjects naturally more or less resilient than others. Breier wanted to test another hypothesis: that circumstances can aggravate or ameliorate stress's impact on the nervous system in a way that affects a person's vulnerability to depression.

After much testing and analysis, Breier found that the strongest predictor of his subjects' mental health wasn't a family history of psychiatric illness (a gauge of genetic vulnerability), age at the time of loss, or even the gender of the parent, but the quality of home life during bereavement. Those who handled the trauma best had been supported by an adult who stayed close to them and addressed their needs. Those who endured the most disruption and got the least support—for days, one child was told only that her dead mother "had to go away"—accounted for 80 percent of the depression prone. Even though they weren't currently ill, moreover, these subjects' basal levels of cortisol, norepinephrine, and other stress-related neurochemicals were elevated. Lack of understanding and support during a crisis seemed to push them over the neurobiological edge into what Breier calls "a naturalistic version of learned helplessness, in which you feel that there's nothing you can do to cope with the stress and no one who can help you."

Just withstanding the loss of a parent might seem to be the best any child could hope for. Breier's resilient group did better than that: they reported that they actually emerged from bereavement feeling stronger and more in control of their lives. In terms of personality, successfully dealing with the potentially devastating experience enhanced their traits of resilience, persistence, confidence, and optimism. Animal research suggests that they might have toughened up on a neurobiological as well as psychological level. Rats who "hold out" before experiencing learned helplessness, for example, last much longer before finally succumbing to seizures or death. Family medical histories notwithstanding, there's no way to be sure that the depression-prone and resilient subjects hadn't to some degree been "born that way." Yet Breier thinks that the key difference in their behavior, both during the trauma and later in life, depended on feeling supported and loved at the time of the loss: "Those who did could undergo the experience and come out okay, which showed them that they'd be able to master other tough situations in life, too."

Throughout history, it has ruefully been observed that we usually learn more from painful experiences than from happy ones. While an inclination to duck the former has obvious immediate benefits, it can also reduce opportunities that used to be called "character building." People who have successfully dealt with conflict, whether by virtue of temperament or acquired grit or both, are more willing to face it again. Those who avoid risk because of natural timidity or experiential bruising are likelier to keep withdrawing from the fray. Because the more often one goes up to bat, the greater one's chances are of scoring—a cornerstone of cognitive therapy—these different approaches to adversity have profound consequences over a life span. "If you overcome a challenge," says Breier, "you'll be stronger and more capable of addressing future ones. If you're overwhelmed by it, your next exposure will be influenced by that response. Denying ourselves or our children the opportunity to overcome a stressor is probably not very helpful." Describing his research as "very optimistic," he says, "if the effects of environmental events are not only very powerful but also able to be mitigated, then you have more control over your fate than if it were simply genetic or determined in utero."

Other intriguing clues about how our experience becomes part of who we are can be picked up from studies of reactive youngsters. Her work with such children at the University of Minnesota leads developmental psychologist Megan Gunnar to redefine temperament as "a set of behavioral predispositions that have physiological substrates *and* experiential components." To observe how different children react to stress, she invites toddlers and their mothers to her lab, where they encounter what psychologists call an "approach/avoidance conflict" in the person of a friendly clown. Confronted by Bozo, certain children rapidly reveal one of the two early temperamental extremes documented by Jerome Kagan, Nathan Fox, and others. "Some kids go, 'Whoopee!'" says Gunnar. "Others go, 'Oh, no!'"

Accumulating evidence concerning genetic influences on behavior sometimes seems to cast experience as but a pale shadow on biology, especially where such extreme temperaments are concerned. When a genetically bold infant monkey from Steve Suomi's population is given to a jittery foster mother to raise, for example, her anxious behavior just rolls off his back and he remains fearless. Researchers who work with children similarly report that bold ones rarely become inhibited. Although the uninhibited children in Gunnar's experiments immediately play with the clown, however, the reactive kids' responses are harder to predict, because they're likelier to be strongly mediated by nurture as well as nature. Those whose mothers don't accept them "as is," worries, warts, and all, are described by psychologists as "insecurely attached"; the more their mothers deny or ignore their temperamental inclinations and push the clown, the greater these children's stress response, measured through the amount of cortisol, a stress-related hormone, in their saliva. The innately anxious children whose mothers accept their disposition and calmly go about helping them feel more comfortable are said to be securely attached; their stress response ebbs, until they, too, might approach the clown. The most important insight from her work with children is that, "regardless of their inborn characteristics, those in good relationships learn to take risks, but at their own pace," says Gunnar. "That point often gets lost in the biological push of the temperament literature."

The idea that the reactive nervous system that's most vulnerable to a negative environment can be toughened up by a positive one gets some impressive support from primate research. When a monkey from Suomi's group that has been bred to be nervous is reared by a bold, easygoing foster mother, the youngster develops not only her ways but even her low-norepinephrine chemistry. In short, says Suomi, "you can push genetic constitution around experientially. The effect is so profound that I'd call it temperament."

Once away from Mother's knee, children continue to develop characteristic strategies for approaching life's challenges. In an experiment that monitored stress in older schoolchildren, Gunnar found that during the autumn, "because they start right out putting themselves on the line, it's the bold, outgoing ones who are pushed to their limits. Because they avoid the most stressful activities, the shy kids' levels don't climb till later, when teachers or parents decide it's time to up the ante for them." In a complementary study that measured the stress responses of children waiting to get a blood test, Gunnar found that, while the littlest ones simply wail, "at a certain age, they try to act big, and *that's* when their stress level goes up. They don't want to cry, but they haven't figured out a coping strategy yet. As they get older—and learn how to deal with that conflict—we don't see the stress reaction anymore."

The best testimony to the fact that experience can toughen up sensitive nerves is that about three quarters of Gunnar's reactive children, fortified by the lessons learned in secure, "good-enough" relationships, learn to handle challenge. Surely not coincidentally, Kagan also predicts that seventy-five out of one hundred of his inhibited two-year-olds will eventually have normal social lives. Neither negating nor overindulging their anxiety, such individuals have found a comfortable way of operating that doesn't invite the stress response. "Reactive kids in good relationships will learn to manage themselves quite well," says Gunnar. "The ones who aren't will anticipate the future differently, experience hormonal consequences, and face some health risks. You may be a certain way, but the big issue is how you manage it—or not."

It sometimes seems that, for reasons ranging from gross incompetence to an overly keen appreciation of individual rights, many modern parents shrink from helping their offspring learn how to handle their temperaments. This hands-off spirit means that fewer children change for the better than might. Nathan Fox observes that, in his studies, "parents usually say, 'This is who my child *is.*' Depending on what they do or don't do, however, that child's biology is either going to express itself or be moderated. Because they're too busy and it's too hard, most parents today don't intervene, so biology mostly creates the kids' environments. But if you expect boys to play football, for example, you're not going to say it's okay for your son to be fearful. That's what changes the children who change."

Most parents of a shy child don't expect him to be a football or movie star, but they don't want him to be a recluse, either. To help him adapt to the real world, they must walk the fine line between seeming to reject his nature and allowing him to duck the very experiences that can help polish his temperament's inevitable rough edges. To Gunnar, the parent's real task is to say, " 'She's shy. How can I help her live happily with that?' With the right support, rather than disliking herself for being quiet, that type of child, who can be very attentive to nuance, might be a great writer or scientist."

The pragmatic father of three grown sons, David Lykken observes that before the timid preschooler faces the thrills and chills of the rough-and-tumble world of school and playground, he can gradually be desensitized to milder excitement. "Swing him between your legs till his eyes widen but aren't scared," he says. "Let him get used to the experience of all those juices surging around. Week by week, as you move through his fear a little at a time, as a therapist does, he'll be able to take more stimulation." Such toughening up is more than skin-deep. When inhibited children figure out how to handle stress, Nathan Fox suspects that the physiological marker associated with fearfulness disappears from their EEGs: "The message of our data is that experience can modify the brain."

Shy temperaments are hardly the only sort that need some modification. "It's important for children to learn to regulate fear and inhibition," says Gunnar, "but maybe more important to handle anger and aggression. Teaching children how to manage frustration is key, because stress reactions aren't only provoked by threats but by the inability to manage a difficult situation."

Happily, time itself can work wonders in the natures of the young. Most of us can think of a candidate for the title of Baby from Hell who turned into everybody's favorite kid. "The study of temperament is an effort to understand how physiology contributes to behavior," says Gunnar, "and physiology changes. A baby is not a tiny grown-up. The brain certainly matures through adolescence, and periods of behavioral discontinuity often coincide with spurts in brain development. A very unregulated, passionate, three thousand percent baby can eventually learn how to control himself with his frontal lobes and end up being as planful as another child who was born so. Our nervous system works in such a way that if you can't do something on one level, you can learn to do it on another. Because he hasn't had to work at those skills, the born-regulated child might actually have, and be, more trouble in adolescence."

Because they're closer to a state of nature, most human temperament research is conducted with babies and small children, but many of its lessons apply to adults. The two great practical principles are the folly of trying to treat different people the same and that of denying, fighting, or punishing a trait rather than accepting and working with it. Whether dealing with others or oneself, it's best to recognize innate strengths and weaknesses, then mostly concentrate on reinforcing the former, taking consolation in the fact that we are who we are and can do so much, but no more, about it.

A sense of how one handles one's own temperament requires some monitoring. "How do you talk to yourself when you're in a stressful situation?" says Gunnar. "Do you say, 'Forget your emotions, they're unimportant, just do it'? Do you become wrapped up in your anxiety and join forty-four support groups? Or are you kind to yourself, able to back off a little and give yourself what you need, neither negating nor overdoing things? Can you let go of stress? Seek help?"

For people who feel shortchanged by nature or nurture in the resilience department, a loving friend or spouse, like a good therapist, can provide what clinicians call a "corrective emotional experience." As a child, for example, Monica learned from the kindly hospital staff that, contrary to her earlier experience, people could love and care for her. Later, from the solid base of a good marriage, she was able to develop long-suppressed parts of her personality that surprised her early mentors. In such secure relationships, says Gunnar, "you learn an adaptive way of dealing with your feelings, and feelings and temperament are very closely linked."

When we think of ties that have helped form us, they tend to be the close personal sort. Our relationship to the larger culture, however, also affects who we are in surprising, and sometimes profound, ways.

CHAPTER 10

CODES OF BEHAVIOR

Ｏne of the great charms of the Monica films is that, like home movies, they ingenuously reveal the changing temper of the times. From the frilly dresses of the 1950s to the androgynous jeans-and-jersey uniform of the 1970s to the sporty shorts of the trim sunbelt grandmother of the 1990s, even Monica's clothes speak to the transitions of her baby-boom generation. Unlike home movies, these have been shot from a scientific perspective, yet that, too, is subjective. The issues that don't come up, as well as those that are emphasized, reveal how culture filters the way in which a person is perceived. For example, Monica's behavior, whether her "orality" or her withdrawal from stress, is always framed in the context of her early trauma—a perspective from the psychoanalytic theory dominant when the study began.

In seeing Monica's story as a "myth for our age" and its heroine as "a twentieth-century 'wild child,' " Myron Hofer puts the case—and his own scientific interest in exactly what mothers supply to development—in yet another, deeper historical perspective. Enamored with notions of "natural reason" and the "noble savage" following its revolution, early-nineteenth-century France was captivated by the Wild Boy of Aveyron, a so-called feral child who somehow survived early abandonment in the wilderness and was captured near that town. Rather than supporting the Enlightenment's notion that a human nature simply unfolds unaided, however, accounts of such children support the modern view of development, in which environment plays a crucial role in the emergence of both individuality and humanity itself.

Contrary to the fond hopes of the French, far from expressing a joyous "natural" emotionality, the wild boy and others of his ilk suffered from severe affective retardation. Moving senselessly from state to state, motivated primarily by food, unable to smile or laugh appropriately, they preferred animal companionship to the human sort. Most walked on all fours, were mute, had remarkable senses of smell, and were strikingly insensitive to cold and pain. In short, lack of nurture had rendered them, by any standard but a strict taxonomic one, animals rather than humans. Despite the intellectual and literary appeal of nineteenth-century ideas about nature's role in who we are, the wild boy never became man enough to leave the institution to which he was confined. In contrast, says Hofer, in a moving expression of the twentieth century's can-do optimism, Monica, whose development had also been deranged, was carefully, patiently remothered and restored to a full life.

Changing concepts and treatment of what Hofer calls "radically altered human beings who embody unsolved philosophical questions of their eras" are just a dramatic example of how culture not only influences who we become, but how we're perceived. It's said that Lord Byron, the hero of the Romantic era, would have been considered a madman in the previous Age of Enlightenment, and different historical periods clearly favor different temperaments and traits. "If you had an obsequious, Uriah Heepy personality during the age of kings," says personality theorist Michael Stone, "you could sign your book, as Galileo did, 'Your most obedient and humble servant.' You were a success then, but you'd be less so in our era."

Long before the era of personality psychologists, the medieval Church discouraged obsessive-compulsive and depressive tendencies by making sins of scrupulosity, hopelessness, and suicide. On the other hand, the long roster of flagellating, persecuting, hallucinating, and hermitic saints testifies to its glorification of the masochistic, paranoid, and schizoid inclinations devalued by modern ecclesiastical reformers. Like religion, modern psychology has its cultural crazes. In the 1950s, the field focused on "the three A's"—achievement, authoritarianism, and anxiety—that preoccupied the America of ulcers, the Cold War, and the buttoned-up Man in the Gray Flannel Suit. Undoubtedly, someone will devise a similarly catchy tag for the therapeutic concerns of the last part of the century—perhaps "the double D's" of depression and dependency.

From a late-twentieth-century perspective, one of the film study's most striking biases comes through in the way it simplistically frames Monica as a passive, compliant "good girl." When he wants to illustrate society's impact on who we are, George Vaillant turns to gender, citing the similar beginnings and very different destinies of the brilliant children of Lewis Terman, the Stanford psychologist who pioneered IQ testing and the longitudinal study of people's lives. As the head of Stanford's engineering school, Terman's son helped establish Silicon Valley. His equally intelligent daughter became a telephone receptionist in one of the university's dormitories. Ironically, Terman's daughter's fate is typical of the female subjects in one of his great works: a study of the lives of very gifted children—their average IQ was 155—followed into old age. "When I finished reading about the Terman women's lives," says Vaillant, "I wanted to burn my bra. Only around retirement does their experience become more exciting than that of, say, the Grant study's men, because society had finally stopped interfering with their ability to create and be happy. You ask, 'Can you make an underclass?' Look at the brilliant, exciting Terman women at graduation from high school and then again after thirty years, and see that all they had developed were survival skills."

For most of history, men's reaction to their anatomy has largely been women's destiny. Ancient scientists first attributed differences between the sexes' behavior to the uterus. According to Stone, a historian of psychiatry, the organ was thought to meander occasionally to the head, where it produced the wild state called hysteria, from *hystera*, Greek for "womb." Later, in bourgeois turn-of-the-century Vienna, Freud focused his view of women's psychology on a different reproductive part. If they wouldn't give up the wish to have a penis, surrender to their husbands', and accept motherhood and family as their only fulfillment, he warned, they would take on the manly traits of competitiveness and lust for females. His disciple Karen Horney was expelled from the New York Psychoanalytic Institute for insisting that culture played a larger role in women's lives than the phallus did.

Outside psychoanalytical circles, differences in male and female ways were attributed to the feebler feminine mind until the invention of the IQ test in the 1930s dispelled this masculine fantasy. Around the same time, psychologist Gordon Allport and others began the democratic and systematic investigations of personality that paved the way for less fanciful theories about what were increasingly viewed as the "traits" of masculinity and femininity. Summarizing some fifty years of data, Hans Eysenck says that, along with differences in sexual behavior and attitudes, "in all the thirty-six countries we've studied, there's a very marked difference between men and women. Men have higher scores in psychoticism—they're more aggressive, impersonal, hostile. Women have higher scores in neuroticism—they're more fearful, depressed, tense. Of course, within each group individuals differ, so these things aren't absolute."

Years of primate research suggest to Steve Suomi that, overall, males are slightly more irritable and active and that after puberty females' response to separation becomes more severe. "Although there may be some hormonal contributions to this," he says, "I prefer the argument, at least where rhesus monkeys are concerned, that after puberty males and females have very different life courses. The males have a much bigger set of challenges to deal with if they are to survive. They have to leave home and get into a new troop, for example, and females don't. Therefore, males may be protected from some of the pain of separation, in that their stress reactions may be blunted. That sort of mechanism could contribute to the gender difference in affect. Postpubertally, females are most sensitive to separation and males to a loss of dominance status." To his colleague J. D. Higley, the substantial gender differences in sociability parallel the development and expression of the sexes' serotonin systems. When monkeys are young and less aggressive, their level is very high, he says; with age, it diminishes until puberty, when it stabilizes. Although there are still individuals who start out and remain high or low, "females tend to have higher serotonin levels that incline them to be more social," says Higley. "Male monkeys spend a lot of time by themselves and females with others."

Like primate research, studies of human infants have turned up little in the way of early gender differences in behavior. Temperament researcher Mary Rothbart doesn't see many, "although some colleagues think that boys tend to be more active. By preschool age, there are some differences in aggression and self-control that favor girls' better modulation—but not much." Among older preschoolers, Megan Gunnar doesn't see big boy-girl differences in temperament, but a "boy culture and a girl culture—not the ones that we create but that *they* do." Research conducted with kids of this age, who are highly preoccupied with who is male and who is female, includes "some disgusting data that show that impulsive, rough-and-tumble boys are admired but such girls aren't," she says. "The girls with those traits can be lovely kids, but they won't be well liked after the age of three or four." Gunnar thinks that testosterone, whose effects on females vary, may play a role in the profile of spunkier girls and concludes that "there should be a third culture for tomboys."

Testosterone is known as the "male" hormone, but females have some too, produced by their ovaries and adrenal glands. The hormone works in two ways: first by "masculinizing" the structure of the pre- and neonatal brain, later by circulating in the bloodstream and probably affecting neurotransmission. If female animals are exposed to too much in utero, they behave like males; in turn, males deprived of such exposure act like females. Almost all men have way more testosterone than they need to develop beards, low voices, and manly behavior. That women's circulating levels differ greatly can help explain their considerable intragender differences in libido and assertiveness—two traits in which intergender differences do seem to be grounded in biology. Women who say they prefer affectionate cuddling to the wilder shores of love or a quiet domestic life to the rat race aren't necessarily repressed, downtrodden, or otherwise psychologically askew but only expressing their own psychobiology.

The story of Eve's creation notwithstanding, basic human anatomy and behavior are female. The more testosterone individuals are exposed to, the more masculine they become. During fetal development, because turning into a male is more complicated and involves more hormonal steps, there's a greater potential for slipups. Men's more complex origins help explain their higher incidences of developmental quirks and glitches, including math genius, left-handedness, nearsightedness, allergies, dyslexia, stuttering, and the aberrant sexual syndromes formerly called perversions.

Were a visitor from another planet to try to assess the broad difference in male and female responses to stress—the great barometer of temperament—he might conclude that, for better or worse, men are more inclined to act and women to feel. Men, who have about ten times more circulating testosterone than women, are demonstrably more aggressive by objective standards: they commit almost all violent crimes. Even among children, behavior problems are much more common in boys. On the other hand, the majority of psychotherapy clients are women. In fact, scientists often qualify the higher female incidence of various mental illnesses by cautioning that many men with the same problems end up in jail or as addicts or vagrants instead of in treatment, where they can be diagnosed and counted.

Despite the differences in neurotransmitters and hormones, however, it's hard to overestimate the impact of the environment on male and female behavior, even the sort that looks very "biological." Referring to a study conducted by psychologists Janice Juraska and Celia Moore of a sexually dimorphic nucleus in the rat's spinal cord whose neurons innervate the penis, William Greenough observes that, not surprisingly, the female's nucleus is much smaller. "At first that sounds like pure biology—not interesting," he says. It turns out, however, that if a male fetus is denied testosterone, his nucleus stays much smaller; if a female fetus is exposed to the hormone, hers becomes much bigger. Moreover, because testosterone ensures that a male pup gives off a certain pheromone, the mother spends much more time licking his genital region than that of her female pups, thus causing his nucleus to grow. If a mother can't smell, she'll lick male and female pups equally, causing the male's nucleus to go in the female direction and vice versa. "That's still biology," says Greenough, "but it's not just mechanical biology or even nonmechanical biology. The loop rests outside the organism, making it biology of an interesting sort that involves experience."

As the fate of the Terman women, who could have been neurosurgeons and senators instead of shop clerks and typists, illustrates so poignantly, many of the differences in men's and women's lives depend on cultural concepts of what's appropriate male or female behavior. Although researchers who study young children don't see big gender differences in temperament per se, they find a sharp contrast in how various dispositions are expressed and nurtured. Depending on whether a shy or aggressive child is a boy or a girl, for example, parents may intervene or not. That society is more, or less, tolerant of different traits in boys and girls mostly accounts for their divergent behavioral paths, according to Rothbart: "If you stop a certain behavior right away, the result will be different than if you let a child take several steps in that direction before intervening."

General George Marshall, the Nobel laureate, soldier, statesman, and author of the eponymous plan to stabilize Europe after World War II, famously observed that feelings were something he reserved for Mrs. Marshall. Especially if they're high achievers, men are often praised for being tough, uncompromising, aggressive, and unsentimental. As the bad press dumped on even semitough women makes clear, the reception a trait or temperament gets can depend on who's expressing it. Women of Marshall's ilk are often described with an unflattering term that, as Barbara Bush said of Democratic vice presidential hopeful Geraldine Ferraro, "rhymes with rich." Less decorously, the mother of Speaker of the House Newt Gingrich declared that her son thought First Lady Hillary Rodham Clinton was "a bitch."

From an evolutionary point of view, it makes sense that female primates would generally be more "field dependent." If their sense of well-being weren't tied to others, they'd be no more interested in the often tedious business of nurturing than males are. A little girl who isn't particularly field dependent, however, may prefer her own company and ways to the group's. Such behavior raises more eyebrows and inspires more correction than it would in a boy, who might be praised for being "his own man." Not surprisingly, although hard-to-handle babies are equally distributed in terms of gender, nurture ensures that boys described as "difficult" are likelier to stay that way than girls with a similar disposition are.

Definitions of masculinity and femininity remain fuzzy and various, belonging to that class of important things that all people, including scientists, feel they understand but have trouble putting a finger on or agreeing with others about. History shows that sex differences expand or contract according to social and economic pressures. In hard times, women have pulled the plow and delivered babies in the field; in prosperous ones, they have been "ladies" immobilized by corsets and hoopskirts. In the course of the 1960s' social revolution, the assumptions that the sexes are very different and that men are better were not just protested but studied. By the mid-1970s, gender differences were considered to be not only few but unimportant. For the next decade or so, there was much interest in the notion of androgyny—a blend of masculinity and femininity supposedly superior to either. By the time the first wave of female lawyers, MBAs, and doctors came pouring out of the graduate schools, many women psychologists were arguing *for* gender differences.

The most important is that, like other female primates, women regard relationships as central to life. Whatever the role of serotonin and other biochemicals in such a broad predilection, experience also powerfully figures. That girls don't have to differentiate themselves from their mothers as dramatically as boys must, for example, helps explain why men are likelier to be characterized by a desire for individuality and separation and women for attachment. To researchers who pursue them as traits, masculinity has much to do with an "instrumental" or "agentic" approach to the world and feminity with an "expressive" or "communal" one. Like other characteristics, however, their expression differs among individuals in terms of intensity and the degree of modulation by other traits. Someone who's temperamentally primed to see life in a highly structured way, for example, may welcome gender as yet another way to sharpen the focus on the big picture—I gotta do what a real man/woman's gotta do—while someone whose perceptions are more diffuse may recoil from such black-and-white constructs.

As the century that had started out explaining male and female behavioral variations with the theories of penis envy and a dull female brain draws to a close, mainstream psychology professes that the sexes sometimes think, feel, and act differently. Regarding women's ways as deficient, however, is an error based on a long history of using men's as the generic human standard. Regarding personality traits, no single one

distinguishes all women from all men. According to Columbia personality psychologist Walter Mischel, "The data are very clear that the intragender differences are greater than the intergender ones. It's exactly
the same with race. The mean is a horrible way to look at people that
has more to do with the sociology of how academic careers are made
than with people's lives."

Individual differences notwithstanding, in the United States, the
tough, pants-wearing, all-for-one, obsessive-compulsive, workaholic
personality traditionally identified with men remains ascendant. Moreover, the self-confidence and aggressiveness long tolerated in men, even
when they border on narcissism and sociopathy, are becoming increasingly acceptable in women. However, the halo that once surrounded
the go-getter's historical complement—the dedicated, tenderhearted,
apron-wearing, one-for-all team player—is fading fast. As social and
economic shifts encourage "masculine" tendencies in both sexes, "the
important question is whether they enrich life or control and distort it,"
says psychiatrist and personality researcher John Oldham, the director
of the New York State Psychiatric Institute. Although many women
have indeed been liberated from restrictive stereotypes, he observes,
"The perfect wife and mother of the family-centered, value-laden '50s,
who put home and children first, is now considered a drone in places
like New York. What was till recently celebrated as the American feminine ideal seems almost pathological. But for some people, life *is* about
caring, and feminism can create conflicts for such women, who may feel
ashamed of their desires."

The changeable way in which even the scientific culture reacts to a behavioral tendency is writ large in the weasely taxonomic history of certain of psychiatry's shifting roster of officially recognized ailments.
Territorial about their awfully similar illness of dysthymia, or chronic
mild depression, many mood researchers are unhappy with the personality disorder currently defined as depressive; because "masochistic" or
"self-defeating" sound less emotional and more cognitive, they would
prefer those descriptors, which have been used for similar problems in
the past. Some personality researchers, however, see fine distinctions

among the three labels, while others feel that the latter two terms have a misogynistic ring, evoking Freud's contention that women like to suffer.

Like it or not, women certainly did suffer more during the era of the early psychoanalysts, long before safe childbirth and birth control, much less dual-family careers. "The family's survival and the whole society were based on the workplace for men and *Kinder, Kirke, und Küchen* for women," says Michael Stone. "In Freud's day, masochism meant an excessive degree of this womanly compliance, which seemed pretty normal then, but is less adaptive in our culture." More important, he says, "perhaps feminists have forgotten, or never knew, that there are just as many if not more male masochists, who chase unattainable women and behave in other self-defeating ways." Moreover, "If a disorder primarily affects females or males, that describes nature, and I'm not responsible for nature. If more men are compulsive, and many, many more men are sadistic and antisocial, and more women are hysterical, why must that be denied?"

As a member of the committee that sorted out and defined the American Psychiatric Association's most recent list of personality disorders, psychologist Tom Widiger recalls feminists' concern "that psychiatry was trying to awaken the archaic notion that women have an unconscious desire for pain. That really wasn't the intention, but calling someone masochistic raises the specter." He allows that depressive is a kinder, gentler term, in that it doesn't imply an unconscious wish to feel crummy, but "it's applied to the same group of people."

For similar political reasons, psychiatry now describes the overheated, capricious personality that the ancients and Freud called hysterical, from the Greek for "womb," as histrionic, from the Latin for "dramatic." When modulated, this affectionate, romantic, spontaneous prototype is, like the nurturing wife and mother, another traditional feminine ideal. Even Freud's friend and colleague Josef Breuer couldn't resist falling in love with his pretty twenty-one-year-old hysterical patient, immortalized in the psychoanalytical literature as Anna O. Among early analysands, the majority of the women were, like Anna, diagnosed as having too much of this good thing, yet in his long career Stone has treated only one such "hysterical neurotic." Just as images of the ideal woman have changed, so have the incidences of female personality perturbations. Many of the women who consult Stone, for example, are afflicted by a combination of self-defeating, dependent, histrionic, and compulsive traits that inclines them to fall for men who won't commit themselves to a relationship.

Very nurturing women probably felt more comfortable in the 1950s than they would in the 1990s, just as the odd "career gals" of midcentury now reign supreme in many places. Because individuals of both sexes are on behavioral bell curves, such cultural shifts mean that "it can never be that a hundred percent of women or men will be comfortable," says Stone. "Some women have more assertive, engineering-type brains than some men, and the most emotive man is more feelingful than the least emotive woman. On average, however, women are more affiliative and dependent on the social field, which is adaptive if you have to care for children and teach them language. Women are more genetically programmed to fulfill those functions, which will never change, as compared to other traditional tasks that aren't so vital anymore. Most women are more comfortable going through life if they fulfill their biological potential to have kids and simultaneously use their brains in the larger society."

How easy it is to pull off that juggling act depends not just on the woman but on her environment. "If she's comfortable in her own skin," says Stone, "a woman who chooses to stay home with her children—or not—thinks, 'It's a big world, there's room for all kinds, and I'm this kind.' She doesn't have a problem." But should she feel troubled by the discrepancy between her desires and society's expectations, she does have one—not so much with her personality as with her difficulty in accepting it. In New York, says Stone, "I see more women who are conflicted because they'd like to have a career but feel they can't. But it might be different if I practiced in Dubuque."

If the same individuals can be regarded differently in two American cities, so can they be in different nations. Americans see the choleric spark as the sign of a hothead or a bad sport, but that same quality is admired and kindled in the Middle East. The inhibition and what-will-others-say attitude that we find sissified is part of the national character of Japan, where our say-anything attitude seems barbaric. While working with Japanese psychiatrists on translating his list of personality traits, Stone observed that their language has no words for certain concepts, such as "inhospitable," because "there are no inhospitable people in Japan. We had to make up a word that translates as 'not kind to guests.' On the other hand, unlike us, they have a term for not being dutiful to parents."

The idea of a so-called national character may not be politically correct, but it has legs. Even those who are philosophically opposed to the hoary concept may find that it influences their choice of vacation spots. Environment, in the form of an economic shift from conquest to trade, made the bloody Vikings into the pacifist, socialist Scandinavians; genocide turned the nonviolent Jews of the European ghettos into the fighting Sabras of Israel. Some researchers, however, think that genes as well as culture figure in ethnic traits. There's some evidence, for example, that people who belong to the type A blood groups are likelier to be more stable and self-sufficient, while those from B groups are likelier to be apprehensive. In a very large study, Hans Eysenck found that the Japanese are significantly lower in extroversion and higher in neuroticism than the British, whose ratio of A to B blood types is significantly higher. Such data presumably help explain why the British speak their minds and value eccentricity, while the Japanese cultivate circumlocution and conformity.

As is the case for the individual sort, one influence on national character, from dolce far niente to "go for it," is the tendency of temperaments to seek their adaptive niches. Observing that in Sweden there are more schizophrenics and schizoids per 100,000 people than in Italy, Michael Stone thinks that "over time, Greta Garboesque, 'I want to be alone' isolates have gravitated to Scandinavia and produced children who are more like Swedes than like Italians." Less speculative colleagues would at least agree with him that "a certain remote type succeeds in that environment of vast open spaces and cold."

Even within the same nation, different personalities select different cultures. Just as armed survivalists are heading to the Northwest in the 1990s, beatniks congregated in Greenwich Village in the 1950s and hippies converged on San Francisco in the 1960s. Since the 1980s, the most recent phase of the ongoing Age of Aquarius has attracted crystal-bedecked mystics and channelers, including many whom John Oldham describes as "idiosyncratic" personalities, to the southwestern meccas of Sedona and Santa Fe. That some of these New Agers strike the hoi polloi as "crazy" reflects their extraordinary receptivity to the novel. Although this characteristic allowed Columbus to follow his hunch that the earth wasn't flat and Galileo to declare that the sun didn't circle it, most eccentrics aren't of this star caliber. Their ability to tune out the external world and focus on a task draws disproportionate numbers to certain professional microcultures, sorting mail at the post office, say, or operating word processors.

Because a personality is considered to be disordered only if it troubles someone, including its owner, what psychiatrists used to dismiss as a mere "geographical cure" can work. By way of analogy, Oldham says, "If you identify yourself as gay and grew up in a very traditional, conservative southern town where that's considered to be horrendous, why torture yourself by staying there, rather than moving someplace where homosexuality is accepted?" Of the crude, aggressive, self-centered Hollywood-mogul stereotypes that we laugh at in the movies, Stone observes that "those traits really do give you an advantage in Los Angeles." Politics too illustrates geography's role in the particular personality contests called elections. The plainspoken, tightfisted, get-off-my-back Bob Dole plays better in the heartland than on the coasts, while Daniel Patrick Moynihan's ruffles and flourishes must seem somewhat suspect in the grain belt. "How adaptive your traits are depends in part on what your situation demands of you," says Kentuckian Tom Widiger. "Agreeableness may be better suited to the South than the East. A degree of antagonism is probably good for a cop but not so good for a priest. And even though antagonism may suit the cop at work, it's not so helpful when he's trying to resolve a conflict with his wife."

As the media transform what was once a big, diverse world into a homogeneous electronic global village and even personality research emphasizes norms and averages, it can be a challenge to accept, much less exult in, who one is. "We give lip service to individuality," says John Richters, "but that isn't really the tone that runs through, say, the child-rearing literature. American parents tend to feel that if a kid is different, that's bad, and they have to get rid of that difference. Labels and categorical approaches to things like shyness and inhibition can make parents think, 'Oops! My kid has it! He's abnormal!' as if traits were diseases. We'd be better off being looser and respecting differences, rather than trying to change kids fundamentally. First, I'm not sure you can, and second, I worry a lot about the cost."

PART III

HOW
WE
COULD
BE

CHAPTER 11

TYPES AND SHADOWS

In a particularly amusing and predictive bit of Monica footage, shot in a playroom when the star was about eight years old, she spills paint on her dress and worries about her mother's reaction. First she attempts to clean the spot. Next she gets Dr. Reichsman to try. When he doesn't succeed either, she doesn't criticize or complain but only says sweetly, "Mom will be so angry at me." He immediately gets another researcher to pitch in, and before long a gaggle of scientists is cheerfully absorbed in a little girl's laundry problem. Even when given explicit directions before a filming that under no circumstances were they to pick up after Monica, these adults could no more resist her ability to get what she wants without seeming demanding or oppressive than they could ignore her engaging smile.

Many years later, shortly after the birth of Monica's third child, the team converges on her small home. The hostess sets out coffee and donuts in the kitchen, but she remains ensconced in the living room, where everyone else, including her two older small children, waits in attendance. Seated on the couch while others pay court and do her bidding, this Monica is the grown-up version of the little iron butterfly who, reclining in her crib, commanded the pediatric ward. Girl or woman, she has a striking ability to get others to do her bidding without making it seem burdensome. Although it's a defining feature of her personality, this special je ne sais quoi isn't on any standard index of traits. Like other qualities that give an individual color and complexity, her uncanny power is a hybrid of several characteristics that resists simple taxonomy.

The attempt to predict behavior and simplify a complex world by categorizing people according to certain characteristics has hardly been limited to scientists. One of the oldest such systems is more popular than ever. "Astrology appears to make sense to some extent, because it's filled with so-called Barnum statements," says Tom Widiger. "They're pretty much true for everybody but, when specifically applied to you, seem to describe you really well. 'You're very assertive when something is important to you'—that's true of all of us. The twelve entries on the newspaper page look different, but they could be scrambled in another order and you'd have still the same reaction of feeling understood." To Auke Tellegen, astrology "fills the modern gap in things that tell us who we are. Like listening to the preacher on Sunday, it makes your life meaningful by linking you and your fate. To the many people who don't feel that connection, it's very gratifying. And like preachers, astrologers give you your marching orders—they tell you what to do." On the other hand, he adds, "astrology doesn't differ from some other personality systems as much in the types of people described as in how they're explained."

For practical reasons from efficiency to safety, we all sometimes rely on labeling, from "good guys" and "bad guys" to "our kind" and "not our kind." The great popularity of the idea that there are certain types of people bespeaks an evolutionary pressure to be able to size others up quickly—a big asset for survival. This capacity takes on a dimension of nearly artistic sensitivity in psychiatric diagnosticians. Just as the best scout can sense things on the savannah that others can't, the most adept clinicians form their impressions from myriad subtle cues. "We wouldn't have believed in types for thousands of years if there were nothing to it," says psychoanalyst Mardi Horowitz. "On the other hand, although there are individuals who seem to fit psychiatry's traditional personality categories, or prototypes, quite well, that's true of tarot cards and astrological signs, too. There's something to the typing theories, but they're not right."

Personality categories aren't "right" for the same reason that the characters in a B movie are really caricatures. We can very quickly identify the bad guy who's going to shoot dogs, not rescue children, rape women, and betray friends, says Horowitz, "and there *are* people who act like that. But it's also a stereotype—an oversimplified formula—because the people who do those things aren't going to be alike in other ways." The same problem applies to real people, most of whom are too complicated to be neatly tagged, at least in Western civilizations that tolerate a lot of individuality. "If a hundred accountants were gathered in the same room," says Widiger, "you'd see a kind of family resemblance to a prototype. But you'd also see that many accountants have some but not all of the features associated with it. Saying someone is the obsessive or dependent type is akin to saying he's an accountant, a man, or a racist. Those so described will have something in common but not much, because people are so complex."

Typing pathological extremes, such as the savage brute who epitomizes the antisocial personality, is easier than trying to pin down someone who's healthy—by definition, flexible and highly differentiated. Although normal personalities have some coloring characteristics and elements that repeat, says Horowitz, "attempts at categorizing these complex patterns haven't been successful." Even the criteria for problematic personalities that doctors have recognized for centuries, such as the paranoid, depressive, and schizoid, go only so far. Although Horowitz has modernized the description of the venerable hysterical type—Scarlett O'Hara is a good example—"it's really only a prototype," he says. "Most of these people are excessively theatrical attention seekers, yet some are shy. Such classifications are beneficial only as a basis for further individualized formulations."

Despite these limitations, doctors must decide whether someone is sick and with what. For thousands of years, they have sorted personalities into various categories: someone is melancholic, say, or paranoid, or he isn't. Taking a very different perspective on the systematic description of the ways that people are, personality psychologists, who are more focused on the normal, have maintained that individuals don't differ in quality but merely in quantity, or the intensity with which they express certain fundamental human characteristics. However, they don't agree about what some of those traits are or what they should be called. As Hans Eysenck, the field's *grand seigneur,* is the first to admit, the lack of an equivalent of the gold standard means that "we now have thousands of personality theories. Each new student makes up his own questionnaire, because his name goes on it. This is ridiculous and not the way you advance science, which is like building a house. Throwing stones on a heap is not building a house. There's a refusal to build on what has been established. Physicists would laugh at this—they don't make up their own temperature scales." Tom Widiger sums up the personality theory wars this way: "If God asked me, 'What is Reality?' I'd say, 'We don't know at present.' If He said, 'You must pick one model now,' I'd take the Big Five, which isn't perfect but is the most compelling in terms of its approach and its consistency."

Dull abstractions in scientific texts, personality models spring to life when used to distinguish real people, even fictional characters. In *Lonesome Dove,* his grand cowboy epic of the Old West, Larry McMurtry creates in Gus McCrae and Woodrow Call two wonderful variations on the prototypical American action hero who populates war, western, cop, and other "buddy" sagas. In the Big Five terminology of extroversion, agreeableness, conscientiousness, neuroticism, and openness to experience, both are fearless, can-do guys who are high on the assertive, active, excitement-seeking aspects of extroversion. Gus's "disregard for danger was so complete that Call initially thought he must want to die. . . . But Gus loved to live and had no intention of letting anyone do him out of any of his pleasures." Just as brave, Call differs from his friend along the same classic lines as the set of male archetypes who move along the plot in *War and Peace.* Like Pierre, Gus is agreeableness squared: a generous, lenient, good-natured Good Ole Boy. Like Prince Andrei, Call is the prickly loner. As Gus tells him, "It's hard for normal men to relax around you."

A trait doesn't exist in a vacuum, but is modulated by its owner's other qualities. Gus's agreeableness is amplified by his negligible neuroticism. "You don't get excited by nothing," Call tells him, "unless it's biscuits or whores." In contrast, Call is high on the trait's self-conscious, touchy dimensions: "Listening to men talk usually made him feel more alone than if he were a mile away by himself under a tree." And as Gus observes, "Once in a while Call would fall into blue spells—

times when he seemed almost paralyzed by doubts he never voiced." Call himself finds it "peculiar to seem so infallible in their [the men's] eyes and yet feel so empty and sad when he thought of himself."

Most often, it's their disparate scores on openness that perturb the two friends. Call wastes little energy on speculation and likes routine: "His purpose was to get done what needed to be done, and what needed to be done was simple, if not easy. The settlers of Texas needed protection, from Indians on the North and bandits on the South." Gus, on the other hand, is interested in anything and everything, from Latin maxims to what's on women's minds to "the finer points of cooking." He drives literal-minded Call nuts with his philosophical and speculative observations: "It's a pity," says Gus, "that cattle can't be trained to carry riders."

The simplest distinction between the heroes of *Lonesome Dove* is that "the men looked to Call for orders and got drunk with Augustus." Gus is better company, but Call is "the Captain": the very definition of conscientiousness—a characteristic that's as American as the Stars and Bars. "Glory don't interest Call," says Gus. "He's just got to do his duty nine times over or he don't sleep good." As the triumphs and trials of the good Lutherans of Garrison Keillor's Lake Woebegon make plain, the hardworking, well-organized, persevering people who share Call's sense of duty and discipline are the backbone of society. They know the right thing to do, and they do it—the right way. Fond as he is of his old trailmate Jake Spoon, Call is not one to let feelings interfere with clear duty; he hangs his friend on the spot after Jake joins a gang of murderous horse thieves.

Conscientiousness comes in handy on the job. In the complex, ambiguous situations that crop up in private life, however, the trait can make things difficult. Call remains uncomfortable with the verdict he passed on the only woman in his life and the mother of his probable only child. Because Maggie made her living by "doing what she could," in Gus's tolerant parlance, by Call's lights it wouldn't have been right to marry her or acknowledge their son, yet the fact that he didn't haunts him after her death. Were it not for Call's conscientiousness, however, there would be no *Lonesome Dove.* The long trail drive that's the novel's narrative spine originates with his need for a new project once the Mexican border has been purged of bad guys. Gus was happy enough hanging around Lonesome Dove, drinking, gambling, and whoring, but the conscientious person can't wait for vacation to be over so he can get back to work.

Despite the contributions of trait theorists, their poor record of using their data to predict what people will do in a given situation suggests that personality is more complex than their formulas would have it. Some scientists insist that the problem is that personality can't be described accurately in a vacuum. If trait-minded theorists locate personality inside the individual, Walter Mischel, whose trenchant criticisms cause some rueful peers to describe him as the personality psychologist who almost did away with the field, puts it somewhere along the fuzzy boundary where person and environment meet. For example, if anxiety is a stable trait, asks Mischel, why is it that often the tensest person in the dentist's waiting room isn't also the most fretful in the classroom right before an exam? Does the anxiety rest in the person, in the situation, or someplace in between? "Trait psychology begins with the shallowest kind of stereotypes," he says. "It ignores the individual's complexity and capacity to change and the fact that he, his situation, and their interaction must be considered together."

Because each person is relatively predictable in some areas of behavior, particularly where intellect and competence are concerned, says Mischel, we're not surprised that the diligent biology student later becomes a doctor and remains hardworking and science minded. Under stress, too, people become more predictable, so that no one is shocked if the six-year-old who was a high-strung baby feels jittery on the first day of school. However, Mischel insists that generally "sensitivity to context is more the rule than the exception. That social situations so often correspond to what we expect from them is provocative."

While discussing a long-term study of the consistency of the social behavior of children aged six to thirteen while at camp, Mischel brings up two kids who had the same summer-long overall score in verbal aggression. On closer examination, however, reports of their behavior in five situations showed that Jimmy is a lamb who goes crazy only when teased about his glasses, while Johnny consistently shoots from the lip. "They are very different children," says Mischel, "and it's the behavioral ups and downs in relation to situations that tell you in what ways. But the kinds of conditionals that give their personalities their particular patinas have been obliterated from most research." Indeed, he says, the similarity in how a subject from the camp study acts in various environments turns out to be "totally trivial," correlating only about .13: "It is the *pattern* of variability—of when and where the child is a lamb or a bully—that's stable and reveals his distinctive 'if . . . then' signature."

To Mischel, the question for personality psychology is "What are the underlying mediating processes in individuals that generate their characteristic patterns and differences?" As far as he is concerned, the organization of behavior seems simpler in theory than it is in reality, personality consistencies seem greater in questionnaires than they are when observed, and the expression of traits across situations is more complex than assumed. But such complexity "is very hard for American psychology to deal with," he says, "not so much because of the nature of the phenomena that have to be understood but because contextual theories aren't as simple and nice as scores averaged across three or five measures that try to predict everything and do so very badly. It's not that behavior is unpredictable but that its nature and locus are not yet pinned down. People would like to make personality much, much simpler than it is. If personality psychologists tried to do what the novelist does, they'd be starting in the right place. A good writer's experiences are always contextualized. Can you imagine Dostoyevski writing a story about a person high in conscientiousness and low in introversion? The real job is figuring out the active psychological ingredients embedded in each situation that trigger an individual's characteristics."

The real problem with trying to portray an individual through a printout of scores on three or five or thirty-five traits may be that personality is just too complex to be codified. After Richard Nixon's death, Lyndon Johnson's daughter Luci offered a surprising recollection: just before he resigned in the wake of Watergate, the beleaguered king of dirty tricks sent her a touching note of congratulations on the birth of a daughter, even remarking on how proud the recently deceased former president, an old political enemy, would have been.

Where that extremely interesting personality is concerned, David Lykken is perplexed by clashing accounts of LBJ's courage. Reliable witnesses have Johnson desperately dodging World War II and cowering on that murderous day in Dallas. Others have him, once the die is cast, behaving with exemplary sangfroid on his lone combat mission and in calming a distraught nation. From Lykken's perspective, a person is constituted to be steady under fire or not; such coolness can't be faked. Yet in *President Kennedy,* Richard Reeves tells stories that suggest that LBJ's characteristic reaction to stress unfolded in two phases. At the height of the Cold War crisis in Berlin, for example, Kennedy told Johnson to visit the German city. " 'Why me?' he said to Kennedy. 'There'll be a lot of shooting and I'll be in the center of it.' " Also present was Sam Rayburn, the legendary Speaker of the House, who "was bucking up his protégé's courage, warning Johnson not to say anything like that again to the President." Once in Berlin, however, LBJ drove and walked the streets, handing out pens and being cheered: "Repeatedly, the man who had been reluctant to go almost leaped into the crowds," writes Reeves. "His guards were terrified, but Johnson was in his element." It might be that, in most cases, a person either has the right stuff or not. However, one characteristic of this enormously complex man, whom Auke Tellegen uses to illustrate independent, coexisting extremes of positive and negative emotionality, was first to respond to an aversive stimulus intensely and then promptly get over it and get on with it. Like Monica's ability to have her way without being bossy, this kind of "trait" is hard to score or even name—reactive boldness?—yet it's such qualities that make interesting people interesting.

"From Hippocrates, all of our theories have been too abstract," says Jerome Kagan. "Our minds prefer to deal with a small number of clear things, but there's little evidence that personality can be approached that way." As far as George Vaillant is concerned, the trait theorist is like "the person who describes the Caribbean as water and sand because he doesn't put on the mask and dive down to see the tropical fish. Maybe there's a taxonomy for personality, but maybe not. We can measure color with angstrom units, but scientists don't talk about it in a very interesting way, and people don't see it the same. The Hopi have no language for colors, and they get along fine." While personality's taxonomy is of limited, or merely academic, interest to some, it's a matter of great concern to many of those who must diagnose and treat its disorders.

CHAPTER 12

"OF ITS OWN BEAUTY
IS THE MIND DISEASED"
–George Gordon, Lord Byron

Early isolation tutored Monica in the terrors of abandonment and the value of attention and care. Throughout her life, people have been awfully important to her. Were this need for others extreme or un-modulated by other traits, it could be emotionally crippling. Someone who's desirous of considerable social support and is also, say, selfish or strident would be called demanding, manipulative, or bitchy; someone lacking in self-esteem, a "doormat." Such unpleasant terms, however, are never applied to a person with Monica's genius for making others feel good about supplying what she needs, from companionship to cleaning spots off her dress to a ride wherever she wants to go. The real achievement of this psychological athlete is that she not only survived her early ordeal but incorporated its lessons into the creation of an adaptive personality. Harmonizing with one another and her environ-ment, her traits are neither rigid nor too extreme—the maladaptive qualities that separate healthy personalities from sick ones.

Monica's gentle way of reaching her goals wouldn't serve very well on Broadway or in Hollywood. In those settings, another complex trait fea-tures in a flashier brand of star quality epitomized by the late comic actor Rex Harrison. In a biography fittingly entitled *Fatal Charm,* vari-ous acquaintances discuss their experiences with the soigné ladies' man, whose appeal was such that even his caddish lapses and flaws—Harrison actually recycled love letters—seemed if not winning, at least amusing. The best testimony to his charm was that most of the women he seduced and abandoned remained fond of him. Indeed, two of his six wives committed suicide rather than face life without "Sexy Rexy"—a handle that, it must be noted in a spirit of fairness, he loathed. Harrison's particular attractiveness involved an astringent element described as "irascible impatience" by *Time* and as impulsivity by psychologists. According to biographer Alexander Walker, his was "the charm of dynamite. . . . He was almost totally lacking in a sense of consequence. He seldom paused to connect cause with effect." Individuals with this my-will-be-done mentality differ, writes Walker, from "the crowd of people who hang back, restrained by mundane things like responsibility. It contributed largely to Rex's charm. Not to be inhibited, not to give a damn; the recurrent triumph of instinct over experience. He never learned from his mistakes and never lacked the boldness to repeat them."

Just as the venues for Harrison's charm were the stage and screen, the setting for breezy big-game guide Baron Bror Blixen's was the African savannah. At the end of her long life, Isak Dinesen, the author of *Out of Africa* (and the Danish baroness Karen Blixen), was asked which of her many fabulous adventures she would relive if she could. To her questioner's surprise, she promptly replied that she would go on safari not with her legendary lover, the quintessential British "white hunter" Denys Finch-Hatton, but with her former husband. Such good fun was Bror that not even the fact that he had infected her with the syphilis that spoiled her health and eventually killed her diminished her affection. The sunny, offhand machismo of the womanizing baron-bwana, who was as nonchalant when facing a charging elephant as when sipping a cocktail, so impressed Ernest Hemingway, no wimp himself, that he made Blixen the model for the sporting hero of "The Short Sweet Life of Francis Macomber."

During the Tudor era, sword-wielding, hand-kissing Sir Walter Raleigh set the standard for political charmers that was upheld in less swashbuckling modern times by John Kennedy. Offering a thumbnail character analysis of JFK, George Vaillant suggests how charm can be both born and made. A good measure of Kennedy's dated back to a strategy learned early in life for coping with its hard knocks. "Their mother didn't love any of the Kennedy children, and the rest turned out mean," says Vaillant. "Instead, Jack learned to have a neuroticism score of zero. When something bad happened, he didn't get upset but tried to figure it out." Then too, he had the genes of his maternal grandfather, John ("Honey Fitz") Fitzgerald, a legendary Boston mayor. "When men like that get through with you," says Vaillant, "they have what they want, and you feel good about yourself. Like Honey Fitz, Jack had humor and took himself lightly." Not all politicians, for example, would delight in the similarities between their profession and the world's oldest. Yet JFK observed that on the campaign trail he'd arrive at a hotel, set up shop in a bedroom, and see the men who were waiting for him in the parlor; after spending a brief time alone with him behind closed doors, they would depart, leaving money. The greatest testimony to Kennedy's charm, says Vaillant, is that "when he competed with people and beat them, except for Nixon, they didn't mind nearly as much as they would had he been someone else, like Bobby."

The smoking-jacketed matinee idol, khaki-clad scout, and dark-suited statesman look different on the surface, but the recipe for their charm is the same: a high level of extroversion that attunes them to the external world and a low level of neuroticism—largely anxiety—that reduces self-consciousness and the sense of vulnerability. Like all traits, however, charm has its drawbacks, just as the unhappily named neuroticism has its benefits. The latter is often misunderstood, says Thomas Widiger, "in that the insensitivity associated with a low score is not necessarily so hot. Because they're unrestrained by anxiety, suave Don Juans and con men can say or do whatever it takes to part us from our money or virtue."

Although extroversion initially draws the charmer to others and vice versa, it can interfere with the building of true intimacy. The party girl and the ladies' man may be unable to keep one true friend or mate. "Politicians remember everyone's name and convey the sense that they're your best buddy after five minutes," says Widiger. "That impresses you because it's so unusual, but there's no real depth to it." In fact, he adds, charm can't fizz by itself, but requires some help from the personality at the receiving end: "Because most people are moderately agreeable and trusting, they just can't believe that there's no real conviction behind what the politician is saying, much less that he's lying through his teeth."

The scintillating combination of lots of extroversion and little inhibition is one thing to fans reminiscing about JFK and Sexy Rexy but another to their wives and others who often sadly trailed in their wake. Not even personality theorists, who should know better, are immune to charm's dangers, from that of a used-car salesman with a lemon to unload to the criminal con man, or psychopath. Although he's an authority on the latter, David Lykken was nonetheless swindled out of $1,000 by one of his research subjects for a share in a putative asbestos mine that "Donald" had discovered on a hunting trip in the Yukon. "You would not think me quite such a fool," he says, "if you had been there yourself and heard Donald's casual, low-keyed pitch, full of circumstantial detail."

While way too much charm creates a psychopath, a little extra has certain advantages in certain environments, from the soapbox to the showroom. So it is with other traits. A David Letterman or Jay Leno should be a bit hyper, a computer programmer a little obsessive-compulsive, a Secret Service agent somewhat paranoid, a night watchman schizoid, and an actor histrionic, says Michael Stone: "Even the antisocial personality stopped in a bit gives you the adventurer and the stuntman." Although people who express extremes of traits can be ranged on a continuum with those whom psychologists call "normals," their unbalanced personalities can sometimes have catastrophic consequences, from Son of Sam's serial murders to the führer's Holocaust.

In the biography of Timothy McVeigh, accused of participating in the 1995 bombing of a government building in Oklahoma City that killed 167 people, Michael Stone sees indications of an antisocial, schizoid—profoundly remote—and paranoid personality: an aggressive loner who feels persecuted. Such perturbation, says Stone, can result when someone "dealt the genetic low card of innate schizoid and paranoid tendencies is then subjected to the stress of maternal abandonment." The larger society, too, can aggravate a dangerous disposition, as apparently happened when the crack soldier who hoped to make a career of the military was rejected as psychologically unfit by the elite Green Berets. Moreover, following a war, even the brief Gulf version in which McVeigh participated, the incidence of violence back home climbs when the troops return, says Stone, "because they've become inured to it and used it as a solution." Such an explosive mixture of problematic traits and external circumstances could so skew an individual's sense of reality that blowing up innocent strangers seems like a reasonable act of revenge on a government that interferes not only with one's own plans but with others': the fiery demise of David Koresh and his Branch Davidians was commemorated by the Oklahoma bombing. To such a mind, the victims become what the Jews, Gypsies, and other *Untermenschen* destined for extermination were to Hitler: not people but, in recent ultra-right-wing parlance, "sheeple."

Following the Oklahoma disaster, there was much debate about the relationship between the perpetrators of the heinous act and the behavior of large numbers of people who hold extremely conservative political views, believe that a sinister power is about to take over their lives, and like to dress up in camouflage, hoard guns, and spin conspiracy theories. To Stone, there's an important distinction to be made: if a person functions adequately and doesn't harm himself or others, he may seem odd but he's not necessarily sick. "Thinking up fantastical notions, like a government plot to control people by implanting microchips in their brains, is symptomatic of true paranoid schizophrenia," he says. "How exactly would these chips *work?*" While the person who first comes up with such an idea may be psychotic, says Stone, "not all those who take up the belief are mentally ill. Many just share in the leader's delusion, as happens in religions."

The point at which any trait becomes pathological depends largely on how adaptive it is. If Monica were so wrapped up with pleasing others that she was habitually unable to think and act on her own, psychiatrists would diagnose her personality as "dependent." If a fear of being criticized, disliked, or ignored prevented her from having a normal social and working life, she would be termed "avoidant." These so-called personality disorders are two of a handful of common, shoot-yourself-in-the-foot behavioral patterns that hamper a person's ability to love, work, and handle stress. They affect 10 to 15 percent of the population, particularly in cities and among the poor; some afflict more men and others more women, but the total is equally spread between them. In most respects, including etiology, these very disparate syndromes are apples and oranges: their unifying theme is being stuck in the same old ruts and vicious circles.

People who are extremely obsessive-compulsive are enslaved by their preoccupation with perfection and control, for example, while the narcissistic and histrionic are compelled to seek the spotlight. The habitually brooding depressive, detached schizoid, suspicious paranoid, and eccentric schizotypal personalities have long populated history and literature, both medical and literary. Other disorders, such as the manipulative passive-aggressive and the emotionally chaotic borderline, are modern constructs. Because a personality disorder is pervasive by definition, those who have one are often blind to it; they see their behavior as a reasonable response to fortune's slings and arrows. To Saddam Hussein, who epitomizes both the domineering sadistic personality and the cold-blooded, risk-seeking antisocial one, problems are caused by Western devils, not his own.

The minority of the population who have seriously troubled personalities interest many of those who don't largely because the symptoms sound all too familiar: they're normal traits turned up too loud or down too low for one's own or others' comfort. The loyal, tenderhearted, homebody aspects of the depressive and avoidant personalities, for example, have traditionally been valued in women. The schizotypal tendencies that enable someone to live in his own world and do his own thing help account for visionaries and geniuses from Crazy Horse to Thomas Edison. Those who have the sort of personality that Freud called hysterical were, he said, "lively, gifted, energetic . . . the flower of mankind, who had difficulty in putting aside conscience and were sensitive, felt neglected and needy for love, but also willful, suspicious, and leery of influence." Too much of this good thing, however, means that a person lurches between feeling like the star of the show and a black hole and goes to inordinate lengths to prove that he's not the latter. Just as a cactus does poorly in a rain forest, a personality's health also depends considerably on its setting; the celebrated diva can get away with more emotional fireworks than the Kansas farmer's wife can.

Most sick personalities, even murderous ones, don't wreak devastation on the scale of Oklahoma City or the Iraqi invasion of Kuwait. As America approaches the millennium, borderline personality disorder is the commonest of these illnesses, accounting for up to a quarter of psychiatric hospitalizations and affecting about three times as many women as men. Here is Stone's "psychological autopsy" of a forty-five-year-old Los Angeles woman who scribbled a will on the back of an envelope that gave half her fortune to an itinerant peddler and then fatally inhaled her Rolls-Royce's exhaust fumes. Before marrying her multimillionaire boss at twenty-eight, she had been an attractive, "bouncy" woman with a normal personality of a rather self-aborbed, dramatic sort. After the birth of the first of three children, she became depressed, then suicidal. She saw a well-known psychoanalyst for a while, but things like showing up for sessions in a bikini interfered with her treatment. Next, she paid $175 per hour to talk on the phone with another therapist for two or three hours a day. Eventually, she completely dropped her roles as mother and wife and took to her bed. Illuminating the cliché "raging out of control," she turned on her children, chasing them with kitchen knives and smearing blood from her slashed wrists on her son's confirmation suit. A few days after her family finally decamped, she finally succeeded in killing herself after eight attempts, each in March.

Despite her wealth, efforts to get help, and "florid derangement," says Stone, the woman had been prescribed Valium but not the lithium that would have stabilized her wild mood swings. Neither of her therapists noticed the seasonal depression manifested by the timing of her suicide attempts nor the striking transition, upon turning thirty and bearing a child, from a normal histrionic personality to that of a character from a horror movie. To Stone, there's no question that the kind of transformation this woman underwent was caused by the sudden explosion of the major psychiatric illness of manic depression, but of a particular "irritable" sort that, he believes, usually underlies borderline personality disorder.

As the ups and downs of Marilyn Monroe's sad biography suggest, life on the borderline's emotional roller coaster is hard on patients, families, and doctors alike. The term has acquired such negative connotations that George Vaillant equates it with "calling someone an asshole." Although he disagrees, his Harvard colleague John Gunderson, who was instrumental in establishing psychiatry's official criteria for the borderline syndrome, says that the great utility of the diagnosis is that it "prepares clinicians for an extremely difficult treatment problem. These patients react with hostility to your caring ministrations and cut their wrists when you don't do what they want. You don't see the symptoms unless you're closely involved with the person. Fear of loss brings out the extraordinary sensitivity to rejection. In *Fatal Attraction,* when the husband wanted to say, 'Thanks, ma'am,' and leave, he found out that the 'other woman' felt that her life depended on his staying. And that's just what happens in real life."

The walking time bomb that is the borderline personality derives from the volatile combination of an inability to regulate emotion and flawed concepts about the self and others. In Big Five terms, the problem is a matter of very low agreeability and conscientiousness and lots of all six facets of neuroticism: in other words, a nasty, undisciplined person who feels anxious, depressed, angry, impulsive, self-conscious, and vulnerable. Adding to the misery, says Paul Costa, the prominent five-factor theorist, are disabling, irrational ideas about the self as being inferior, which further undermine resistance to stress. All this adds up to what he describes as "an affective and cognitive storm that keeps the person functioning at a borderline level of self-organization." To Auke Tellegen, borderlines are "highly negatively emotional, poor in constraint, and variable in positive emotionality. Impulsive and stress reactive—that's what you can say about them in terms of temperament." He too remarks on the disorder's cognitive dimension: "Along with being prone to excessive, labile self-assessment, they have an extravagant sense of being both evil and excellent. Many borderlines report that they were sexually abused by their parents, but they blame themselves because they're bad but special—fatally attractive. They have this sense of drama because, to them, the world doesn't contain ordinary people who are neither particularly excellent nor evil."

Although the etiology of the borderline is various, one important element is often an underlying biological, perhaps partly heritable, problem such as alcoholism, attention deficit disorder, or manic depression. In fact, Stone and Hagop Akiskal argue that the borderline's wild swings in emotional stability, self-image, impulsivity, and sociability are often best understood and treated as "bipolar disorder of the irritable type." This diagnosis, which is not universally accepted, links the severe mood sickness with an extreme of the "explosive," or angry, irritable temperament recognized by Hippocrates, Kraepelin, and many contemporary clinicians. While discussing the disposition of some individuals who as infants are easily startled and are later demanding, prone to tantrums, and ultimately aggressive, Stone recalls a fourteen-year-old boy who, after beating a private-school classmate with a baseball bat, was diagnosed as having manic depression of the irritable type. His family history showed that the youth's father, grandfather, and uncle were all on lithium. In short, the portrait of the borderline that Stone and Akiskal paint shows a habitually angry person in a really bad mood. "Irritability is the red thread that runs through all the borderline definitions," says Stone, "whether manifested as unreasonableness and tantrums or the murderous outbursts of the serial killer John Gacy."

If some of the borderline's great difficulty in modulating emotions is inherited, many have also endured harsh, even brutal childhoods. Seemingly environmental risk factors, such as child abuse or the maternal abandonment experienced by Monica and the young Timothy McVeigh, can perturb biology as surely as genes can. After analyzing the biographies of 212 murderers, Stone determined that, of the 39 women, 13 were borderlines; 7 of these had been subjected to incest. Both of the male murderers who were borderlines, including the recently executed Gacy, had been brutalized by their fathers. In some dreadful transformative process, their own childhood agony had turned into a rage and hatred expressed in innocent blood.

Troubled men are often described in antisocial rather than affective terms: as criminals, not patients. Stone recalls a conversation with the woman who had been serial killer Jeffrey Dahmer's date at his high school senior prom about thirteen years before he was finally arrested—but just two weeks before the first of his seventeen murders. She described him as aloof and "nerdy"—J. D. Higley's term for his aggressive primate troublemakers. It's doubtful that the young woman would have gone to the dance had she known of her escort's fondness for cutting off dogs' heads and putting them on sticks in the backyard. Similarly, long before he became a serial murderer, the "quiet" teenager David Berkowitz, later known as Son of Sam, recorded in his diary that he had set 1,488 fires in the Bronx. Such relatively rare, gravely deranged persons suffer from a hardwired defect in their ability to interpret others' emotions and motives, says Stone: "With a healthy personality, what you see is what you get, but with a sick one, it's something very different." By his lights, those who best know, albeit briefly, the world's Berkowitzes and Dahmers are their victims.

There are no statistics to prove whether certain personality disorders are more common today than in yesteryear or whether their overall incidence is higher. Learned opinions on these matters vary. The business of relating certain traits to particular social and economic conditions is similarly iffy, if time-honored even in psychology. In the wake of World War II, for example, personality researchers tried to figure out why Germans had supported Nazism: Was there something in the "national character" that inclined the citizenry toward fascism? In 1950, *The Authoritarian Personality,* the classic text on the subject, claimed that rigid people attracted to polarizing stereotypes and external explanations for behavior have a greater propensity for fascism; it was pointed out that astrology was very popular in Germany between the two world wars. According to more recent thinking, what seems like an increase in the number of people who express certain tendencies, whether fascist or liberal, is usually the result of a convergence of social and economic factors—whether they affect the threatened German working class of the 1930s or the American one of the 1990s—which simply encourages such people to speak up (or shoot) and be counted.

Although the historical epidemiology of personality disorders is uncertain, America is in the throes of an epidemic of depression that is also increasing worldwide. One contributing factor that's often mentioned is a simultaneous rise in people's expectations and decline in social support, values, and controls. Perhaps because they have been spared these twin scourges, pretechnological tribal groups that preserve tight bonds and promote hands-on practices of grooming and stroking seem to be exceptions to the depressive trend. During the Pleistocene era, Auke Tellegen observes, "people had no place to go. Because practical constraints kept them with the tribe, they didn't need, and didn't evolve, an instinct to stay attached." Then, too, the band raised the children. Now that Western parents do so in pairs or alone, life is harder for them and their young. "Children are exposed to an extremely limited sample of people," says Tellegen, "which gives them a skewed view of humankind. In the old days, even if your father was crazy or criminal, an older brother, uncle, or neighbor could be your model or mentor. Now that there's no community, parental incompetence is no longer compensated for. Gene-environment correlation ensures that a rugged kid will find what he needs, but others may not."

Where the forming of character is concerned, much depends on whether a society values primarily "me" or "us." Asian cultures have traditionally stayed closer to our evolutionary roots as deeply social organisms. In the East, a person is inextricable from the fabric of his relationships; the main goal is the maintenance of social bonds, not expressing oneself. Just as America's emotional plague is depression, in Bali, one of many societies organized around communal duty rather than individual rights, the predominant psychological disorder is a form of what psychologists call social phobia and others call stage fright. In Japan, the national ethic of cooperation begins at home: physical contact between mother and offspring lasts years longer than in the United States, and the child who misbehaves is likelier to be briefly exiled than grounded. American kids, however, are encouraged to be autonomous and individualistic—to do their own thing like folk heroes from Johnny Appleseed to Elvis Presley—even when in groups, from the peace-loving dropouts of the 1960s to the gun-toting survivalists of the 1990s. However attractive this heroic me-myself-and-I Western self may be on a literary or philosophical plane, it doesn't jibe with behavioral research on well-being. Given a choice of being free or being connected, Tellegen thinks many members of modern urbanized society choose "more isolation than is good for us. Today, we can go where and do what we want, but we don't have good social instincts that would tell us to stop by at the coffee hour or invite the neighbors over. For children, certainly, life is better when the street is a social network, but we may even make a point of not knowing our neighbors, because that means losing some of our freedom."

Where culture and personality disorders per se are concerned, Drew Westen has similar concerns. "These days, if one parent is nutty, the other often gets out of the marriage and may leave the children behind. If you want to create a personality disorder, leave a child alone with a parent who's seriously troubled." Regarding the nation's most common such illness, he adds that "a central issue for borderline patients is that they can't find meaning, which is harder still in a society whose values are increasingly pluralistic." That technology and urbanization require a lot from the individual is adaptive for some resilient personalities, says Westen, but disastrous for vulnerable ones who need lots of old-fashioned, small-town support: "If you know you're going to spend your life in a big family within a close community, how vulnerable to rejection can you be? Can you even *be* borderline?"

Theorists who have a more sanguine view of contemporary society doubt that more personalities are perturbed than before. Every generation thinks the values of the younger one have sadly deteriorated, says Thomas Widiger: "There have been a hell of a lot worse times than now. How about the worldview at the fall of Rome or during the Black Death? Children are treated far better today. People may be a lot more agreeable. Women are freer to express ambition and men their nurturing side. This may be one of the most civilized times in history." John Gunderson observes that people were once left to suffer from many psychological problems, including depressive illnesses and the sequelae of child abuse, that are now recognized and treated. Where personality is concerned, the excessive reliance on others that's a characteristic of both the dependent disorder and various forms of "codependency" was actually praised, in women at least, back in the good old days. "There may have been a lot more masochism in previous generations because it was socially valued," says Gunderson. "It wasn't called that, but people didn't suffer any the less."

In the course of trying to ease emotional suffering, Mardi Horowitz "often finds that the person has had the same kind of maladaptive relationship over and over." He offers the example of someone trapped in a self-defeating career pattern: without being aware of it, he first woos the boss with dazzling work, then procrastinates; when the supervisor finally protests, the employee counterattacks, gets fired, and blames the boss. "He wasn't planning to do any of that," says Horowitz, "but some inner plan is repeating for some reason that he doesn't understand. If you study the stories he tells, you'll see that he's constantly dealing with a particular configuration of relationship models that mean that no matter what he starts out doing, he ends up following an obligatory script." Psychotherapy offers an opportunity to rewrite it.

CHAPTER 13

"WHERE THE NAIL STICKS UP . . ."

Just as a Gothic cathedral can't be turned into a modern skyscraper, the architecture of a personality can't be totally transformed. It can, however, be renovated. "When I sense that a patient's personality needs to change," says Michael Stone, "it has less to do with one of the Big Five traits than with whether he's imperious, say, or pushy or cheap. As the Japanese say, 'Where the nail sticks up, you pound it down.'"

Among the patients who have sought Stone's benign hammering is a man who "will take a woman to a restaurant—not the best one, either—and get into an argument over a dime with the waiter. He could be right, but inevitably the woman gets the picture that this is one cheap son of a bitch, and she'll never go out with him again." His cheapness, tendency to feel taken advantage of, propensity for shooting from the lip, and need to police others bespeak a combination of maladaptive obsessive-compulsive and paranoid characteristics exacerbated by being reared in a family that had, says Stone, "very little oil in its social machinery." Eventually, the man's "panoply of negative traits" obstructed his personal relationships and professional advancement enough to cause him to seek Stone's help.

Things are gradually looking up for the abrasive cheapskate. When Stone responded to an account of his disastrous dinner date by saying "Gee, I guess that woman was only worth a dime to you," the man replied, "What do you mean?" Twice a week for two years, doctor and patient have chewed over similar incidents in a way that allows the latter to "step out of himself" and consider hitherto unquestioned automatic behavior in a new light. Because his rigid character nonetheless has a certain degree of flexibility, he's able to accept his doctor's authority and see things from another's point of view—prerequisites for successful therapy. When Stone pushes him to frame the restaurant debacle from his date's perspective, he can say, "I never realized it seemed that way." Because he has the capacity to reconsider his ways and accept help, he's able to change. On his next date, "even if he's overcharged, he'll hold his breath and white-knuckle it," says Stone. "The woman will go out with him again, and the pleasure of continuing a relationship is now, thank God, worth the dime. Even though the rest of his personality retains its usual adamantine hardness, that's a significant change in an area that was causing great trouble."

Just as his tight fist has loosened, this prickly patient has also become somewhat more tactful. By nature—a paranoid one—he thinks that people are out to get him. Stone often helps him figure out whether, in a particular situation, that's really so and how he should respond. "He takes great pride in telling it like it is," says Stone, "but there are a zillion situations in life when that's not a good idea and you have to muffle your point." At the office, for example, the man chewed out a higher-up for not operating the security door correctly. She responded by filing an official complaint about his rudeness. "He was right about the door," says Stone, "but he made a gaffe. Every week he presents such an incident, and I take out my sandpaper and file him down a bit. He's learning that even if he thinks someone scowled at him or is trying to tick him off, he's better off giving the benefit of the doubt." As this long-ornery man acquires easier new ways, his world is expanding along with his personality. He has not only a new social life but a more collegial profile at work. Peers complain about him less, and his supervisor smiles more. "As therapy moves him a little further into his personality's comfort zone," says Stone, "he's becoming less difficult. He'll always be suspicious, though. He'll always be a bit resentful of waiters and be the one who checks the bill. But society needs some people like that."

"The human mind, moving in a sea of detail, is compelled like a questing animal to orient by a relatively few decisive configurations," writes sociobiologist E. O. Wilson. "There is an optimum number of such signals. Too few, and the person becomes obsessive-compulsive. Too many, and he turns schizophrenic. Configurations with the greatest emotional impact are stored first and persist longer. Those that give the greatest pleasure are sought on later occasions." The kind of formative experience that Wilson alludes to makes it unlikely that a cheapskate will become lavish, a shy person the life of the party, or a compulsive one casual about details. Such 180-degree changes don't happen, says Stone, "because personality is embedded in the warp and woof of the brain, not just in one neurotransmitter system or another. That's why someone who has been a Catholic for thirty years can't become a wholehearted Buddhist who feels the same way about sticking little pieces of gold on an icon as he had about receiving the wafer at the altar. In terms of the intensity of feeling *right,* nothing can replace the tracks laid down in the first six years of life."

Each person's combination of biology and experiential saturation means that basic traits such as extroversion don't often alter much after adolescence. As the case of the ill-mannered tightwad shows, however, subtler yet important modifications can significantly improve one's own and others' quality of life. In fact, their greater experience with such positive shifts inclines researchers who treat the troubled personalities most motivated to change to be more sanguine about that possibility than those who study only "normals."

Although relatively few personalities *require* treatment, everybody could benefit from it, says Tom Widiger. "There's no one who couldn't be more flexible. Whether to enter psychotherapy is a cost-benefit decision. How much you're willing to do about your myopia depends on the degree of your nearsightedness and on how much you value clear vision. The same process applies to traits. Your solution to dealing with your shyness may be to find a more comfortable niche and tolerate the tendency or to make some internal changes and adjustments."

Because tinkering with personality is both difficult and expensive, it's only prudent to consider whether one's own is okay as is. As John Oldham says, we are who we are, which isn't perfect but usually isn't the worst, either. Sometimes any necessary renovations can be the do-it-yourself sort. The first hurdle in that process is identifying troubling tendencies; others' consistent complaints bear thinking about. Next comes some behavioral modification. Although you can't change everything, says Oldham, "you can fine-tune rough edges by practicing being a little different. If you're very conscientious and put everything into your work, you can remind yourself to tell your spouse that she's pretty or he's handsome. If you're too self-sacrificing, you can learn to set limits. Most people know themselves pretty well and have this kind of capacity."

Of several psychotherapeutic approaches to change, the simplest is Hans Eysenck's treatment of choice. In behavioral therapy, a patient is exposed to what he most fears or dislikes in a supportive setting until the response is "extinguished." Thus, someone whose very shy, avoidant personality makes a social life difficult gradually learns to tolerate one-on-one chatting, then small groups, and eventually, parties. As Eysenck says, "Behavioral treatment doesn't change personality, but just one particular reaction."

Often, the behavioral approach is combined with another brisk technique: cognitive therapy, developed to treat depression by psychiatrist Aaron Beck. According to its tenets, certain things in the environment automatically trigger reactions in one's brain, so that every time a particular stimulus appears, out pops a specific cognition, adaptive or not. Were Walter Mischel seated across from a man whose depressive personality had mired him in a series of crummy relationships that never panned out, he'd first seek "an elaboration of what sucks the man into that behavior. What is he getting out of it that makes him repeat it?" This needn't particularly involve what his father did to his mother, says Mischel; it may be that he doesn't really want a real relationship or that he's not willing to do much for himself or that he wants to be the kid on the outside looking in. "The important point is that the problem is a living, breathing thing *now*," says Mischel, "not something that happened when he was three." To change, says Mischel, "a person has to rework those brain circuits by rethinking and reexperiencing the way he wants to construe and feel about the things that spark his problematic thoughts and emotions. Altering the cognitive system changes the affective system, because it's really a single one." Mischel agrees that changing who we are "is very hard. Even the most miserable people say they don't want to change, because it's difficult. But who says it should be easy?"

From a different perspective, at the heart of troubled personalities is what psychoanalytically oriented Drew Westen calls "a five-year-old's solution" to handling certain difficult issues. "As kids, we make a lot of decisions about how we're going to handle wishes, fears, and other emotions," he says. "If they were discouraged or not talked about at home, we may have learned to shut off or ignore tender feelings. If traumatic things happened to a child during the first five years, such as abuse or neglect, or if his match with a parent was really poor, it's as if he had been asked to solve a calculus equation in kindergarten. The answer he came up with at the time—repression, shutting off his emotions, fighting authority figures, chronically acquiescing—was the best he could do then. But later, he may not be able to rework that solution because it has been unconsciously stored. As adults, we're in a position to come up with a better solution."

One hard truth regarding the difficulty of personality change is that what used to be called "neurotic" wishes and needs—to hurt others, say, or be hurt—become associated with pleasure, "not so much in the sense of feeling good," says Westen, "as in feeling 'right.'" Westen recalls one patient, whose maladaptive traits kept her involved with men who merely used her. First she became aware that these experiences weren't random events but parts of a pattern. Next she saw that her need for uncaring men re-created her girlhood relationship with her father. Then she actually had to change her behavior, which was hard because nice men weren't attractive to her: the wrong guys felt right.

Psychoanalysts once thought that when patients gained insight into the source of their troubles, they'd be home free, but things proved to be more complicated. Just telling a patient what is wrong—or what to do about it—doesn't work, because not just a few ideas, but a long-entrenched system of largely unconscious, emotion-laden schemas, must change. To find simpler, more conscious paths to pleasure and satisfaction, a person needs to form new schemas about what kind of relationships are possible and then practice them, which won't feel right at first. Starting with her therapeutic relationship with Westen, the self-defeating woman began to link men who treated her well with good feelings. She also began to associate her old, unhealthy urges with unhappiness rather than gratification: "Changing wishes is the hardest part," says Westen, "because it means giving up important things before you have anything to replace them with." Finally, the patient needed to accept the parts of herself that weren't going to change and learn to minimize the drawbacks: she might always have a certain hankering for a heel on a Harley, but she doesn't have to go out of her way to find one. Had she not sought help, the woman who was her own worst enemy wouldn't have noticed her predilection for cads or the pleasures of gentlemanly company and would have kept forlornly gazing at happy couples from the deep rut of a troubled personality.

Just as our early ideas about how the world works were based on our experience with our parents, Daniel Stern thinks that the therapeutic key to changing those constructs is the patient's experience with the clinician. "Without ever naming it, the therapist can let someone *do* something differently in the course of the treatment process," he says. Conjuring up a hypothetical session with a patient whose aggressive personality pits him against authority, Stern says, "Suppose he reacts to something I say in a belligerent way. But suppose that my response isn't counteraggressive but something like 'I didn't really get what it was that ticked you off right then. What happened inside you at that moment?' Curiosity. I might even go to the physical realm and say, 'Did I look like I was jumping back at you with my body or face? Did you see it that way?' I'm not slapping him back, but I'm not just lying there taking it either. When he goes back to the office, the man may see something different in his boss's behavior that's different from what his old schema says is happening, because he just experienced it in mine. You don't say it's different but construct a situation so that it *is* different."

The idea that a person should confront and wrestle with his demons and thereby strengthen and even transcend himself runs deep in Western culture. A man in an unhappy marriage becomes depressed and insomniac. Eventually he leaves his wife, and his good spirits return. If he had taken an antidepressant and stayed in the marriage, would his depression have remitted? If so, should his troubles be attributed to a "chemical imbalance"? Or was it "better" that he relieved his distress without recourse to drugs?

Now that doctors and patients have a choice of tools, the type of treatment doesn't necessarily depend on whether a problem began with a biological or experiential etiology. Kenneth Kendler describes a young mother "whose aorta was the size of a balloon that could burst at any moment. The doctors couldn't operate. I would have been depressed in her situation. She said, 'I think about this all the time. I cry. I'm no good to my kids. Can't you make me feel better so I can enjoy my family in the time remaining?' She had a clear antidepressant response." Where the causes and cures of mental illness are concerned, such experiences incline Kendler to "argue against the dangers of falling into a mind-brain dichotomy." In a study that vividly supports his argument, people suffering from a form of anxiety known as obsessive-compulsive disorder who were successfully treated with either therapy or drugs showed the same brain changes on a PET scan, suggesting that the treatments affected the central nervous system in a similar way. "If a situation can cause biological changes that affect behavior," says Kendler, "why shouldn't a drug treat them?"

CHAPTER 14

OF PILLS AND PERSONALITY

Not since Timothy Leary, a leading personality psychologist, left Harvard, convinced that LSD would eliminate the need for things like universities and psychotherapy, has a drug gotten the rave reviews Prozac has. No one but a misanthrope could dispute that the psychopharmacological relief of depression, which affects one in ten Americans, is one of the twentieth century's great medical advances. Despite some halfhearted caveats, however, much of Prozac's press has less to do with treating an illness than with titillating intimations of a psychic pep-up tonic that's good for what ails you.

Throughout history, people have incorporated various legal and illegal substances into their efforts to change: to become zippier or calmer, smarter or sexier, holier or happier. Many of the questions about personality that the new and improved antidepressants, notably the serotonin reuptake inhibitors such as Prozac and Zoloft, have made au courant in the agora are not new in academe; psychiatric researchers such as Hagop Akiskal and Columbia psychiatrist Donald Klein, who is the director of psychiatric research at the New York State Psychiatric Institute, have discussed them for years. As is always the case with psychoactive drugs, however, culture plays an important role in how they're perceived and used. The advent of antidepressants that don't make people feel "doped up," as older ones could, combined with belt tightening in the health care and insurance industries that increasingly makes psychotherapy, like art and travel, a luxury, mean that more and more people take psychiatric medicines. Moreover, just as psychedelics suited the experimental temper of the 1960s, Prozac fits America nearing the millennium, hunkering down, and looking to the right: Who couldn't use some more resilience, confidence, cheerfulness? This confluence of technological, economic, and social elements has raised the most interesting philosophical and practical questions in psychiatry, particularly considering the milllions of people involved. Can drugs change personality? Should they be used only to treat the sick? Or can they ethically be employed to help "normals" become better than that?

When discussing how to change personality, psychiatrists reveal different understandings of it. To those who regard it largely as a matter of an individual's emotional patterns, saying that a drug that relieves affective symptoms doesn't change personality not only makes no sense but also undermines biology's role in making us who we are. In *Listening to Prozac,* Brown University psychiatrist Peter Kramer reasons that if neurotransmitters underlie temperament as they do mood, how could it be that the drug changes only the latter? Moreover, "it's virtually certain that experience is encoded not just in cognitive memory but also in the sort of biology that medication affects," he says. "Medication can also have broad mood-modulating effects that impact on many parts of the self, including those that are experience-derived."

To illustrate his contention that "partly correctly and partly in an exaggerated way, we are letting pills tell us about the structure of personality," he describes the drug reaction of an erstwhile roué. After being prescribed Prozac for depression, the patient's mood lifted and he performed better at work, but the man who had faulted his wife for not watching X-rated videos was no longer interested in pornography. " 'Gee, Doc,' he said, 'it's disturbing that that was a biological obsession,' " recalls Kramer. "He had felt his 'continental sensibility' was very much a unique part of his character and was embarrassed that the pill agrees with his wife." Kramer stresses that antidepressants aren't the only chemical agents of personal change. Another man confided that until his drinking finally overcame him, he had been a better writer as an alcoholic. When he dried out, he suddenly changed his subject matter, because the eccentrics who had once fascinated him now seemed merely annoying. "That his whole beat became uninteresting to him really is a matter of personality change on 'medication,' " says Kramer, "but here it was alcohol—or the things in his brain that he has to deal with when he's not on alcohol."

Endlessly informed that our futures depend on whether we're on or off the technological bus, it seems more chic to talk about "chemical imbalances" than character. Yet psychiatrists who regard affect and its underlying neurotransmission as just part of personality, albeit an important one, deny that drugs can change it. Of some six hundred traits, only the few that concern mood, such as pessimism or cheerfulness, respond to drugs, says Michael Stone. Although antidepressants slow the borderline's emotional pendulum, for example, it usually takes years of psychotherapy before such a patient gets a handle on problematic traits such as manipulativeness. "Medication may drive the affective needle from where it has been stuck to some other place in the spectrum, so the depressed person is less gloomy or more assertive," says Stone. "But that isn't in any way a fundamental personality change. Such a person remains conscientious or crooked, abrasive or polite. Those things don't change. What drug would make the cheap man liberal? It's absurd. Pills don't change character. After enough listening to Prozac, the depressed, pessimistic, ingratiating, dishonest, egotistical patient becomes euthymic, less pessimistic, ingratiating, dishonest. . . . Cyclothymics may become less boisterous and extroverted upon listening to lithium, but they remain self-centered and devious. The mood has gotten better, but the basic character, alas, stays the same. The little bit of personality that we can modify with lithium or Prozac is not much more than South Carolina in the context of the USA."

The researcher who has arguably done the most to advance the psychopharmacological treatment of anxiety and depression, Donald Klein, also doubts that drugs change personality. Although no one would expect antidepressants to alter, say, an antisocial streak, Klein was surprised to find that those that relieve obsessive-compulsive disorder, a form of anxiety that drives its victims endlessly to think certain thoughts and repeat certain activities, are useless for easing the constrictions of the rigid obsessive-compulsive personality. "When we say a drug treats a personality disorder," he says, "it really just treats an affective element of it."

Offering a provocative example, Klein observes that although extreme sensitivity to rejection "sounds so psychological," it's a symptom of a subtype of depression that's "outstandingly modifiable" by antidepressants. The same tendency figures in the avoidant personality, whose symptoms overlap with those of social phobia, an anxiety disorder that also responds to the same medicines; the arguably overfine distinction between them resembles that between depressive personality disorder and dysthymia, or mild, chronic depression. "Is rejection sensitivity a personality trait?" asks Klein, "Or is it an affective vulnerability that makes these patients prone to a maladaptive lifestyle? The latter makes more sense to me, because if we stop the drug, the problem comes right back. That's a fact, and it must be paid attention to. A lot of this debate about personality change is taking place in a fact-free arena. We have to narrow down which aspects of a disorder respond to drugs."

Saying that antidepressants don't alter personality doesn't mean that an improvement in mood can't look and feel like a more fundamental change, particularly when dysthymia's gray cloud has hung over a person's head for years on end. Testimonials to the new drugs, however, often go far beyond their salubrious effect on mood. John Oldham describes the now-familiar scenario in which "someone says that his identity finally came into being on Prozac. Things were fine for six months, when he stopped taking the drug. After another six months, his identity wasn't so good anymore, so he went back on Prozac and felt better again. Now, come on. That's depression, treatment, the return of depression, and more treatment. The most offensive claim being made about these drugs, which has a great deal of cachet, is that they can liberate your real self."

The most controversial aspect of the new "cosmetic psychopharmacology" concerns whether powerful medicines designed to alter neurotransmission in aberrant brains can or should be used to jazz up basically healthy ones. Regarding the notion that Prozac can make someone feel 110 percent well, Kramer says, "I think that it may help a person go from one temperament to another that, if he had been born with it, would be a hundred percent." To Klein, "The simplest way to answer the question of drugs and personality change is to treat normals. But for some reason, the pharmacology companies are not too enthused about such research."

There are no credible estimates of how many people are taking Prozac and its ilk for what reasons. But, says Hagop Akiskal, "I assure you that most people don't go to psychiatrists because they feel well and want something to make them feel better. They are either functioning at a deficit or so excessively that they're disorganized, or alternations of the two. When it comes to people who are functioning in an average way but are dissatisfied with that . . . I don't think we can answer this question of improving the normal with the current level of knowledge in psychiatry."

Distinguishing the normal from the sick is not always easy. According to Klein's definition, mental illness is "the subset of all illness that presents evidence in the cognitive, behavioral, affective, and motivational aspects of organismal functioning. It must be believed that something has gone wrong to attribute illness. For functional disorders, involuntary impairment is a key inference, supported by a range of evidence including lack of response to self-instruction, evidence of instrinsic suffering, clear incapacity, the likely production of overriding negative consequences, etcetera." Such definitions notwithstanding, psychiatry has traditionally maintained that a condition that responds to medicine is a disorder. This rationale has been mostly based on the fact that just as aspirin lowers temperature only if you have a fever, the older tricyclic antidepressants lift the spirits only of the depressed. Even where their sophisticated successors are concerned, Philip Gold says that "people whose arousal systems are not perturbed do not respond to these agents. The idea that healthy people who take Prozac feel better is absolutely ridiculous." Kramer, however, describes the argument that medications can restore only the ill to a normal state as "specious." Noting that Prozac relieves the symptoms of many women who suffer from serious premenstrual mood changes, he asks, "Do all such women therefore have an illness?" Other than tricyclics, he says, "it's almost the rule rather than the exception that psychoactive medication affects people whether they have an illness or not. Amphetamine improves concentration whether a person is hyperactive or not, just as alcohol makes everyone, shy or not, less inhibited." If psychiatry reexamines its drug-response-proves-disease stand, says Kramer, it will face "a morally complex situation in which, through medication, a person can change from one normal state to another."

Since Hippocrates, the devoted, sensitive melancholic temperament has been considered, when not extreme, to be one of several normal ways that people can be. Now that the possibility of changing it exists, some individuals who have this disposition, pathologically or not, may wish to do so. As to whether the criteria for illness will be lowered until anyone who's not "happy" can get treatment, Kramer says, "We certainly accept that where psychotherapy is concerned. The gap between how ill you need to be for medication as opposed to psychotherapy is narrowing. Psychopharmacology is looking a little more like therapy than it has in the past."

Unquestionably a great humanitarian boon, psychopharmacology nonetheless has its frightening dimensions. Some are purely practical. There are simply no studies on Prozac's safety or effectiveness when used for long periods, as antidepressants increasingly are, nor of what it does to personality. While a person who's clearly ill might find that the drug's benefits outweigh potential risks, someone less distressed might not. "What are we doing when we give six million brains this powerful, highly specific medication for five years?" asks Kay Jamison. "Particularly the million that are not depressive brains but essentially normal, slightly off-margin ones that belong to people who'd like to be a little quicker, brighter, more chipper? What happens when you put a brain in overdrive? It's a large experiment, and we simply don't know what's going to happen."

In addition to these clear-cut health concerns, medicines such as Prozac raise subtler issues. Suppose a drug blocks pain that's less a symptom of disease than a signal that a person needs to make a change in his relationships, say, or career? Suppose it deprives him of depth by blunting his response to one of the upsetting experiences that are part of life? Or makes him care less about something that should be important? When two of Kay Jamison's depressed male patients lost their libido upon taking Prozac—a relatively common reaction in both sexes—she was "struck not so much by the side effect as by the fact that they were so blasé about it. My concern is their nonchalance and relative lack of responsiveness to something that they'd normally react to by saying, 'Are you out of your mind? You think I'm going to give that up?' "

The concept of medication that can make people emotionally wrinkle free strikes Gold as repellent as well as unrealistic. "To respond to the loss of a loved one or a cherished dream casually is grotesque. To 'feel better' means to feel one's feelings better, including sadness or anger, without getting stuck in them." Addressing colleagues in Japan, Gold said, "The tragic and ironic visions facilitate the process of grieving in a way that the comic and romantic cannot. Neither espouses a perfectionistic ideal where triumph over adversity and attainment of a relatively unambiguous, pain-free existence is seen as the ultimate and perhaps only appropriate aim of living. An aesthetic of the tragic and ironic visions is that individuals can continue to celebrate the beauty of existence and the wonders of an interior life and external connections despite being surrounded by unanswerable questions, ambiguous dilemmas, and the certainty of loss and death. Viewed in this way, each life is infinitely valuable despite and perhaps even because of its immense vulnerability."

Long before Prozac, when he first began to prescribe antidepressants, John Gunderson found it "rather scary to think that people's views about themselves and their social patterns could be affected by medication. The basic principle of psychodynamic therapy is that you should feel what's there to be felt, learn from it, and put it into perspective. The sadness and fear that are often desirable responses to life are easily medicated. But suffering can be good for one's identity, and where the diagnostic line is drawn can be fuzzy and variable." Psychoanalysts used to say that a patient who becomes depressed during treatment shouldn't be given a drug, says John Oldham, "because it could take away his motivation to work. I think that's unethical where true depression is concerned, but not for dark moods and rough weeks. We want the depressed to be treated but not to say that drugs can help everybody."

The notion of cosmetic psychopharmacology also raises the specter of drug abuse. Oldham observes that, on college campuses, "Prozac is a very hot item. I'm worried about that, because those are tumultuous years in which identity hasn't yet been formed. Working through difficult times increases your capacity to cope, because you've triumphed over something." Drew Westen, who has treated many university students, is concerned that "practitioners who don't know how to take a social history or make a psychodynamic formulation are dishing out Prozac" and cites as examples young men given antidepressants to ease symptoms of an undisclosed conflict over homosexuality. "I don't think that taking the edge off their feelings is doing them a favor," says Westen, "because they haven't resolved what they need to resolve. That's not to say that Prozac can't help, but medicating instead of talking is becoming the norm." Kramer, who treats students at Brown University, is dismayed, however, when young people who have a serious problem that requires medication become "very upset at the thought of 'polluting' their bodies. They'll take every drug except the one that might help." He does agree, however, that abuse of such medicines is possible. Although she's very successful, Tess, the star patient in Kramer's best-seller, came up hard in a classic drug abuser's milieu. "Some of her less successful peers are out in the streets medicating themselves for perhaps the same post-traumatic effects that she's being treated for," says Kramer. "By virtue of her new social class, she's able to get a cleaner, better version."

There may be a more interesting question than whether drugs can or should change personality: Can drugs adapt a personality to an environment to which it's temperamentally unsuited? Are they psychic equivalents of scuba gear or a space suit? Certainly, different personalities prosper and languish in different times and places. The obsessive-compulsive one that drives the American success story seems deranged to the denizens of more relaxed, pleasure-loving places that Bostonians and Chicagoans regard as vacation spots. A young Indian woman who lets her parents arrange her marriage and then moves in with her mother-in-law might strike a Western peer as having a dependent personality. Were she to become a widow, this woman might even retire from the world and, with her community's approval, devote the rest of her life to prayer and good works, but an American who reacted that way would be offered an antidepressant.

During the Victorian era, even the formidable Isabel Burton, Richard's wife, delighted in submitting to her husband and spent much of her life obeying his commands to "pay, pack, and follow" him from one exotic posting to another. She approvingly described her still bolder friend Jane Digby el-Mezrab "serving her husband, preparing his food, sitting on the floor and washing his feet, giving him his coffee, and while he ate she stood and waited on him, and glorying in it." If these energetic, adventurous women lived today, they might still enjoy the pleasures of male company yet be too busy with their own careers for much following and foot washing. However, the modern women who resemble Jane and Isabel's sentimental, dependent Victorian peers, whose homebound natures conformed to the era's feminine ideal, would be likely candidates for Prozac. Their normal neurochemistry and temperament have fallen into social disfavor.

Within the male and female cultures, there are some striking differences in the desirability of certain personality characteristics and the incidence of mental illnesses. Depression, for example, affects twice as many women as men. The traits emphasized by Prozac have a butch ring to them: confidence, assertiveness, resilience, toughness. At first glance, Prozac seems "like a feminist drug," says Kramer, in that it emboldens certain women to ask for promotions and leave destructive relationships. After taking Prozac, Tess, who had spent a lifetime rescuing members of her big, troubled family, became a little less responsible; she felt better because she was not so concerned about everyone else's welfare. Whether that's entirely a good thing, and for whom, is not a simple matter.

Imagining a sci-fi scenario in which someone *has* to be more resilient, say, to get ahead on the job, Kramer says, "If drugs create pressure on people to change and homogenize temperament and society, which I don't think will happen, that would be bad. There's an implicit coercion in medications that can make you quicker or more adaptable, in that they so strongly mimic certain societal ideals. Prozac made me wonder how much our society rewards, even demands, the hyperthymic temperament, with its assertiveness, decisiveness, and flexibility. At a societal level, maybe we'd be better off taking a broader view of desirable temperaments, having different ideals than the masculine one, and suffering more."

Most discussion about personality change focuses on the effects of psychotherapy or drugs. The degree to which we can alter personality on our own is also a matter of opinion that depends considerably on how one defines personality.

CHAPTER 15

TIMES OF CHANGE

In the most recent film of Monica, it's hard to believe that the attractive, outspoken forty-two-year-old woman who casually dandles a grandchild on a shapely knee was ever that desperate baby, diffident girl, or uptight Barbie bride. She has recently seen, for the first time, all the movies of her life, and she tells Lynne Hofer, her interviewer, that she's annoyed by suggestions that she was ever in some way "a pushover." Lacking the benefits of hindsight and several decades' worth of scientific advances, some of the study's early observations and predictions, offered in the film's narrative, inevitably seem misguided now, particularly those that underestimated Monica. Certain scenes, too, have upset her. In one sequence, in which she sat near a younger sister who repeatedly prodded her shin with a teasing toe, teenage Monica shrank back in a modified version of her old withdrawal. After watching this incident, Monica tells Hofer that she got so mad that she "had to walk away." Later, she phoned her sibling and bawled her out as if the episode had happened yesterday, rather than nearly thirty years before. Whether it's because she's trying to counter her old pushover image, feels more comfortable dealing with a woman researcher, or has undergone some important internal changes, the assertive person in the latest film is, as Hofer says, "a very different Monica" who tells it like it is and relies far less on her smile.

In most of the early films, the heroine is the classic 1950s prefeminist sweetie pie: a Mommy's little helper who doesn't make waves. Yet there are occasional hints of a very different Monica. Her triumph over the fate to which most severely traumatized babies succumb depended on not only her dynamite smile but also an innate fighting spirit. During her long early hospitalization, she periodically had tantrums complete with enraged yelling, pinching, and even biting, which her paternal mentors didn't deem suitable for filming. In contrast to their starlet's sweetheart image in most of the footage, however, in one early sequence, Monica withdraws from a stranger who misses her overture of offering him a plaything and aggressively cootchy-coos at her, but she's clearly mad as hell, too. She waves him away, saying "No! No!" Her reaction has less to do with stranger anxiety than with the fact that "the man ignores and interrupts her game plan," says Hofer. "She wants to do things *her* way." This show of mettle in such a frail, beleaguered child speaks of the broad bold streak that runs through Monica's adventurous parents to her spunky siblings to her own free-spirited daughters. The valiant little girl defending her bit of turf summons thoughts of Elizabeth I, fortified by bold Harry's blood coursing through her veins. "I know I have the body of a weak and feeble woman," she told her troops as they faced the Spanish Armada, "but I have the heart and stomach of a king, and a king of England too; and think foul scorn that Parma or Spain, or any prince of Europe, should dare to invade the borders of my realm."

Like Elizabeth I, Monica shares her feisty family's gene pool, but her personality also depends on the environments in which her heredity is expressed. For a sickly, immobile, hospitalized baby entirely dependent on the kindness of strangers, smiling is a better survival strategy than throwing tantrums. After her recovery, she faced the further challenge of reestablishing a niche for herself in a lively, populous household. Trying to compete with her scrappy siblings on their terms would have been far less adaptive than emphasizing her unique sweetness and minimizing risks. Past the early films, the mad-as-hell Monica vanishes. On the surface, at least, her goal seemed to be to please, to be the model child. Her smiling charisma and self-protectiveness remain her personality's twin pillars over time. As the most recent film shows, however, the reemergence of a healthy aggressiveness represents Monica's capacity for growth and change.

———

Although who we are, as measured by our test scores on a handful of basic traits, largely seems "set" by early maturity, documenting an individual's behavioral continuities from infancy to that point is the sword in the stone of temperament research. Those joined in the struggle have a rueful saying: the child may be the father of the man, but the baby is not the father of the child. Intuitively, this doesn't seem right, because a strong trait that appears early and is enmeshed in physiology should endure. When such stability can be demonstrated at all, however, it usually involves individuals who express the extremes of traits; for example, Nathan Fox reports stable behavioral and EEG patterns among very inhibited and uninhibited children, particularly the latter.

When Steve Suomi analyzed two decades' worth of data on twelve of his monkeys, he found that the only measurement that predicted adult behavior right from infancy was a characteristic of inhibition called the "passive stare": how much time an individual sits on the sidelines and just watches. Neurochemical development seems to play a role in the primates' general behavioral discontinuity. Between their early infancy and first birthday, which is equivalent to a human's third, Suomi finds that the monkeys' levels of serotonin, the neurotransmitter involved in so much emotional and social behavior, are quite unstable. At one year, however, the levels become not only steady but also predictive of sociability right up to the multiple transformations of adolescence.

Pressed to explain the difficulty in proving their conviction that early temperament nevertheless somehow endures, researchers offer various hypotheses. Jerome Kagan suggests that temporal stability need not rest in a single characteristic, but may appear in a number of related ones that seem to cluster together. Thus, the fearfulness of an inhibited baby or the tantrums of an irritable one may mellow into reflectiveness or assertiveness, yet still "count" as a persistent trait. This flexible approach makes sense when linking the child's persistence in completing a task to the adult's drive to achieve, or even early derring-do in the playground to later larking in the bedroom, but some connections get Jesuitical.

The most intriguing explanation of temperament's seeming lack of stability from early life is that we "grow into it" over time. Describing the relevant literature as "interesting and surprising," John Gunderson says that "the expectation would be that temperament would be most evident in childhood and then get absorbed somewhat through acculturation. You'd think that the genetic component of, say, shyness would be more evident at six months of age than at thirty years. But twin studies show that older identicals are more alike than younger ones on some temperamental measures." Kagan attributes this effect to the flaws of data gathered from questionnaires rather than from more direct methods, but to Gunderson, "that we change less past our twenties suggests that temperamental heredity is most fully expressed in maturity." The possibility that we become more like ourselves over time is supported by psychiatric research that traces the connection between certain early traits and later disorders. The high anxiety level that's the hallmark of the trait of neuroticism and seems linked to early reactivity, for example, is "quite unstable in the teens and only becomes [stable] around the age of thirty, when someone is clearly a worrier or not," says Gunderson. "In fact, none of the Big Five traits, which aren't simple temperamental ones, may be stable till that point." The tendency, even among behavioral scientists, to confuse temperamental and character traits when discussing personality change contributes to the impression that it doesn't occur after the age of twenty-five. Yet the fact that most personality disorders don't endure over long periods makes Gunderson wonder, "At what point are you looking at temperament as opposed to character? The literature has few indices that you can identify as temperament as opposed to an amalgam, even early in life, that includes environment." Even when the technology and methodology of the study of temperament are far more advanced, environment will likely remain a confound in determining stability and change. From the moment we're born, the disposition that was our embryonic personality starts becoming just part of it: less important in itself than as a filter that affects how we choose and sort, tint and interpret our experience.

In *Gentlemen Prefer Blondes,* Anita Loos writes that "fate keeps on happening." For a different audience, personality psychologist Henry Murray observed that "an individual displays a tendency to react in a similar way to similar situations, and increasingly so with age." A personality evaluation made between the ages of eleven and thirteen, just before the tempest of adolescence, is usually a pretty accurate augury of the mature model. From a different perspective on continuity—how we cope with stress—our manner of handling the transition from elementary school to junior high is a good predictor of adaptation to important changes later in life (by way of consolation, we tend to recall our adolescent selves as having been worse than they were, as well as more different from the adult version than they are). Twin research, too, supports personality's persistence: generally, aged identicals are no less similar than they were in youth. Each member of a pair changes over a lifetime, says David Lykken, "but they do so according to similar trajectories."

Yet even the high levels of stability in adult personality that many researchers report—correlations of .7 or .8—mean that a not-inconsiderable amount of change goes on. The simple passage of time accounts for some of it. Psyches as well as bodies alter according to certain schedules set by biological clocks. "As you become an adolescent and young adult, new things that simply weren't there before kick in and change you," says Auke Tellegen. "With the kind of biological change that occurs in women after menopause, and perhaps similarly but more gradually in men, there might also be personality change. For lack of hormones, a man might be a Zen monk at seventy." By their forties, even thrill-seeking psychopaths lose some of what Lykken calls their "lustful vigor," which can open a window onto a more tranquil way of life.

Middle age also brings a different perspective. Thinking in terms of how much time is left rather than how much has elapsed makes even an extrovert more introspective. Although adults don't develop in the classic biological sense that children do, one mature characteristic suggests a kind of parallel. German research psychologist Paul Baltes has found that a trait he simply calls wisdom—the ability to deal with complexity, uncertainty, and conflict and to frame events in a larger context—doesn't emerge in those who have it till about the age of forty and peaks only at about sixty. Jerome Kagan, too, thinks that certain subtler characteristics are late bloomers: "Some people are either very good or bad at reading other people's minds. Bill Clinton is good at it, and George

Bush wasn't. You don't have that propensity as a baby, but it could still be a temperamental trait that's something like, say, an artistic skill."

Along with the psychological and biological shifts wrought by age, the experience we acquire changes us. Describing the improvement in a young girl's very negative personality "upon sailing into the harbor of a good marriage," Auke Tellegen observes that some of us go through more changes than others simply because "certain things happen." Lamenting the common misunderstanding that an inborn trait can't change and an acquired one can, he says, "Someone who's born with, say, an aggressive temperament can learn to suppress or redirect it. On the other hand, the post-traumatic stress response that affects some combat veterans and abused children is acquired, yet it's very resistant."

Although few people undergo such traumatic transformative experiences, most of us assume two private roles in adulthood that profoundly alter our perspective on life. Just as her innate social appeal had bloomed only in the nurturing atmosphere of the hospital, after Monica married, she gave a strikingly different response on one of the standard psychological tests she had taken periodically throughout her life. Previously, she had interpreted a deliberately ambiguous drawing as a cold, bleak house lashed by a blizzard; by the age of twenty-five, the same image had become a cozy cottage with a fireplace. Nor was this new sense of contentment and security the only way in which Monica changed. In the movie of her wedding, the dutiful bride who performs so carefully seems destined to play out in her marriage the good-daughter role she had long perfected. However, the study's first official, and somewhat surprised, mention of Monica's true grit comes just after the arrival of her first baby. Despite much contrary advice, the young mother feeds little Adele *her* way, which feels as "right" and natural to her as it did when she mothered her dolls long before. In the secure atmosphere created by her and her steady, sensitive husband signs of Monica's long-buried assertiveness increase with the years.

Monica's reaction to marriage and motherhood is a classic example of the way in which adults change. Like travel abroad, becoming a spouse or parent forever alters how one sees the world. Rites and the personal changes they forge continue to shift later in life, as Carl Jung presciently observed: when domestic demands subside, women no longer have to suppress their aggressiveness and emphasize their nurturing side, nor men the reverse, which can release long-stifled aspects of personality. Where women are concerned, some research supports Jung's intuition: one longitudinal study shows that in their late twenties, women increase in measures of self-discipline and traditional femininity; later in life, their confidence, dominance, and coping skills increase. The mature Monica still wouldn't rank among the more aggressive female subjects in a personality data bank, but compared to her bridal self, she's a tiger.

A flamboyant example of someone who transformed his life by shifting professional roles, Timothy Leary believes that people have great potential for change, "even though most are wired up to be normal, dull humans who are most comfortable in the middle of the road. They've also been saturated with this static, Newtonian idea that personality is permanent—the way it's represented in astrology." Those who are content with the personal status quo that Leary decries are the least likely to change. In one long-term study, the subjects whose personalities stayed the same had been successful as teenagers and were better adjusted later in life; those who became different tended to be late bloomers whose personalities had called for some adjustment. According to Leary, aside from drugs, the best way to shake up personality is to "change the people you hang out with and your setting."

The stable settings that do indeed make for consistent personalities were much commoner before the social revolution of the 1960s in which Dr. Leary played such a colorful part. What continuity most people experience in urbanized America no longer comes from the traditional small-town social institutions of school and church, club and playing field but from a small circle of kindred spirits, sometimes connected electronically. "When our primates are kept in the same environment, we get wonderful temperamental stability, particularly with some traits, such as reactivity," says Steve Suomi. "If we start moving things around, our shy individuals go off in different experiential patterns, and their continuity starts to disappear. Both our nervous systems and social habits are sensitive to what's around us, so that the more constant the environment, the stabler we are."

Much of the transformative power of a new environment lies in the new roles it can afford. If her own home set the stage for Monica's private expressions of assertiveness, moving from the North to the South, far from the supports and restrictions of her old social network, inaugurated her more public forcefulness. When her husband decides to transplant the family in search of greater economic opportunity, despite her preference for the familiar and deep ties, Monica packs and follows. At first, living with in-laws and caring for their children as well as her own, she passes some weepy months of the sort the Rochester doctors had anticipated. After her initial distress, however, just as she had done at various crossroads throughout her life, Monica surprised the experts. While her husband traveled about looking for work, she not only rented them an apartment but moved the family into it before he returned. Next she found work as a dishwasher, was soon promoted to cook, and ended up with a good job at a manufacturing company in which she takes much pleasure and pride. Considering her evolution, it's no wonder that Monica gets annoyed at being thought a pushover.

Just because a personality change, such as Monica's after the move, follows an environmental one doesn't necessarily mean it lacks genetic roots. A new job, marriage, or city might work its magic by coaxing the expression of certain dormant genes—perhaps Monica's aggressive ones. Then, too, certain characteristics incline a person to switch careers or opt for early retirement, to leave or stick with a bad marriage, to move to the country or stay in the city. "People think that if something is hereditary, it never alters," says Robert Plomin, "but molecular genetics is about change—both short-term gene regulation and long-term developmental differentiation. The reason I do longitudinal twin and adoption studies is to get at the genetic contribution to change, and you find it in personality rather than, say, cognition."

New roles and settings have the potential to shake up our personalities because they push us toward the new learning that by adulthood most of us mightily resist. On separate tracks from both psychoanalytical theory and personality psychology a third group of scientists has approached the study of why we are the way we are from the very different perspective of learning theory. According to psychologists J. B. Watson and B. F. Skinner, just like Pavlov's dogs, people can be motivated or, in their parlance, reinforced or conditioned, to do anything. Watson famously declared that, regardless of the child's genes, given a baby and a specified setting, he could raise a doctor, lawyer, beggar, or thief. (No fan of Watson, Michael Stone observes that the behaviorist's son, who was raised according to his father's principles, committed suicide.) Going beyond austere stimulus-response behaviorism, modern learning theory focuses on social influences on motivation. According to theorist Albert Bandura, who we are and what we do depends not only on our "competencies," or abilities, but also on "expectancies" based on our experience. Not surprisingly, people who feel competent and expect to succeed are likelier to do so than those who don't.

Monica's early experience of being unloved and learning to withdraw is an extreme example of a phenomenon that causes all of us some degree of trouble. After taking some tests, say, or going to some parties, we devise some rules—right or wrong, adaptive or disastrous—for handling such situations in the future, and we keep on playing by them. Because they cause us to "encode" ourselves and our experiences in a certain way—"I test badly" or "I'll never meet Mr. Right"—these mind-sets shape us as surely as heritable traits do. A stunning example is what psychiatrist Aaron Beck describes as the "hopeless and helpless" thought pattern shared by many people who are vulnerable to depression. In short, by the lights of modern learning theory, Monica's personality changed when her old negative expectancies, based on her early encoding of traumatic experiences, were challenged by her new competencies as a wife, mother, and productive worker.

That who we are is bound up with expectancies and competencies, victories and defeats, and other shifting dimensions of an individual's experience seems beyond question to social psychologist Orville Gilbert Brim, the director of the MacArthur Foundation Research Network on Successful Midlife Development. "People who are shy in childhood may remain that way or get over it, and that interests some researchers," he says. "Others are interested in how, from day to day and over longer periods, a person changes in his motivation and self-evaluation of his worth, roles, bases for comparisons, aspirations. We don't think that shyness, say, makes any difference to the really important things in life, such as happiness, well-being, interests, achievement, power, money, fame, and sex, and how they change over time."

To give a sense of his more expansive perspective on personality, Brim brings up a fellow who graduated from college wanting to be a famous musician. "After eight or ten years of little cues coming in, there comes a day when he says to himself, 'It's never going to happen, so you might as well adjust your sights.' " In most such cases, says Brim, the person doesn't sit down and decide to be off with the old and on with the new. Instead, accumulating experience and subconscious processing bring a slow dawning that culminates one morning in the realization that he's no longer interested in musical fame, but something else. A similar process seems to be involved in the most common of what Brim and his colleagues describe as adulthood's "deep psychological experiences": religious conversion. "Someone may be struck while walking down the road," says Brim, "but I don't think that it's the finger of God. Rather, it's the resolution of some conflict that has been going on, without too much conscious awareness, for a long time."

Deciding to give up on rock stardom and join the family firm or to leave the stock exchange and take up organic farming doesn't mean that an individual's traits have changed. He may nonetheless feel and seem like a different person. In the course of discussing why we do what we do, Brim observes that "there's not much new in human behavior. You have to remember to ask yourself, 'What did they used to call it?' William James called it 'will.' "

From a very different perspective than Freud's, philosophers sacred and secular, including his peer William James, have described an individual's seeming ability to prevail over the forces of nature and nurture in the pursuit of an important goal as simple, old-fashioned "will." That Mohandas Gandhi, Martin Luther King, and Nelson Mandela fixed their eyes on the prize and persisted in their efforts to win justice in the face of daunting odds testifies to what will can do on a heroic scale. In more prosaic settings, from twelve-step meetings to weight-loss programs, millions of ordinary mortals gather to pump up their "willpower."

Despite the vaguely supernatural aura that clings to a term that's variously defined, "will is part of nature," says Jerome Kagan. "It's part of consciousness. Many scientists hope to win the Nobel Prize for finding the brain circuit that's responsible for the fact that I can start reaching for my coffee mug, then stop. I can stop—that's will. Just as the web is special to the spider, will is a special characteristic of Homo sapiens that allows us to control our behavior. As Freud said, the fact that there is a conscience is nature. *Nature!* "

To biologically minded psychologists, will and motivation are rooted in traits, particularly the one often called conscientiousness or constraint. Long before it's reasonable to talk in such terms, three-month-old infants vary in their temperamental ability to shift their attention and concentrate. Because the distractable baby is easier to help out of unpleasant states, he's a more congenial companion. Later on however, the less active, more highly focused child is the apple of the teacher's eye; along with many a parent of a bright but wriggly little boy, Mary Rothbart thinks that overly valuing these "good child" traits can lead to an unfair assessment of ability. Very small children also differ in their capacity to delay gratification—a crucial aspect of will that accounts for big differences in our individual evolution. A child's growing self-image figures in his willpower quotient, too. On failing at a task, children who see themselves as "helpless" blame their lack of ability and nurse self-defeating thoughts. Their "mastery-oriented" peers chalk up the difficulty to not trying hard enough, pull up their socks, and do better next time.

In a sequence in which eight-year-old Monica's vigorous siblings accompany her on a visit to the Rochester doctors, the decorous heroine is soon elbowed away from the playroom's paints and easel—usually hers alone—and left to carry out their orders or stand forlornly on the sidelines. At first, will or its lack can look like very little or too much inhibition. Because inhibition dampens impulsivity and expressiveness, the trait can make it easier to focus, but not all self-disciplined children are inhibited, nor are all inhibited ones self-controlled. To underscore this distinction, Rothbart refers to deliberate self-regulation as "effortful control." That this capacity is generally not influenced by an individual's boldness or timidity is, she believes, an important illustration of our flexibility: "We can act in ways that don't necessarily correspond to the temperamental differences that initially predispose us to seek the least pain and most pleasure possible."

Pain and pleasure, punishment and reward bring up another aspect of who we are that's associated with will. Conscience has traditionally been considered one of the most important applications of learning. From Kagan's viewpoint, however, conscience develops in the child's maturing brain, unfolding just as intelligence and traits like sociability and empathy do. He believes that, by the end of their second year, all neurologically normal children have the innate sense that harming others is wrong; parents and teachers don't instill this moral capacity but only provide settings that support or discourage it.

Other temperamentally inclined psychologists relate conscience to an individual's vulnerability to fear. The lower one's threshold for feeling anxious, the likelier one is to perceive the cause as internal and to use moral concepts to buffer stress. In Rothbart's experience, "good" girls like Monica outnumber boys in this regard. Partly because they're not as fearful of disapproval, the woodshed, or even hellfire, conventional moral appeals are less effective with bold children, more of whom are male. When adults resort to harsh forms of discipline, young naturally tough guys may become uninterested in internalizing morals and adopt an externally based what-can-I-get-away-with code instead.

From a very different perspective, Walter Mischel says, "That will depends on learning doesn't even seem debatable to me. Trait theorists wait for someone to find a 'will gene,' because they don't deal with the processes of self-regulation that strongly influence personality." Like William James, Mischel considers will to be the central and most fascinating problem in psychology. Its crucial elements are the ability to set a distant goal, he says, and "to resist all kinds of distractions and frustrations in the pursuit of it. How does one conquer temptation, from outside and within? It's a story as old as Prometheus and Adam and Eve."

Whether a child decides to finish his homework or watch TV or an overweight adult opts for the gym or the snack bar depends on what James called "preliminaries," or sets of skills, mental transformations, and self-distractions that we learn over time. Largely acquired from models such as parents and teachers, these cognitive strategies—making a persistent effort or thinking before one acts—underlie our ability to regulate our own behavior. It's these preliminaries, says Mischel, that predict whether someone will or won't keep a New Year's resolution, "even one that involves survival, such as quitting smoking."

That personality researchers don't record much change in adulthood doesn't mean it can't happen, says Mischel, but rather that often one of two necessary ingredients is missing. "If you bring the motivation," he says, "I'll give you the willpower, which is a strategy we can work out. Until you're determined to make new friends, lose weight, or stop going out with losers, there's not a thing anyone else can do for you. Given that, you next have to know what you must do. Then you have to break that strategy down bit by bit, taking the mystery out of it to make it easier." Whether one is a thrill seeker trying to give up an addiction or a shy violet who wants to speak in public without dread, the path to transformation is traversed in "little teeny, weeny steps," says Mischel. "That's hard for people who can make big leaps, but the process of change rests in making the stages manageable, tolerable, and doable. About a hundred years ago, James said that desire with no expectation is mere wishing. When you have both ingredients, however, and if certain preliminaries or strategies are made accessible, you can exercise will."

To Robert Cloninger, will involves both the biological and social dimensions of a person's heritage. He considers persistence to be a basic temperamental trait enmeshed in automatic emotional responses involved in the procedural memory system; regardless of circumstances, the naturally persistent person is neurophysiologically primed to keep on keeping on. Not just a matter of biologically grounded habits and skills, however, will also involves character, specifically or a trait that Cloninger calls "self-directedness," which depends on the learned ideas and values that enable us to discipline ourselves to work toward a goal. Although the naturally persistent can acquire willpower more readily, anyone who cultivates self-directedness can do so. To parents who feel helpless before their children's strong temperamental inclinations, says Cloninger, the need to instill the good values that underlie character "means that at least there's *something* they can do for their offspring! It's the combinations of the child's genes and the family's environment that yield the wonderful permutations that make each person so interesting."

In *Henry V,* the duke of Exeter warns the king of France not to mistake his monarch for the erstwhile wastrel prince: "And, be assured, you'll find a difference, / As we, his subjects, have in wonder found, / Between the promise of his greener days / And these he masters now." Once king, Henry puts the juvenile delinquent's thrill-seeking oppositionalism to a different end and invades France. Even his familiars, however, mistake what is merely Hal's new focus for a whole new temperament.

A more contemporary textbook example of how we change yet remain the same is Jerome Kagan's midcareer decision to drop the study of nurture and take up that of nature, which he pursues with the very same innate zeal. Yet the experience that has accompanied this professional shift has caused a personal one: Kagan now views himself and others "with a new set of lenses," he says. "With my closest relatives and friends, I now acknowledge that they can't help a lot of the behavior that annoys me, so I've become more permissive." Yet not entirely indulgent: "This is the most important thing for people to understand. Don't go all the way and assume that just because a person has a temperamental quality, he has no conscious control over it. That's going too far. A genetic influence doesn't mean a person has no choice. There's no question that male primates, including men, have a strong biological urge to be promiscuous. Therefore, we should excuse all men for adultery? No, because even though they have a powerful natural impulse, they can master it. This biological determinism business has become ridiculous."

Just as King Henry *seems* different from Prince Hal, David Lykken recalls a research subject of the heroic-psychopathic sort who passed much of his earlier life in prison, then succeeded in business and bought a plane. After Lykken accepted an invitation to go flying, he wondered " 'What am I doing? He's going to stand the plane on end and scare me to death.' But he flew like a transport pilot, because his self-esteem is now involved with being licensed to fly jets and do all sorts of things the average amateur can't." John Dean, an aide to Richard Nixon who played a part in the Watergate cover-up, has presumably always possessed the character trait that Cloninger calls self-directedness. In the White House, Dean used this quality, which he has come to disparage, to drive his "blind ambition." "Now the same trait is molded by more mature ethical values," Cloninger says. "If that's a trivial change, then those of us who are concerned about and working to improve the quality of our society are wasting our time."

Like the ex-con turned high-flying entrepreneur and several reformed Watergaters, the new John Wetteland, a relief pitcher on the New York Yankees who's perhaps the best closer in baseball, appears to have precious little in common with the old one. Now a devout bornagain Christian who keeps a Bible in every room, Wetteland listens to Jesus rock and votes ultraconservative. Not so long ago, this son of a beat musician–amateur pitcher was a hard-drinking, drug-abusing California Deadhead whose ideas were far out rather than far right. Two elements have remained constant in Wetteland, and both come naturally: he has always been a great athlete, and he always takes things to the limit. Auke Tellegen's favorite example of temperamental camouflage also concerns religion and an extreme individual: "Charles Colson would have beat his grandmother to death when he was with Nixon, but then he was 'born again.' He probably always had a very emotional, intense temperament, but now he has different enemies and friends. His nature didn't change—he just does something else with all that zeal. One's *mode* of engagement with life may not alter much. But one's focus can, which in itself allows for significant change."

The seventeenth-century philosopher Sir Francis Bacon wrote that "Nature is often hidden, sometimes overcome, seldom extinguished." His observation remains pretty much state-of-the-art.

ACKNOWLEDGMENTS

For their contributions to the study of why we are the way we are and their generosity in sharing their great learning and reviewing its applications in the following pages, I express my heartfelt gratitude to Hagop Akiskal, John Bates, Alan Breier, Orville Gilbert Brim, C. Robert Cloninger, Scott Dowling, Hans Eysenck, Nathan Fox, Philip Gold, William Greenough, John Gunderson, Megan Gunnar, J. D. Higley, Myron Hofer, Mardi Horwitz, Kay Jamison, Kenneth Kendler, Donald Klein, Peter Kramer, Walter Mischel, John Oldham, Robert Plomin, Alvin Poussaint, Frank Putnam, John Richters, Mary Rothbart, Daniel Stern, Stephen Suomi, George Vaillant, Theodore Wachs, Drew Westen, Thomas Widiger, and the many other scientists whose works have made this one possible. The contributions of the many people involved over the years in the "Monica" study, particularly those of the subject herself, the original research team of George Engel, Vivian Harway, D. Wilson Hess, and Franz Reichsman, and Lynne Hofer, the most recent investigator, merit special mention.

For their particular insight, kindness, and patience in reading and commenting on the entire manuscript, I thank Jerome Kagan, David Lykken, Auke Tellegen, and Michael Stone.

SUGGESTED READINGS

An academic bibliography of the scientific literature on why people are the way they are would be a book unto itself that wouldn't serve the general reader for whom this one was written. With that person in mind, the following publications have been selected, many of them by the scientists who particularly figure under the chapter in which their research initially appears in detail.

CHAPTER 1

Engel, G. L., F. Reichsman, V. Harway, and D. Hess. "Monica: Infant-Feeding Behavior of a Mother Gastric Fistula-Fed as an Infant: A 30-Year Longitudinal Study of Enduring Effects," *Parental Influences in Health and Disease,* ed. E. J. Anthony and G. H. Pollock. Boston: Little, Brown, 1985.

———, and A. H. Schmale. "Conservation-Withdrawal: A Primary Regulatory Process for Organismic Homeostasis," *Physiology, Emotion and Psychosomatic Illness* (Ciba Foundation Symposium 8) ed. R. Porter and J. Knight. Amsterdam: Elsevier-Excerpta Medica, 1972.

Harlow, H. F. "The Nature of Love." *American Psychologist,* 1958.

Hofer, M. A. "An Evolutionary Perspective on Anxiety," *Anxiety as Symptom and Signal,* ed. S. P. Roose and R. A. Glick. Hillsdale, N.J.: The Analytic Press, 1995.

———. "Hidden Regulators: Implications for a New Understanding of Attachment, Separation and Loss," *Attachment Theory: Social, Developmental, and Clinical Perspectives,* ed. S. Goldberg, R. Muir, and J. Kerr. Hillsdale, N.J.: The Analytic Press, 1995.

———. "On the Nature and Function of Prenatal Behavior," *Behavior of the*

Fetus, ed. W. Smotherman and S. Robinson. Caldwell, N.J.: Telford, 1988.

———. *The Roots of Human Behavior.* San Francisco: W. H. Freeman, 1981.

Spitz, R. A. "Hospitalism: An Inquiry into the Genesis of Psychiatric Conditions in Early Childhood." *Psychoanalytical Study of the Child,* 1945.

CHAPTER 2

Allport, G. W. *Pattern and Growth in Personality.* New York: Holt, 1961.

Buss, A. H., R. Plomin, and L. Willerman. "The Inheritance of Temperaments." *Journal of Personality,* 1973.

Cloninger, C. R. "A Systematic Method for Clinical Description and Classification of Personality Variants." *Archives of General Psychiatry,* 1987.

———. "Temperament and Personality." *Current Opinion in Neurobiology,* 1994.

———, D. M. Svrakic, and T. R. Przybeck. "A Psychobiological Model of Temperament and Character." *Archives of General Psychiatry,* 1993.

Costa, Paul T., Jr. and Robert R. McCrae. *Personality in Adulthood.* New York: Guilford Press, 1990.

Clancy, F. "The Flight Stuff." *American Health,* 1992.

Eysenck, Hans J. *The Biological Basis of Personality.* Springfield, Ill.: Charles C. Thomas, 1967.

———. *The Decline and Fall of the Freudian Empire.* Washington, D.C.: Viking, 1985.

———. *A Model for Personality.* New York: Springer-Verlag, 1981.

———, and M. W. Eysenck. *Personality and Individual Differences.* New York: Plenum Publishing, 1985.

Gray, Jeffrey. *The Neurophysiology of Anxiety.* London: Oxford University Press, 1982.

Hastings, Selena. *Evelyn Waugh.* Boston: Houghton Mifflin, 1995.

Higley, James D., and Stephen J. Suomi. "Temperamental Reactivity in Nonhuman Primates," *Temperament in Childhood,* ed. D. Kohnstamm, J. E. Bates, and M. K. Rothbart. West Sussex, UK: John Wiley, 1989.

Hippocrates. *Works of Hippocrates,* ed. W.H.S. Jones and E. T. Withington. Cambridge, Mass.: Harvard University Press, 1923.

Kagen, J. "Biology and the Child," *Handbook of Child Psychology,* ed. W. Damon. New York: John Wiley, in press.

———. *Galen's Prophecy.* New York: Basic Books, 1994.

———. *Unstable Ideas.* Cambridge, Mass.: Harvard University Press, 1989.

Lykken, David T. "Fearlessness: Its Carefree Charm and Deadly Risks." *Psychology Today,* 1982.

———. "A Study of Anxiety in the Sociopathic Personality." *Journal of Abnormal and Social Psychology,* 1957.

Patton, Robert. *The Pattons.* New York: Crown, 1994.

Pavlov, I. P. *Conditioned Reflexes and Psychiatry.* New York: International Publishers, 1941.

Pervin, L. A. *Handbook of Personality: Theory and Research.* New York: Guilford Press, 1990.

Plimpton, George. *The Writer's Chapbook.* New York: Viking, 1989.

Reeves, Richard. *President Kennedy.* New York: Simon & Schuster, 1993.

Rice, Edward. *Captain Sir Richard Francis Burton.* New York: Scribners, 1990.

Suomi, Stephen J. "Early Stress and Adult Emotional Reactivity in Rhesus Monkeys," *The Childhood Environment and Adult Disease,* ed. D. Barker. Chichester, UK: John Wiley, 1991.

———. "Influence of Bowlby's Attachment Theory on Research on Non-Human Primate Behavioral Development," *Attachment Theory: Social, Developmental, and Clinical Perspectives,* ed. S. Goldberg, R. Muir, and J. Kerr. Hillsdale, N.J.: The Analytic Press, 1995.

———. "Uptight and Laid-Back Monkeys: Individual Differences in Response to Social Challenges," *Plasticity of Development,* ed. S. Brauth, W. Hall, and R. Dooling. Cambridge, Mass.: MIT Press, 1991.

Tellegen, Auke. "Folk Concepts and Psychological Concepts of Personality and Personality Disorder." *Psychological Inquiry,* 1993.

———. "Modeling and Measuring Environment." *Behavioral and Brain Sciences,* 1991.

———. "Personality Traits: Issues of Definition, Evidence, and Assessment," *Thinking Clearly About Psychology,* ed. D. Cicchetti and W. Grove. Minneapolis: University of Minnesota Press, 1991.

———, D. T. Lykken, T. J. Bouchard, K. J. Wilcox, N. L. Segal, and S. Rich. "Personality Similarity in Twins Reared Apart and Together." *Journal of Personality and Social Psychology,* 1988.

Queen Victoria's Highland Journals, David Duff, ed. Exeter, UK: Webb & Bower, 1980.

CHAPTER 3

Akiskal, Hagop S. "Delineating Irritable-Choleric and Hyperthymic Temperaments and Variants of Cyclothymia." *Journal of Personality Disorders,* 1992.

———. "Temperaments on the Border of Affective Disorders." *Acta Psychiatrica Scandinavica,* 1994.

———, and K. Akiskal. "Reassessing the Prevention of Bipolar Disorders: Clinical Significance and Artistic Creativity." *European Psychiatry* (ex *Psychiatrie et Psychobiologie*), 1988.

Jamison, Kay Redfield. *Touched with Fire: Manic-Depressive Illness and the Artistic Temperament.* New York: Free Press, 1993.

———. *An Unquiet Mind.* New York: Knopf, 1995.

———, and Frederick K. Goodwin. *Manic-Depressive Illness.* New York: Oxford University Press, 1990.

Owen, David. "The Straddler." *The New Yorker,* January 30, 1995.

Rothbart, Mary K. "Social Development," *Atypical Infant Development* (2d ed.), ed. M. H. Hanson. New York: Oxford University Press, in press.

———. "Temperament and Development," *Temperament in Childhood,* ed. G. Kohnstamm, John E. Bates, and Mary K. Rothbart. Chichester, UK: John Wiley, 1989.

———, and H. A. Ruff. *Attention in Early Development: Themes and Variations.* New York: Oxford University Press, in press.

CHAPTER 4

Archer, J. "The Influence of Testosterone on Human Aggressiveness." *British Journal of Psychiatry,* 1991.

Cleckley, Hervery. *The Mask of Sanity.* St. Louis: Mosby, 1964.

Cloninger, C. Robert, et al. "Predisposition to Petty Criminality in Swedish Adoptees." *Archives of General Psychiatry,* 1982.

Coccaro, E. F. "Cebtral Serotonin and Impulsive Aggression." *British Journal of Psychiatry,* 1989.

Dabbs, J. M., et al. "Saliva Testosterone and Criminal Violence Among Women." *Personality and Individual Differences,* 1988.

Dodge, Kenneth A., John E. Bates, and Gregory S. Pettit. "Mechanisms in the Cycle of Violence." *Science,* 1990.

Epstein, S. "Anxiety, Arousal, and the Self Concept," *Stress and Anxiety,* ed. I. G. Sarason and C. D. Spielberger. Washington, D.C.: Hemisphere, 1976.

Foote, Shelby. *The Civil War: A Narrative,* vol. 3. New York: Random House, 1974.

Friend, Tom. "A Nonconformist in a League of His Own." *The New York Times,* April 20, 1995.

Higley, J. D., W. T. Thompson, M. Champoux, D. Goldman, M. F. Hasert, G. W. Kraemer, S. J. Suomi, and M. Linnoila. "Paternal and Maternal Genetic and Environmental Contributions to CSF Monoamine Metabolite Concentrations in Rhesus Monkeys *(Macaca mulatta).*" *Archives of General Psychiatry* 50, pp. 615–23, 1992.

———, P. T. Mehlman, D. T. Taub, S. B. Higley, B. Fernald, J. Vickers, S. J. Suomi, and M. Linnoila. "Excessive Mortality in Young Male Nonhuman Primates with Low CSF 5-HIAA Concentrations." *Archives of General Psychiatry,* in press.

————, P. T. Mehlman, R. E. Poland, I. Faucher, D. T. Taub, J. Vickers, S. J. Suomi, and M. Linnoila. "A Nonhuman Primate Model of Violence and Assertiveness: CSF 5-HIAA and CSF Testosterone Correlate with Different Types of Aggressive Behaviors." *Biological Psychiatry,* in press.

Linnoila, Markku, et al. "Biochemical Aspects of Aggressiveness in Man," *Clinical Neuropharmacology,* ed. W. E. Bunney, E. Costa, and S. G. Pottsm. New York: Raven Press, 1986.

Lykken, David T. *The Antisocial Personalities.* Hillsdale, N.J.: Erlbaum, 1995.

Olweus, D. "Familial and Temperamental Determinants of Aggressive Behavior in Adolescent Boys." *Developmental Psychology,* 1980.

Poussaint, Alvin F. "Black Suicide," *Textbook of Black-Related Diseases,* ed. R. A. Williams. New York: McGraw-Hill, 1975.

————. "Interracial Relations and Prejudice," *Comprehensive Textbook of Psychiatry* (3rd ed.), ed. H. I. Kaplan, A. M. Freedman, and B. J. Sadock. Baltimore: Williams and Wilkins, 1980.

————. "Looking Ahead: Problems and Solutions." *Journal of Health and Social Policy,* 1990.

Richters, John E., and D. Cicchetti. "Toward a Developmental Perspective on Conduct Disorder." *Development and Psychopathology,* 1993.

————, and ————. "Mark Twain Meets DSM-III-R." *Development and Psychopathology,* 1993.

————, and P. E. Martinez. "Violent Communities, Family Choices, and Children's Chances." *Development and Psychopathology,* 1993.

————, and ————. "The NIMH Community Violence Project: Children as Victims and Witnesses to Violence. *Psychiatry: Interpersonal and Biological Processes,* 1993.

Schachter, S., and J. E. Singer. "Cognition, Social, and Physiological Determinants of Emotional State." *Psychology Review,* 1962.

Shedler, J., and J. Block. "Adolescent Drug Use and Emotional Health." *American Psychologist,* 1991.

CHAPTER 5

Fostinger, T. *No One Ever Asked Us . . .* New York: Columbia University Press, 1983.

Kendler, K. "A Longitudinal Twin Study of One-Year Prevalence of Major Depression in Women." *Archives of General Psychiatry,* 1993.

————. "A Longitudinal Twin Study of Personality and Major Depression in Women." *Archives of General Psychiatry,* 1993.

————, et al. "Stressful Life Events, Genetic Liability, and Onset of an Episode of Major Depression in Women." *The American Journal of Psychiatry,* 1995.

————, et al. "Symptoms of Anxiety and Symptoms of Depression: Same Genes, Different Environments?" *Archives of General Psychiatry,* 1987.

Lykken, David T. "The Genetics of Genius," *Genius and the Mind: Studies of Creativity and Temperament in the Historical Record,* ed. A. Steptoe. Oxford: Oxford University Press, in press.

————, T. J. Bouchard, M. McGue, and A. Tellegen. "Emergenesis: Genetic Traits That May Not Run in Families." *American Psychologist,* 1992.

————, and A. Tellegen. "Happiness Is a Stochastic Phenomenon." *Psychological Science,* in press.

Plomin, Robert. *Genes and Experience: The Developmental Interplay Between Nature and Nurture.* Newbury Park: Sage, 1994.

————. *Nature and Nurture: An Introduction to Human Behavioral Genetics.* Pacific Grove, Calif.: Brooks/Cole, 1990.

————, and J. Dunn. *Separate Lives: Why Siblings Are So Different.* New York: Basic Books, 1990.

CHAPTERS 6 AND 7

Angier, Natalie. "Heredity's More than Genes, New Theory Proposes." *The New York Times,* January 3, 1995.

Edelman, Gerald. *The Remembered Present: A Biological Theory of Consciousness.* New York: Basic Books, 1990.

Freud, S. *Standard Edition of the Complete Psychological Works of Sigmund Freud,* ed. and trans. J. Strachey. London: Hogarth Press.

Godden, D. R., and A. D. Baddeley. "Context-Dependent Memory in Two Natural Environments." *British Journal of Psychology,* 1975.

Horowitz, Mardi. *Introduction to Psychodynamics.* New York: Basic Books, 1988.

————. *Personality Styles and Brief Psychotherapy.* New York: Basic Books, 1984.

————. *Person Schemas and Maladaptive Interpersonal Patterns.* Chicago: University of Chicago Press, 1991.

————. *States of Mind* (2nd ed.). New York: Plenum Publishing, 1987.

Janet, P. *L'Etat Mental des Hysteriques.* Paris: Alcan, 1911.

Loftus, E., and K. Ketchum. *The Myth of Repressed Memory.* New York: St. Martin's Press, 1995.

Stern, D. N. *Diary of a Baby.* New York: Basic Books, 1990.

————. *The First Relationship: Infant and Mother.* Cambridge, Mass.: Harvard University Press, 1977.

————. *The Interpersonal World of the Infant: A View From Psychoanalysis and Developmental Psychology.* New York: Basic Books, 1985.

Vaillant, G. *Adaptation to Life.* Cambridge, Mass.: Harvard University Press, 1995 reprint.

———. *The Wisdom of the Ego.* Cambridge, Mass.: Harvard University Press, 1993.

Westen, Drew I. "Psychoanalytic Approaches to Personality," *Handbook of Personality,* ed. L. Pervin. New York: Guilford Press, 1990.

———. *Psychology: Mind, Brain, and Culture.* New York: John Wiley, in press.

———. *Self and Society.* New York: Cambridge University Press, 1985.

Wilson, E. O. *The Naturalist.* Washington, D.C.: Island Press, 1994.

Chapters 8 and 9

Bates, John E. "Applications of Temperament Concepts," *Temperament in Childhood,* ed. G. A. Kohnstamm, J. E. Bates, and M. K. Rothbart. Chichester, UK: John Wiley, 1989.

———, and K. Bayles. "The Role of Attachment in the Development of Behavior Problems," *Clinical Implications of Attachment,* ed. J. Belsky and T. Nezworski. Hillsdale, N.J.: Erlbaum, 1988.

———, and T. D. Wachs, eds. *Temperament: Individual Differences at the Interface of Biology and Behavior.* Washington, D.C.: American Psychological Association Press, 1994.

Breier, A., et al. "Early Parental Loss and Development of Adult Psychopathology." *Archives of General Psychiatry,* 1988.

Cooper, R. M., and J. P. Zubek. "Effects of Enriched and Restricted Early Environments on the Learning Ability of Bright and Dull Rats." *Canadian Journal of Psychology,* 1958.

Csikszentmihalyi, M. *Flow.* New York: HarperCollins, 1990.

Dowling, S. "Abstract Report from the Literature on Neonatology." *Psychoanalytic Quarterly,* 1981.

———. "A Piagetian Critique." *Psychoanalytical Inquiry,* 1985.

———. "Seven Infants with Esophageal Atresia." *Psychoanalytic Study of the Child,* 1977.

Eysenck, H. J., and D. Fulker. "The Components of Type A Behavior and Its Genetic Determinants." *Personality and Individual Differences,* 1983.

Goodwin, Doris Kearns. *No Ordinary Time—Franklin and Eleanor Roosevelt: The Home Front in World War II.* New York: Simon & Schuster, 1994.

Greenough, William T. "Brain Adaptation to Experience: An Update," *Brain Development and Cognition,* ed. M. H. Johnson. Cambridge, Mass.: Blackwell, 1993.

———, and J. E. Black. "Induction of Brain Structure by Experience," *Behavioral Developmental Neuroscience* (Minnesota Symposia on Child Psychology), vol. 24, ed. M. Gunnar and C. A. Nelson. Hillsdale, N.J.: Erlbaum, 1992.

———, et al. "Development of the Brain: Experience Affects the Structure of

Neurons, Glia, and Blood Vessels," *Proceedings from the Third International Workshop on the At-Risk Infant,* ed. N. Anastasiow and S. Harel. Baltimore: Paul H. Brookes Publishing Co., 1993.

———, et al. "Determinants of Brain Readiness for Action: Experience Shapes More Than Neuronal Form." *Brain Dysfunction,* 1992.

Gunnar, M. "Psychoendocrine Studies of Temperament and Stress in Early Childhood," *Temperament: Individual Differences at the Interface of Biology and Behavior,* ed. J. Bates and T. Wachs. Washington, D.C.: American Psychological Association Press, 1994.

———, et al. "The Stressfulness of Separation Among Nine-Month-Old Infants." *Child Development,* 1992.

Kelley, Virginia, with J. Morgan. *Leading with My Heart.* New York: Simon & Schuster, 1994.

Lewis, M., and L. Rosenbaum, eds. *The Effect of the Infant on Its Caregiver.* New York: John Wiley, 1974.

———. *The Development of Affect.* New York: Plenum Publishing, 1978.

Nachmias, M., M. Gunnar, et al. "Behavioral Inhibition and Stress Reactivity." *Child Development,* in press.

Putnam, Frank W. *Diagnosis and Treatment of Multiple Personality Disorder.* New York: Guilford Press, 1989.

———. "Altered States." *The Sciences,* 1992.

———. "Are Alter Personalities Fragments or Figments?" *Psychoanalytic Inquiry,* 1992.

———, and M. D. De Bellis. "The Psychobiology of Childhood Maltreatment." *Child and Adolescent Psychiatric Clinics of North America,* 1994.

Scarr, S., and K. McCartney. "How People Make Their Own Environments: A Theory of Genotype-Environment Effects." *Child Development,* 1984.

———, et al. "Personality Resemblance Among Adolescents and Their Parents in Biologically Related and Adoptive Families." *Journal of Personality and Social Psychology,* 1981.

Seligman, M.E.P. *Helplessness: On Depression, Development, and Death.* San Francisco: W. H. Freeman, 1975.

Spiegel, David, et al. "Effect of Psychosocial Treatment on Survival of Patients with Metastatic Breast Cancer." *Lancet,* 1989.

Stern, D. N., L. Hofer, et al. "Affect and Attunement," *Social Perception in Infants,* ed. T. Field and N. Fox. Norwood, N.J.: Ablex Publishing, 1984.

Temoshok, Lydia, and Henry Dreher. *The Type C Connection.* New York: Random House, 1992.

Thomas, A., and S. Chess. *Temperament and Development.* New York: Brunner/Mazel, 1977.

Wachs, Theodore D. "Determinants of Intellectual Development." *Intelligence,* 1993.

————. "Genetic and Family Influences on Individual Development." *Psychology Inquiry,* 1995.

————. *The Nature of Nurture.* Newbury Park, Calif.: Sage Publications, 1992.

Williams, R. B., and J. C. Barefoot. "Coronary-Prone Behavior," *Type A Behavior Pattern,* ed. B. K. Houston and C. R. Synder. New York: John Wiley, 1988.

CHAPTER 10

Adorno, T. W., et al. *The Authoritarian Personality.* New York: Harper, 1950.

Belenky, M. F., et al. *Women's Ways of Knowing.* New York: Basic Books, 1986.

Bem, S. L. "Theory and Measurement of Androgeny." *Journal of Personality and Social Psychology,* 1979.

Eysenck, Hans J. "National Differences in Personality as Related to ABO Blood Group Polymorphism." *Psychological Reports,* 1977.

Geertz, C. "Person, Time, and Conduct in Bali," *Interpretation of Cultures.* New York: Basic Books, 1973.

Gilligan, C. *In a Different Voice.* Cambridge, Mass.: Harvard University Press, 1982.

Itard, J. "On the First Developments of the Young Savage of Aveyron," (1799), reprinted in *Wolf Children and the Problem of Human Nature,* ed. L. Malson. New York: Monthly Review Press, 1972.

Kluckhohn, C., et al., eds. *Personality in Nature, Society, and Culture.* New York: Knopf, 1953.

Maccoby, E., ed. *The Development of Sex Differences.* Stanford, Calif.: Stanford University Press, 1966.

————, and C. N. Jacklin. *The Psychology of Sex Differences.* Stanford, Calif.: Stanford University Press, 1974.

Oldham, J. M. "Personality Disorders: Current Perspectives." *Journal of the American Medical Association,* 1994.

————, E. Hollander, and A. E. Skodol, eds. *Impulsivity and Compulsivity.* Washington, D.C.: American Psychiatric Press, in press.

————, and L. B. Morris. *The New Personality Self-Portrait.* New York: Bantam Books, 1995.

————, A. E. Skodol, H. D. Kellman, E. S. Hyler, N. Doidge, and L. Rosnick. "Comorbidity of Axis I/Axis II Disorders." *American Journal of Psychiatry,* 1995.

Reinisch, T. M., et al., eds. *Masculinity/Femininity: Basic Perspectives.* New York: Oxford University Press, 1987.

Chapters 11 through 14

American Psychiatric Association. *Diagnostic and Statistical Manual of Mental Disorders,* 4th ed. Washington, D.C.: American Psychiatric Association, 1994.

Beck, A. T., and A. Freeman. *Cognitive Therapy of Personality Disorders.* New York: Guilford Press, 1990.

Gunderson, John G. "Severe Personality Disorders: Diagnostic Controversies," *Annual Review of Psychiatry,* vol. II, ed. A. Tasman and M. B. Riba. Washington, D.C.: American Psychiatric Association, 1992.

———, et al. "Personality and Vulnerability to Affective Disorders," *Personality and Psychopathology,* ed. C. R. Cloninger. Washington, D.C.: American Psychiatric Association, in press.

Klein, D., and P. H. Wender. *Mind, Mood & Medicine.* New York: Farrar, Straus and Giroux, 1981.

———, and ———. *Understanding Depression.* New York: Oxford University Press, 1993.

Kraepelin, E. *Psychiatry.* Leipzig: J. A. Barth Verlag, 1909.

Kramer, Peter D. *Listening to Prozac.* New York: Viking, 1993.

Kretschmer, E. *Physique and Character.* New York: Harcourt Brace, 1926.

McMurtry, Larry. *Lonesome Dove.* New York: Simon & Schuster, 1985.

Mischel, W. "Toward a Cognitive Social Learning Reconceptualization of Personality." *Psychological Review,* 1973.

———, and Y. Shoda. "A Cognitive-Affective System Theory of Personality: Reconceptualizing Situations, Dispositions, Dynamics, and Invariance in Personality Structure." *Psychological Review,* 1995.

———, and ———. "Delay of Gratification in Children." *Science,* 1989.

Stone, Michael. *Abnormalities of Personality: Within and Beyond the Realm of Treatment.* New York: Norton, 1993.

———. *The Borderline Syndromes.* New York: McGraw-Hill, 1980.

———. *Essential Papers on Borderline Disorders.* New York: New York University Press, 1986.

———. *The Fate of Borderline Patients.* New York: Guilford Press, 1990.

Walker, A. *Fatal Charm.* New York: St. Martin's Press, 1992.

Widiger, Thomas A. "The DSM-III-R Categorical Personality Disorder Diagnoses: A Critique and an Alternative." *Psychological Inquiry,* 1993.

———. *Understanding the DSM-IV* (monograph and audio tapes). Keystone Heights, Fla.: PsychoEducational Resources, 1994.

———, et al. *Personality Disorder Interview IV.* Odessa, Fla.: Psychological Assessment Resources, 1995

Chapter 15

Block, J. *Lives Through Time.* Berkeley, Calif.: Bancroft, 1971.

Brim, O. G. *Ambition: How We Manage Success and Failure Throughout Our Lives.* New York: Basic Books, 1992.

————, and J. Kagan, eds. *Constancy and Change in Human Development.* Cambridge, Mass.: Harvard University Press, 1980.

Caspi, A., and D. Bem. "Personality Continuity and Change Across the Life Course," *Handbook of Personality,* ed. L. A. Pervin. New York: Guilford Press, 1990.

Feldman, S. S., and B. G. Aschenbrenner. "Impact of Parenthood on Various Aspects of Masculinity and Femininity." *Developmental Psychology,* 1983.

Helson, R., and G. Moane. "Personality Change in Women from College to Midlife." *Journal of Personality and Social Psychology,* 1987.

James, William. *The Principles of Psychology.* New York: Henry Holt and Co., 1890.

INDEX

WINIFRED GALLAGHER has written about human behavior for *The Atlantic Monthly, Rolling Stone, The Sciences, Discover*, and other publications. She is the author of *The Power of Place: How Our Surroundings Shape Our Thoughts, Emotions, and Actions*. With her husband and children, she lives in Manhattan and Long Eddy, New York.

This book was set in Garamond, a typeface originally designed by the Parisian type cutter Claude Garamond (1480–1561). This version of Garamond was modeled on a 1592 specimen sheet from the Egenolff-Berner foundry, which was produced from types assumed to have been brought to Frankfurt by the punch cutter Jacques Sabon (d. 1580).

Claude Garamond's distinguished romans and italics first appeared in *Opera Ciceronis* in 1543–44. The Garamond types are clear, open, and elegant.